Cases 'n' Places

Global Cases in Educational and Performance Technology

A volume in
Educational Design and Technology in the Knowledge Society
Stewart Marshall and Wanjira Kinuthia, *Series Editors*

Cases 'n' Places

Global Cases in Educational and Performance Technology

Edited by

Wanjira Kinuthia
Georgia State University

Stewart Marshall
University of the West Indies Open Campus

IAP

INFORMATION AGE PUBLISHING, INC.
Charlotte, NC • www.infoagepub.com

Library of Congress Cataloging-in-Publication Data

Cases and places : global cases in educational and performance technology / edited by Wanjira Kinuthia, Stewart Marshall.
p. cm. – (Educational design and technology in the knowledge society)
Includes bibliographical references.
ISBN 978-1-60752-314-7 (pbk.) – ISBN 978-1-60752-315-4 (hardcover) –
ISBN 978-1-60752-316-1 (e-book)
1. Educational technology–Case studies. 2. Computer technology–Case studies. 3. Computer science–Study and teaching (Higher)–Case studies. I. Kinuthia, Wanjira. II. Marshall, Stewart.
LB1028.2.C38 2009
371.33–dc22

2009039171

Printed and bound by CPI Group (UK) Ltd, Croydon, CR0 4YY

CONTENTS

SECTION 2

PROGRAM DEVELOPMENT

SECTION 3

TEACHER EDUCATION AND DEVELOPMENT

SECTION 4

PROFESSIONAL DEVELOPMENT

SECTION 5

TECHNOLOGY IMPLEMENTATION AND ADOPTION

ACKNOWLEDGEMENTS

This book would not have been possible without the contributions of the authors, and we thank them for their hard work, both as authors and as peer reviewers, and also for their patience as they responded to our endless requests for information and changes. We also wish to thank the Information Age Publishing staff for their support and encouragement throughout the whole publishing process.

And of course, we wish to acknowledge the hard work and diligence of our Editorial Assistant Roxanne Russell, especially for the long days and late nights that she had to endure in order to meet our deadlines.

We also thank others who, though not directly concerned with the book, provided the enabling environment for our work on it. We thank our parents and siblings for their support and influences on our lives. And we thank our friends and colleagues for their support.

ABOUT THE EDITORS

Dr. Wanjira Kinuthia is an assistant professor of Learning Technologies at Georgia State University. She worked as an instructional designer in higher education and business and industry for several years. She also worked in and conducted research on faculty development and e-learning. Dr. Kinuthia received her PhD degree in Instructional Design and Development; a master's degree in International Affairs, focusing on African Studies and Women's Studies; and a master's degree in Computer Education and Technology. She has a bachelor's degree in International Business. Before that she attended the University of Nairobi. Dr. Kinuthia has a special interest in international and comparative education, focusing on educational technology in developing countries, and conducts research and teaching in this area.

Professor Stewart Marshall, PhD, is the Director of the Academic Division of the University of the West Indies Open Campus (UWIOC) and holds the UNESCO Chair in Educational Technologies. Although originally an electrical engineer with the Central Electricity Generating Board in the UK, Professor Marshall has worked in higher education since 1973. He was the foundation Professor of Communication at the Papua New Guinea University of Technology, foundation Professor of Communication Studies at Monash University in Australia, and foundation Coordinator of Academic Studies and Professor of Distance Education at the Institute of Distance Education at the University of Swaziland in Southern Africa. Professor Marshall's research interests are in the role of ICT in education, especially in developing countries. He has published several books and over 90 other publications, including book chapters, refereed articles, and conference papers.

Cases 'n' Places: Global Cases in Educational and Performance Technology, page xi

ABOUT THE CONTRIBUTORS

Rachael Adlington is an academic in the Faculty of the Professions, University of New England. She works with Education students to become proficient users of information and communication technologies to enhance teaching and learning. Ms. Adlington is also an experienced primary-school teacher, specializing in the teaching of literacy, technology, and music. Her current research interests include the role of technology in education and the new literacy practices emerging alongside new technologies.

Sausan Al Kawas has a DDS, PhD from McGill University, Postdoctoral fellowship from Royal Victoria Hospital in Canada. Dr. Al Kawas was assistant professor then associate professor and occupied the position of Head of Department and Deputy Dean at the Faculty of Dentistry, Ajman University, UAE. In 2005, she moved to participate in the foundation of the new College of Dentistry at the University of Sharjah. Currently she is the Chairperson of the Department of Oral and Craniofacial Health Sciences. She participated in several international conferences and published many scientific research papers. She won several awards as the Biennial Research Award from the Canadian Dental Association and the Young Investigator Award from the American Society of Bone and Mineral Research. In 2007, she became a Fellow of the International College of Dentists (FICD) in the United States.

Nor Aziah Alias, PhD, is currently an Associate Professor of Instructional Technology and the Deputy Dean (Academic, Quality, and Research) of the Faculty of Education, Universiti Teknologi MARA (UiTM), Malaysia. She holds a first and second degree in Physics and a Graduate Certificate in Open and Distance Learning. Her involvement in the field of distance

Cases 'n' Places: Global Cases in Educational and Performance Technology, pages xiii–xxi

education and online learning spans more than 10 years, where she has served as an instructional designer and has conducted research, mainly on the motivation of adult online learners. Dr. Nor Aziah's research interest is basically in the integration of technology in learning and instruction, especially in the context of adult and online learning. She has published book chapters, refereed articles, and conference papers in the area and is actively involved in design and developmental research.

Dr. Payal Arora has conducted extensive research in education and communication technologies in the United States as well as internationally. Her works have been and are being published in several peer-reviewed journals including the *International Journal of Cultural Studies*, the *Information Communication and Ethics in Society Journal*, the *Association of Advancement in Computing in Education Journal*, *International Journal of Education & Development using ICT*, *Education Philosophy and Theory Journal* and others. She holds a master's in Education from Harvard University and a doctorate from Teachers College, Columbia University. She is currently an assistant professor in communication and media at Erasmus University Rotterdam, The Netherlands.

Judi Baron has a Master of Education (Distance Education) and is presently enrolled in a doctorate investigating academic staff readiness for, and effective delivery of situated online learning environments. Judi has a special interest in cultural values and beliefs and learning styles and the online educational implications for staff development purposes. Judi has more than 20 years experience working in higher education and has conducted extensive research into flexible learning including the evaluation of online role-play simulations within a community-of-inquiry framework. Judi is the Convenor of a Graduate Certificate in Online Learning (Higher Education) and is also the Online Learning Coordinator at The University of Adelaide, South Australia. She is also a Fellow and South Australia's Network Leader for Project ENRoLe, a nationally funded initiative, which encourages role-based learning environments within university education.

Danilo M. Baylen, EdD, is an Associate Professor of Media and Instructional Technology in the College of Education at the University of West Georgia. Baylen received his doctorate in instructional technology and a master's degree in counseling from Northern Illinois University, and in elementary education from Florida Gulf Coast University. His research interests include technology integration across the curriculum, media literacy, online learning and teaching, and instructional design. Previous work experiences include posts in faculty development, instructional technology services, instructional design and development, and English as a second language teaching.

Bev Bramble has 15 years of experience in private-sector e-learning instructional design and project management. He is currently an instructional designer with Teaching and Learning Services at the University of New Brunswick in Canada.

Jason Caudill is an Assistant Professor of Business at Carson-Newman College. Jason holds a PhD in Instructional Technology from the University of Tennessee as well as an MBA and a bachelor's degree in Business. Jason's primary interests are in technology management and open source software.

Teresa Connolly is a lecturer in Open Educational Resources at the Open University. She has extensive experience in delivering face-to-face, distance, blended, and open educational materials in a variety of subject areas. Teresa has a degree in Geography and has developed a number of map-based e-learning resources.

Susan Crichton is an associate professor in the Faculty of Education at the University of Calgary. Her research focuses on the effective uses of ICT to inform teaching, learning, and e-training. She developed an innovative preservice course that prepares novice educators to teach in blended and online environments.

Hanan Salah El-Deen El-Halawany is an instructor of Comparative and International Education with an interest in the field of ICT and Education. Another field of interest is gender and education. In this arena she places herself among Middle Eastern feminists, who believe in the power of a well-educated Arab woman with her roots fixed in her local authentic culture, her arms outstretched to embrace the world in peace, and her brain absorbs and appreciates diversity, believing that all men are created equal and what makes the difference is their individual ability to spread peace and contribute to secure a better future for our children.

Giselle Ferreira is a lecturer at the Faculty of Maths, Computing, and Technology at the UK Open University. She was seconded to the OpenLearn Academic Team throughout the Pilot Stage of the Project. Giselle has a long-standing interest in the concept of "boundaries," and her current research explores boundary issues that arise in relation to curriculum and pedagogy for online learning as well as discourses and technologies of "openness." Her ongoing research into the impact of Open Educational Resources is based on an ethnography of learning situations across the "informal learning/formal learning" continuum afforded principally by the OpenLearn project.

John A. Gedeon holds a doctorate (EdD) in Instructional Technology & Distance Education from Nova Southeastern University, Fort Lauderdale, Florida. He is currently working as an Educational Technologist in the Instructional Development Unit at the University of the West Indies in Trinidad & Tobago. He also possesses a master's degree in Public Administration specializing in Public Sector Reform, has taught in the MBA program, conducted numerous business workshops, and has been a management consultant for 29 years.

Joan Glacken, EdD, is a founding faculty member of Florida Gulf Coast University and serves as associate dean, curriculum and assessment and chair, Division of Health Sciences in the College of Health Professions. She earned her graduate degrees in health professions education from Rutgers University. She received her undergraduate degree in medical technology from Douglass College in New Jersey. Past work experiences include serving as supervisor for AccuMed Diagnostic Laboratory and adjunct faculty at Rutgers University and the University of Medicine and Dentistry of New Jersey.

Dr. Jamiliah M. A. Grant received her PhD in 2004 from Boston College. Her research interest is technology in education. She published her first article on the use of technology to teach reading in 2004: "Are Electronic Books Effective in Teaching Young Children Reading and Comprehension." While the work was based on a review of current research in the field, her concept for the work was based on her personal experience in the American classroom. Subsequently, Dr. Grant accepted a position at the University of the West Indies (UWI), Barbados, as an Instructional Development Specialist. During her stay at the UWI, Dr. Grant formed the research group Scholarship of Teaching through Action Research on Teaching (START). The group produced, piloted, and administered a survey that captured the technical skill and capacities of students at the university. The group produced several collaborative research publications, such as *Are Students Ready for a Virtual University; Toward a Policy for a Computer Literacy Programme; Helping New Faculty to Document their Scholarship through the Creation of e-Portfolios; New Directions in University Education: Perspectives from the Caribbean; Teaching French in the Anglophone Caribbean;* and *Let the Games Begin!*

Heather Leona Gray is a PhD candidate in the Department of Management, Griffith University. She has been widely published in book chapters, journal articles, and has presented papers at international conferences. Ms. Gray's research areas include information technology research, human-computer engagement, and IT engagement and motivations in developing and developed countries. She is also the Research Associate for the federal governmentally funded Mobile Staff Productivity Project, spanning two universities in Queensland, Australia.

Dr. Shironica Priyanthi Karunanayaka is a Senior Lecturer in the Faculty of Education in the Open University of Sri Lanka (OUSL). Currently she is the head of the Department of Secondary and Tertiary Education. She has been serving at the OUSL for over 15 years. Dr. Karunanayaka holds a first class in the bachelor's degree in Science from the OUSL and obtained the Gold Medal for Best Performance. She obtained the Postgraduate Diploma in Education from the University of Colombo. She also holds the degree of Doctor of Education from the University of Wollongong, Australia, specializing in the area of information technology in education and training. She is an active researcher and author/co-author of over 30 refereed journals, conference, and other publications appearing in both national and international fora. Her research interests are in the areas of information and communication technology in teaching and learning and instructional design.

Professor Andy Lane has a BSc in Plant Sciences and a PhD from the University of London. He has been in the Systems Department of the Technology Faculty at the Open University since 1983 and held various offices in the faculty including head of the Systems Department, as well as Sub Dean (Courses) and from 2000–2006 Dean of the Technology Faculty. He was promoted to Professor of Environmental Systems in 2005 and in 2006 he was appointed as Director of the Open University's OpenLearn Initiative. He has authored or co-authored many teaching texts and research papers dealing with systems and environmental management and also the use of diagramming to aid systems thinking and study, including the Sciences Good Study Guide. He has personally used systems diagrams to assist development and change within the complex organizations and projects he has led and is now extending his interests to Open Educational Resources.

Patrick McAndrew is Senior Lecturer in the Open University's Institute of Educational Technology. He has led a range of research projects addressing how materials and environments can support learning through the use of learning design and the provision of tools for learners. Patrick has a degree in mathematics from the University of Oxford and a PhD in computer science from Heriot-Watt University in Edinburgh. He is currently the Research and Evaluation Director of OpenLearn, a major initiative to provide open content for free education supported by the William and Flora Hewlett Foundation.

Ewa McGrail is Associate Professor of Language and Literacy Education at Middle and Secondary Education and Instructional Technology, Georgia State University. She is a coordinator of a master's in English education program and teaches English methods and literacy and technology courses. McGrail is an ardent supporter of innovation and newer technology applications in both research and instruction. She experiments with newer technologies and newer literacies in her own instruction. In research, McGrail examines literacy and technology connections as well as teacher education, technology, and professional development.

Grady Mclean is a 25-year Navy veteran who led the development of a 27-week computer-controlled engineering propulsion course at the Great Lakes Naval Station, Great Lakes, Illinois. He has also taught electronics and technical math at the 2-year college level in addition to teaching history and geography in public high school. Grady also led the development of the Master Craftsman training program for a major gulf coast shipyard, which included both basic and advanced skill training for 16 shipyard crafts. Some of Grady's accomplishments in the program were the in-house development of over 200 computer-based technical, safety, and management training courses. This project proved the values of computer-based training in reducing training cost and reduction of accidents. He is currently President of DiMac Educational Consultants, Mobile, Alabama, specializing in rapid development of computer-based training programs for Gulf Coast shipyards.

Dr. Iwona Miliszewska is a senior lecturer in computer science at Victoria University, Melbourne, Australia. She has led and participated in research projects involving transnational education, effective teaching methods, lifelong learning, and women in computer science, and has published in these areas. Iwona is currently leading a grant-funded research project aimed at testing and refining a multidimensional model for effective transnational education programs.

Dr. Som Naidu is currently Associate Professor and Director in the of Teaching & Learning Quality Enhancement and Evaluation Services in the Division of Learning and Teaching Services at Charles Stuart University, NSW, Australia. From 1997 to 2008 he was Associate Professor of Educational Technology at the University of Melbourne, Victoria, Australia. He possesses undergraduate qualifications in education and graduate qualifications in educational technology from Montreal, Canada. His career in the field of educational technology dates back to the early 1980s, during which period and since he has worked in various roles in the fields of educational technology, e-learning, and distance education in Canada, Australia, the United Kingdom, and the United States. More recently, he has been working on several educational development projects in India, Sri Lanka, Malaysia, and Singapore. Dr. Naidu has been Executive Editor (since 1997) of the international peer-reviewed journal *Distance Education* and series co-editor of the Routledge Falmer book series on Open and Flexible Learning, also published by the Taylor and Francis Group.

Dr. Thanh T. Nguyen is Associate Professor and Graduate Program Coordinator for an online hybrid master's degree in the Instructional Technology program at Bridgewater State College in Massachusetts. Dr. Nguyen has advocated a paradigm shift for online learning and teaching from lecturing to self-directed learning; from a self-contained classroom to social constructivism environment; from answering exam questions to engaging learners in examining their own beliefs and culture; from sharing their own understanding of new materials to accepting different interpretation of others; from looking for an answer from the instructor to searching for more answers from classmates and research. Teachers teach diverse populations and should be trained to work with unpredictable challenges.

Jennifer Nicholls is Senior Lecturer at Macquarie University where she teaches theater and educational drama courses. Jennifer has worked as a theater director, teacher, and consultant for theater companies and arts and educational institutions. For the past 10 years she has been designing the integration of Web-based technology to support and extend the teaching of drama for students.

Robyn Philip is an educational consultant with a background in education and the humanities. She is a consultant for the Australian Learning and Teaching Council (ALTC), working on engagement and user support for the ALTC Exchange, an initiative to support networks and reuse of educational resources in Australian higher education. She also lectures and undertakes educational design for the School of Indigenous Health Studies at the University of Sydney.

Aaron Powell, PhD, is an assistant professor at Valdosta State University and serves as the Academic Director of Georgia ONmyLINE, graduate distance programs for the College of Education. Dr. Powell recently finished his dissertation at Virginia Tech. He studied the use of a course-management system for online support of a teacher community of practice. He's very interested in supporting professional knowledge networks and learning communities by design, and exploring the implementation of various technologies to serve the purposeful sharing of learning resources and knowledge artifact in such communities.

Ellen Rose has 15 years of experience as an e-learning instructional designer and project manager. She is an associate professor at the University of New Brunswick, where she holds the McCain-Aliant Telecom Chair in Instructional Design and Multimedia.

L. Roxanne Russell is an instructional technology and design consultant and PhD student. Her professional and research focus is providing training solutions for organizations with global personnel challenges. She is currently serving as a Research Fellow for the India, China, & America Institute, where she is glad to have the opportunity to help foster conversation among a global audience on the impact of the market relationship between America and the world's two largest emerging markets. Her current research interests are indicated in her latest publication: "Training for Innovation in India: Cultural Considerations and Strategic Implication," *Performance Improvement Quarterly*, June 2008.

Dr. Louis Sanzogni is the Head of Department, Department of Management, Griffith University. He has been widely published in book chapters, journal articles, and has presented papers at international conferences. Dr. Sanzogni's research areas include information technology research, Internet research, and organizational intelligence technologies. He is also on the steering committee for the federal governmentally funded Mobile Staff Productivity Project, spanning two universities in Queensland, Australia.

Lesley Steele is currently the Program Manager, School of Dentistry, University of Adelaide. Her role is to oversee the development of an existing dentistry curriculum into a contemporary online format for delivery and implementation at the University of Sharjah, Bachelor of Dental Surgery program. Her previous areas of work have been with developing curricula and teaching resources for indigenous oral health programs, dentistry, and dental hygiene programs. She holds qualifications in dental hygiene, business, teaching, and postgraduate qualifications in public and international health.

Cherry Stewart is consultant with OnQ Learning, an independent organization specializing in educational design and development, particularly for online learning. In addition, Ms. Stewart provides academic development services to the Faculty of the Professions for the University of New England, where she is currently supporting the redesign of online learning programs in education and nursing. Over the past 25 years, Ms. Stewart has held senior management positions in NSW TAFE, and advised business and government in educational design programs for rural and remote learners. Ms. Stewart's current research activity is focused on educational design, professional development, and transformational learning in organizations.

David Edwin Stone serves as the Director of the Instructional Technology Services Group at Southern Polytechnic State University (SPSU), where he has guided technology selection for distance learning and instructional technology at SPSU and developed a variety of faculty development programs since 2001. David has been active in Science, Technology, Engineering, and Mathematics (STEM) outreach programs for middle and secondary students in the State of Georgia, including the Georgia BEST Robotics competition, Future City, and Science Olympiad. David has conducted international research in the area of English as a second language via the use of virtual environments in China, and has focused his research primarily on organizational change and development within the context of higher education.

Dr. Paul Walcott received his PhD in Information Engineering from City University (UK) and is a Lecturer of Computer Science at the University of the West Indies (Barbados). He was the winner of the 2007 UWI/Guardian General Premium Teaching Award and is the current Chairman of the Scholarship of Teaching through Action Research on Teaching (START) group. Dr. Walcott is the Editor-in-Chief of a new open access journal called the *Electronic Journal of Computing for Undergraduates in Developing Countries.* He teaches courses in software engineering, information systems and e-commerce; and research interests include computers and education, e-commerce, e-portfolios and e-learning.

Tina Wilson, a lecturer in Open Educational Resources at the Open University in the UK, has experience teaching in both face-to-face and distance learning modes. Her research interests include e-learning, open content, human computer interaction, computers and education, new media, and education. A particular focus for exploration is the interactivity and interaction aspects of online communities of learners and the use of structure, organization, and support in such environments. Though this research is mainly related to adult e-learning, students' supervisions have focused on using e-learning to assist young children and those with learning difficulties such as dyslexia.

Kay Xuereb is a PhD candidate at the University of the West Indies, Jamaica. She successfully completed her Bachelor of Education degree with qualified teacher status at the University of Warwick in the United Kingdom and taught in England before continuing her teaching career in Malta. She was one of the coordinators for the National Strategy for Information Technology in Malta and contributed to the development of the National Minimum Curriculum. She completed her Master of Education in Information Technology at the University of Exeter. Her research interests focus on information and communications technology in education in small island states.

ACRONYMS

ADB	Asian Development Bank
AECT	Association for Educational Communications and Technology
CD	Compact Disc
CD-ROM	Compact Disc: Read-Only Memory
COL	Commonwealth of Learning
CPD	Continuing Professional Development
DVD	Digital Video Disc
eSim	Electronic Simulation
HTML	HyperText Markup Language
ICT	Information and Communication Technology
IT	Information Technology
LMS	Learning Management System
MDGs	Millennium Development Goals
MOE	Ministry of Education
ODL	Open and Distance Learning
OECD	Organization for Economic Cooperation and Development
OER	Open Educational Resources
OU	Open University (United Kingdom)
OUSL	Open University of Sri Lanka
PDA	Personal Digital Assistant
PDF	Portable Document Format
PRC	People's Republic of China
SME	Subject Matter Expert
UAE	United Arab Emirates
UiTM	Universiti Teknologi MARA
UN	United Nations

Cases 'n Places: Global Cases in Educational and Performance Technology, pages xxiii–xxiv

UNDP	United Nations Development Programme
UNESCO	United Nations Educational, Scientific, and Cultural Organization
USA	United States of America
UWI	The University of the West Indies
UWIDEC	The University of the West Indies Distance Education Centre
WYSIWYG	What You See Is What You Get

INTRODUCTION

CASES 'N' PLACES

Global Cases in Educational and Performance Technology

Wanjira Kinuthia and Stewart Marshall

RATIONALE FOR CASES 'N' PLACES: GLOBAL CASES IN EDUCATIONAL AND PERFORMANCE TECHNOLOGY

As with many business-school programs, many educational technology instructors recognize the added advantage of using case studies in instruction. However, there are few existing resources to assist them in the process. Additionally, they do not have the time to create cases for their courses, yet many would incorporate them if they were available. The goal of *Cases 'n' Places: Global Cases in Educational and Performance Technology* is to make a variety of cases available as follows:

1. Cases as exemplars;
2. Cases as opportunities to practice analysis, assimilation of differing perspectives, and the contemplation of action; and
3. Cases as simulations for reflection.

Cases 'n' Places: Global Cases in Educational and Performance Technology, pages xxv–xxviii

This book presents cases with dilemmas that the learners will have to decipher, interpret, judge, analyze, and discuss in order to draw their own conclusions in solving the problems that are identified in the cases.

Solutions to the problems will include technical information, knowledge, and skills to bridge the gap. The approach of the cases is to present cases that are problem-centered descriptions of design situations and developed from the actual experiences of Instructional Design and Technology (IDT) practitioners. The cases are dilemma oriented, where each case ends before the solutions are presented. Learners will analyze, discuss, synthesize, reflect, and report on the cases. In doing so, they will identify problems in the field and determine the importance of context in implementing solutions.

The goal of the book is to help the learners identify existing and potential problems, issues, and situations in educational technology and to subsequently develop potential solution plans. Some of the cases identify how different contexts apply theories, models, and approaches to transform education and assist developing communities to close the knowledge divide. The book provides coverage by using scenarios in both developed and developing nations by providing examples of best practices and principles.

CASE FEATURES

The cases in the book exhibit most of the following features:

1. *Cases appear authentic and realistic:* The cases develop real-life situations and provide as much factual information as possible. Quotes, conversations, graphs, tables, and such have been included to add realism to the case.
2. *Cases use basic case structure in writing:* Most of the cases open up with broad issues and then move into the specific situation. Most of the cases are written in narrative style, using storytelling techniques that provide details about actions and persons involved.
3. *Cases fit with learners' and practitioners' needs:* The topics and content of the case are appropriate, relevant, and important to learning objectives and end-user needs.
4. *Cases pose complex, controversial issues rather than theories:* The cases generate debates, especially when there are no clear simple solutions. The theories behind the issues will emerge in the discussions and instruction.
5. *Cases provide sufficient background information:* The cases allow learners to address the emerging issues from their own perspectives and also from the perspective of the case characters. Cases provide enough description in the prose for learners to be able to situate the case

problem and understand the context. The cases also provide ample information about the case characters to help learners situate the cases better.

6. *Chapters have discussion questions at the end of narrative.* These questions serve to generate possible solutions and case outcomes.

THE ORGANIZATION OF THE CASES 'N' PLACES

The *Cases 'n' Places Facilitator Guides* collection is divided into five sections to match the corresponding book of cases: Course Design, Program Development, Teacher Education and Development, Professional Development, and, Technology Implementation and Adoption.

Section 1: Course Design

The cases described in this section are drawn from very different countries and settings. They demonstrate the need to include cultural awareness and diversity in course design; that is, in relation to the provision of technology-based courses to mature adult learners. They also seek to provoke innovative educational approaches with new tools such that genuine learning takes place.

Section 2: Program Development

The cases in this section deal with program development. They demonstrate that the difficulties faced in program development are very often not educational at all, but instead are such issues as finance, institutional politics, staffing, and staff development. They also demonstrate that very often the program developer is working with incomplete data and impossible deadlines.

Section 3: Teacher Education and Development

The cases in this section deal with developing the skills required in the teaching process, whether it be preservice teachers or university lecturers. They are designed to engage teachers in reflection and in-depth analysis of teacher decision making, and in designing, developing, implementing, and evaluating appropriate educational technologies. They also demonstrate that a teacher will very often face multiple challenges in a single class and an environment that is out of their control.

Section 4: Professional Development

The case studies in this section deal with professional development in the use of ICT in education in several contexts: university faculty, education officials, teachers, and head teachers.

Section 5: Technology Implementation and Adoption

This section looks at issues of technology implementation and adoption in various contexts, from the specific level of a university program to the very general level of cross-sector, cross-border training; and from the introduction of a specific technology to "mainstreaming" the educational-technology process on campus. In several of the cases can be seen the necessity to consider cultural differences and using strategies that consider their fit in the global and local context at the same time. All the cases demonstrate the need to engage the services of an educational-technology specialist early in the planning process.

SECTION 1

COURSE DESIGN

CHAPTER 1

THE SITUATED COGNITION PARADIGM IN AN *A PRIORI* SETTING

A Case in a Multicultural Classroom

Louis Sanzogni and Heather Gray
Griffith University, Australia

PROBLEM

Like most tertiary institutions, Griffith University offers the subject Project Management, which attracts students from a variety of backgrounds ranging from experienced project managers looking for tertiary qualifications to students who move from undergraduate work straight to a postgraduate degree and who have limited or no work experience, as well as international postgraduate students. In a review of the course, which includes updating material from the latest academic research as well as recent practitioner experience, a need to include cultural awareness and diversity was identified. In order to utilize the multicultural diversity and experience in the learning process, *a priori* learning and situated cognition are being investigated.

Cases 'n' Places: Global Cases in Educational and Performance Technology, pages 31–8

ORGANIZATION

Griffith University has five dispersed campuses across the southeast corner of Queensland in Australia. The institution is a multicampus, complex organization where staff members, both academic and general, are often required to work across campuses. It is technologically sophisticated, with high quality fiber optic networks, expanding wireless coverage, and an increasing use of laptops. While the technology exists to support a more flexible, mobile workforce, and take-up of laptops is strong, take-up of emerging mobile devices and collaborative technology is slower and not being leveraged for improved productivity, improved decision making, reduced consumption of paper, and reduced travel. Project Management is taught within the Schools of Management and Communication and Information Technology. The course is a one-semester postgraduate subject and is offered to students as an elective in alternate semesters. It is part of the Graduate Certificate of Information Systems, Graduate Diploma of Business, Computing and Information Systems, and the Master of Information Systems programs. The participants in this course consist of students from India, China, Turkey, northern Europe, Australia, and the Gulf region (United Arab Emirates, Saudi Arabia, Oman, Egypt, etc.).

THE CASE

Situated cognition is a multifaceted concept that sits well in postmodernism. Critical realists like Mingers (2000) allude to it not so much in words but through the hints of nonreductionist metaphysics still in their infancy. A concise and well-laid-out position for situated cognition has been expressed by Greeno (1998). This position places situated cognition at the crossroads of skill acquisition, knowledge, and conceptual understanding within the context of development of identities and meaningful, active, influential engagement in social activities related to learning communities as a whole. Moreover, Marsh and Gabora (2008, p. 104) suggest "cognitive agents do not just learn from one another, but 'put their own spin on' what they learn, make sense of it in their own terms, and then express or implement their 'take' on the ideas back to others."

Situated cognition still remains very much a concept that is well-researched but not very well applied, lacking in clear, agreed-upon definitions and practical methods of application where "its principles are also less specific in their prescription for the design of learning environments" (Wilson & Myers, 1999, p. 70). What seems appealing about the concept is its ability to encompass "individual and social scales of study" (p. 73). From this premise the situated cognition paradigm is well-placed to embrace behaviorist as well as cognitive concepts in its framework. These concepts have contributed and continue to contribute a great deal to educational models but have (perhaps unjustly) been portrayed in the literature as opposing views. Situated cognition provides an environment where these concepts can coexist in a larger, situation-dependent context. Positions assumed by information-processing/symbolic-cognition theorists like Clancey (1991) also contribute to make the view of the concept appear to be on a united front:

> The situated cognition hypothesis is that all processes of behaving, including speech, problem-solving, and physical skills, are generated on the spot, not by mechanical application of scripts or rules previously stored in the brain. (p. 110)

Situated cognition proponents however appear not to have satisfied critics on a number of issues, especially those concerning the lack of clear guidance on how knowledge can be transferred across contextual boundaries. Another issue regards the concept of self-directed learning and the possibility of "fossilization," where the knowledge-acquisition process can lead to the formulation of false axioms that become rooted in the psyche and prove difficult to remove. Recognizing these drawbacks is useful, as it can prevent the establishment of erroneous practical applications of the concept.

While situated cognition can be viewed in prescriptive terms, leading to a structurally predefined environment, it can also be used as a descriptive base for an accommodating framework of practices for instruction. There appears to be cautious agreement in the literature, noting that applications of the concept in practical settings should not be dismissive of a more extensive view and not be restricted by individual opinions. Within this context, situated cognition is said to provide a more encompassing ontology, where the "physical context is being reunited with the social, within the thought process" (Light & Butterworth, 1992, p. 1).

There is a need to transform this promising concept into something concrete that can deliver. In practical terms, the student's interpretation of a situation is based on relevance and experience, gathered during a timeline extending from the present into the past (Lemke, 1997). Therefore, to teach in a way that encourages changes in conception, instructors must recognize how students already think about phenomena—they must make themselves aware of, and use, the conceptions students already have (Ramsden, 1988). An alarming body of literature reports that although a majority of students appear to comfortably satisfy assessment requirements, surface learning remains predominant, with little evidence of conceptual understanding of the subject matter.

Therefore, using Ramsden's (1988, p. 24) assertion that "perhaps the most significant single influence on students' learning is their perception of assessment," we see an opportunity to engage situated cognition by modifying or adapting the assessment material of a chosen subject for its implementation. Further, the use of past experiences appears to be congruent with Laurillard's (2002, p. 30) position that "It makes no sense to remediate a faulty procedural skill with reference to the procedure alone; we have to appeal to the conceptual apparatus that supports it as well. We have already established that knowledge is situated in action" and, therefore, what better premise to allow students to work out where they can locate themselves in an academic debate but through their experiences.

In order to utilize the multicultural diversity and experience in the learning process, *a priori* learning and *situated cognition* are being investigated.

Current Situational Application

The method was implemented through the course assessment items. The assessment consisted of three stages:

1. A reflective essay on a particularly vivid, relevant, substantial past experience.
2. A reflective essay on the association of a major theoretical discourse with a relevant past event.
3. A reflective essay on the whole of the theoretical discourse and misalignment of the theory taught.

The instructor solicited and encouraged discussions (regarding the assessment items) based upon the cohort's experiences (i.e., *a priori* situated cognition).

The first assessment item sets the foundation and is essential for the success of the following two. This is where an appropriate past experience is selected and described in detail with the assistance of the tutor. A great deal of thought goes in to this formulation in terms of the participant's involvement, technical details, human resource issues, planning issues, management issues, legislation, and so on. Indeed, if this part is handled well, the student will have a sound, relevant experience upon which to base the delivery of the subject matter.

The second assessment item allows the student to bring forth a particular aspect of the chosen past experience and compare it with a substantial theoretical discourse delivered during lectures. The students here are given a choice, as not all of the theoretical discourses are appropriate. The usual reason for inappropriateness is that not all aspects of the chosen past experience directly match theoretical discourse. At this juncture, the benefits of *a priori* experiential learning begin to emerge; in other words, the linking of theory with experience.

The third assessment item uses all the aspects of the chosen past experience in order to highlight gaps in the appreciative entity's knowledge or the theoretical discourse in its entirety. Students are asked to pay particular attention to their knowledge gap in view of the theory and are also asked to criticize the theoretical discourse in view of their past experience.

Issues regarding the preparation of the students for the use of their past experience in an *a priori* learning context were resolved by contextualizing past experiences to the needs of the current course. Possible tools that could be used in achieving this would be guided interviews, blogs, and wikis, where students are given the opportunity to relate their past experiences to the subject matter. In this instance, to determine success of this updated learning structure, a voluntary survey of students was undertaken to qualitatively determine the students' opinion of this style of learning.

It is useful to note that certain themes persisted throughout the study. For instance, students have difficulty, at times, contextualizing past experiences to the task at hand. As the significance of these experiences becomes clear, the students find it easier to relate them to their theoretical underpinning, thus, providing a sense of empowerment and making room for open, critical appraisal of the theories. This, in turn, leads to a more in-depth understanding of the subject matter and a more pronounced cognitive experience.

Discussion Questions

Using the publications identified in the case study, develop a three- or four-part assessment for a project-management course, which enables the sharing of knowledge from diverse cultures as well as prior experience from practitioners that are also students in the course.

Some items to consider or be included in the assignment are:

1. Describe in detail an appropriate past experience with the class. Consider sharing technical details, human resource issues, planning issues, management issues, legislation, and such that have influenced your learning and development experience.
2. Discuss how you would enable participants to use a chosen past experience. Compare this with the theoretical discourse in the publications discussed in this case study.
3. Are there past experience examples that directly match any of the theoretical discourse topics?

4. Identify the benefits of *a priori* experiential learning and how and where these would begin to emerge (linking theory with experience).
5. Identify and consider some gaps that have emerged between participants' knowledge or the theoretical discourse.
6. Consider any knowledge gaps, in view of the theory, and explore how the participant can criticize the theoretical discourse in view of their past experience.

REFERENCES

Clancey, W. J. (1991). Situated cognition: Stepping out of representational flatland. *IAI Communications: The European Journal on Artificial Intelligence, 4*(2/3), 109–112

Greeno, J. G. (1998). The situativity of knowing, learning, and research. *American Psychologist, 53*(1), 5–26.

Laurillard, D. (2002). *Rethinking university teaching* (2nd ed.). London: Routledge Falmer.

Lemke, J. L. (1997). Cognition, context, and learning: A social semiotic perspective. In D. Kirshner & J. A. Whitson (Eds.), *Situated cognition: Social, semiotic and psychological perspectives.* Mahwah, NJ: Lawrence Erlbaum Associates.

Light, P., & Butterworth, G. (1992). *Context and cognition: Ways of learning and knowing.* Hillsdale, NJ: Lawrence Erlbaum Associates.

Marsh, L., & Gabora, L. (2008). The cultural evolution of socially situated cognition. *Cognitive Systems Research, 9,* 104–114.

Mingers, J. (2001). Embodying information systems: The contribution of phenomenology. *Information and Organization (formerly Accounting, Management and Information Technology), 11*(2), 103–128.

Ramsden, P. (1988). *Improving learning: New perspectives.* London: Kogan Page.

Wilson, B. G., & Myers, K. (1999). Situated cognition in theoretical and practical context. In D. Jonassen & S. Land (Eds.), *Theoretical foundations of learning environments.* Mahwah, NJ: Erlbaum.

CHAPTER 2

TECHNOLOGY-BASED LEARNING EXPERIENCE OF MALAYSIAN OLDER ADULT LEARNERS

Nor Aziah Alias
Universiti Teknologi MARA, Malaysia

INTRODUCTION

Technology is ubiquitous and becoming more accessible; it penetrates one's life in various ways, be it at home, at work, or at school. As a driving force of globalization, technology is rapidly transforming how and with whom we learn. Knowledge can now be generated and transmitted within and across nations in a matter of seconds. People of all ages are pursuing continuing education to learn and relearn in order to compete in the globalized world. Higher education institutions need to display more flexibility and variation in curriculum design and implementation to meet the increasingly diverse and changing needs of the learners. These needs may differ according to the background of the learners, including their education, socioeconomic milieu, culture, value systems, and preferred learning styles. Moreover,

Cases 'n' Places: Global Cases in Educational and Performance Technology, pages 37–19

learning can be made more enthralling as the learners are now exposed to various resources from the Internet and other technologies.

This chapter presents a Malaysian case in which there is a distinct departure from the commonly discussed face-to-face or online instruction in terms of the nature of the learners and the context of the course. This chapter illustrates the provision of a technology-based course to a group of older adult learners who are in reality changing the demographics of higher education. In the context of this chapter, the learners are nontraditional in that they have left formal schooling and are now back to pursue new knowledge and learn new skills.

Preamble

With education being the keystone of a learning society, the quest for knowledge has moved beyond formal schooling and continues well into the adult working years. The former Malaysian premier once addressed the matter:

> Lifelong learning will and is becoming increasingly important in the knowledge based economy where knowledge and skills need to be continuously updated and upgraded... the old idea that once you are trained for something then you continue to do the same thing over and over again for years and years is no longer tenable. (Mahathir Mohamad, October 28, 2003)

The Malaysian government has in fact, initiated efforts to promote and implement lifelong learning through the provision of affordable training courses and education programs through the Internet or other ICT-related media. The Malaysian Multimedia Super Corridor project is an example of how serious the intention of the government is to embark on an ICT-capable society. Table 2.1 displays some of the ICT-related programs undertaken by the Malaysian Ministry of Education

The policies for ICT in Malaysian education include:

1. ICT for all students; ICT as an enabler to reduce the digital gap between the schools
2. ICT in education as a teaching and learning tool, as part of a subject, and as a subject by itself
3. ICT to increase productivity, efficiency, and effectiveness of education management

With governmental effort and technology infiltrating the lives of people from all levels and communities worldwide, it is only apt that it is exploited

TABLE 2.1 Ministry of Education ICT Related Programs

Year	Program
1986	Introduction to computers
1990	Computer-Integrated Learning System project (MOE-MIMOS)
1992	Computer literacy
1994	Computer-Assisted Instruction and Learning (CAIL)
1995	Education Network
1996	Electronic Resource Centre
1999	Malaysia SchoolNet (MySchoolNet)
1999	The Smart School project
2000	Introduction of Information Technology subject at high school level
2003	Introduction of Computer Graphic and Multimedia subject at the high school level
2003	Policy on using English to teach Mathematics and Science; Teachers are provided laptops and computer-based instructional materials

Source: Chan, F.M. (2002), ICT in Malaysian schools: Policies and strategies.

to the best of the educators and the learners' advantage. The pervasive forms of technology enable instructors to create learning experiences that will engage learners in relevant activities and to support learning in context. How the instructors can best bring technology into the adult learning environment is still a challenge. This is especially vital when it concerns older adults. As Selwyn, Gorard, and Furlong state:

> Key questions of who is using ICT for what purpose and with what outcomes remain largely unanswered by current literature.... Beyond recognizing the promise and potential of new technologies, mapping how ICT and ICT based learning fit with the everyday lives of adults is a vital task for the research community. (p. 1)

The same scenario applies to the Malaysian educators and educational administrators. As technology progresses and schools and campuses are drawn into the potential of technology, higher-education administrators and school heads need to understand what technology can and cannot do. The rest of the chapter will illustrate the provision of the technology-based program at one particular higher-education institution in Malaysia.

THE PROGRAM

As part of the national effort to promote and implement lifelong learning, the Malaysian Ministry of Education has provided opportunities for education administrators to upgrade their skills and knowledge by awarding scholarships and partnering with public universities to establish programs for primary school teachers and primary school heads. The Special School Heads Certification Program is one such program. It is initiated by the ministry for school heads who have passed the age of 45 years old and are yet to possess a higher-education degree. Most are certified Malaysian educators who underwent basic teacher education courses at a level not amounting to a degree level. The program seeks to assist the school heads in upgrading their educational achievement to a Bachelor in Education (Educational Management) before they retire. Without a higher-education degree, they will be left with a small amount of monthly stipend for the rest of their retirement years. Participants of the program are given full pay throughout their study during which time they attend intensive sessions at several institutes of higher learning. The participants join the mainstream, stay in dormitories, attend face-to-face classes during the week, and leave for their respective hometowns to be with their families on weekends.

The school heads study with several faculties of education in various higher-education institutions in the country. A typical session or phase lasts 5 weeks; they are back in their respective schools to attend to their jobs in between the sessions (Table 2.2). In order to graduate, they have to go through a number of phases, which will ultimately add up to the learning hours needed to fulfill the graduation requirement. The medium of instruction is English.

The courses are predominantly determined by the Ministry of Education and the Higher Education Institution where they are registered. For instance, the school heads who are attending the program in Universiti Teknologi MARA (UiTM) will go through 12 phases. The courses taken during the first 5 phases are listed in Table 2.3. The first cohort will be graduating in July 2009.

The school heads are expected to register for three courses per phase. The contents of the course are expected to fulfill a similar full-time course requirement that normally involves 14 weeks of study. However, as mentioned earlier, the school heads and the instructors are constrained by the

TABLE 2.2 A Typical Schedule for the Special School Heads Certification Program Cohort

Year	Jan	Feb	Mar	Apr	May	Jun	July	August	Sept	Oct
1										
2										
3										

TABLE 2.3 A Typical Plan of Study for the First 5 Phases of the Special School Heads Certification Program

Phase 1	Ethnic Relations, Report Writing, Theories and Principles of Educational Management
Phase 2	Meetings, Educational Leadership, Curriculum and Instruction
Phase 3	Arabic Language 1, Information Management in Education, Action Research
Phase 4	Arabic Language 2, Curriculum Management, Project
Phase 5	Arabic Language 3, IT in Educational Management, Microcounseling

5-week period as stipulated in their study plan. Hence, each course is taught at the rate of 8 to 9 lecture hours per week.

THE TECHNOLOGY-BASED COURSE

The Special School Heads Certification Program includes the latest technology as one of its curricular components. The provision of the Internet or other information and communication technologies in the universities warrants these school heads to trudge into the current technology-laden learning environment and become technology proficient. They not only learn the content through technology, they are also required to learn about technology and develop the skills to use it. In this case study, the focus is on a technology-as-curriculum approach, which is the provision of the ICT in Educational Management course. It is a three-credit course; the instructor is expected to spend 42 hours of contact with the learners. There is no prerequisite to the course. The instructor is given the independence to design the instruction based on the objective that the course components will assist the school head in school management.

Similar to other courses, an ICT in Educational Management course should comprise the basic KSA (knowledge, skills, and attitude) components. Typically, the learners should be able to gain knowledge of the latest ICT tools and systems relevant to their workplace and to develop an understanding about the implementation of the national education ICT policy and the impact of ICT on administration and management. The learners should also be able to synthesize, apply the relevant ICT knowledge, and assess its use to support administration of their schools.

THE PARTICIPANTS

In the case of the first cohort of school heads studying at the UiTM Faculty of Education, there are 28 participants, with an equal number of males and females. The participants' average age is 49.9 years, and they come from different parts of the country. Some travel 7 to 8 hours by bus to the university each week. They attend lectures, engage in discussions, and are involved in various hands-on activities throughout the duration of their courses. They are given access to the Internet in some of the classrooms; they are brought to the computer labs for computer-based tasks. Their English language competencies are varied; a few speak fluent English, while others are of a mediocre level. Most have had more than 25 years of experience as an educator. As primary-school heads, they have a wealth of administrative experience. Each of them manages an average of 45 academic and administrative staff in his or her school. In terms of health, they are generally of good health except for a few cases of hypertensive school heads. They are all Muslims and they belong to the Malay race (Malaysia boasts a multiracial society with Malays accounting for over half the population).

There is the pertinent need to address the characteristics of adult learners, and in doing so, highlight the andragogical characteristics, those that differentiate them from the pedagogical characteristics. Andragogy is basically the art and science of helping adults learn. As they seek to relate content to their lives, adult learners tend to be pragmatic learners. They study to improve their performance in other social roles; they will let their schoolwork take a back seat to other responsibilities, such as jobs and families. Adults depend upon themselves for material support and life management, thus adult learners are often time-conscious learners. Adults carry well-developed personalities and a broad range of life experiences to the learning situation. This reservoir of experience enables the adult learner to better grasp, process, and apply new information.

These characteristics are prominent in the case of the school heads studying in UiTM. Paradoxically, they tend to underestimate their own ability. They raise doubts about their ability to learn new things. In terms of learning approaches, a study by Tan and Pillay (2007) indicated that Malay adult learners who have the intention of acquiring meaningful learning are less likely to adopt a deep approach. Adult learners are also prone to having previous negative educational experiences and need special orientation, counseling, and tutoring. This is not only true for Westerners (Conner et al., 1996) but also for the Malaysian adult learners. Deferment of study often arises from personal problems, financial constraints, lack of encouragement from family, and from poor academic performance.

Despite the various ICT programs organized by the Ministry of Education, most school heads in this case study are novices and are not being sufficiently prepared for new technology. At the onset of the course, some have never heard of Bluetooth technology or seen a Personal Digital Assistant (PDA). In terms of technology ability, only one of the school heads is highly competent. Some possess laptops and are able to use the basic features of a word processor. Two school heads term themselves as "computer illiterates," while another has initial problems using the mouse. Most do not use e-mail; they do not generally employ the Internet for communication purposes or for academic resources without assistance. Some express their concerns, as they find it daunting to learn the various tools in a limited time period. They are required to fill out a technology-skills checklist on the first day of class to gauge their basic skills as a technologically independent user. Figure 2.1 illustrates some of the checklist elements and the number of responses from the participants.

Some have been shying away from technology; they see little need to learn as there will always be "people doing things for them." They are school heads; they see the responsibility of learning new technology to be that of the younger teachers and the administrative staff. This cultural trait is explicated in Strother's (2003) analysis of cross-cultural issues for Asian e-learners based on Hofstede's four cultural dimensions of power-distance, collectivism versus individualism, uncertainty avoidance, and masculinity

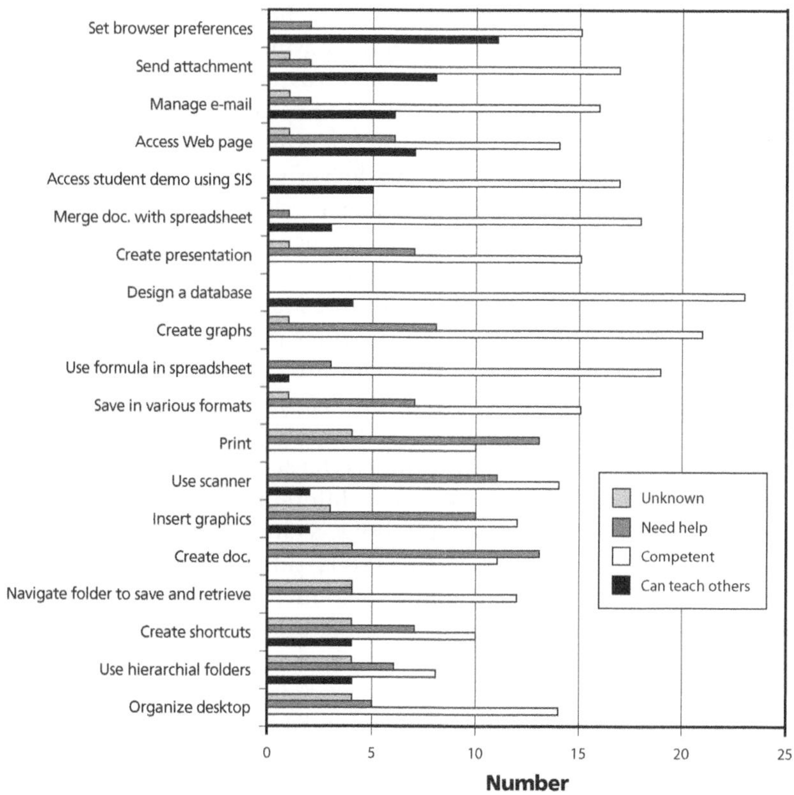

Figure 2.1 Technology skills of the adult learners.

versus femininity (Hofstede's original work includes a fifth dimension of long-term/short-term time orientation). Interestingly, Malaysia ranks first out of 53 nations in the power-distance dimension. This implies a high degree of acceptance that power and authority can be distributed unequally. In relation to this, the school heads have the authority to instruct his or her subordinates to assume the task of acquiring technology skills and putting it to good use in their respective schools. Despite the equal number of males and females in the group, males are appointed to lead the cohort during the different phases.

Another dimension to consider is teacher reverence among Malaysian learners. Ziguras' (2001) examination of the utilization of educational technologies to increase the flexibility of learning in Singapore, Vietnam, and Malaysia is one study to be considered. His site visits, analysis of promotional materials, and semistructured interviews gave an account of the tendencies of Malaysian learners at three higher-education institutions to be "spoon-fed," to expect more direction, and closer supervision from locally available teaching staff, to "not want to be left alone" and to have a high regard for lecturers. These findings signify teacher-centered education with the flow of information considered to be moving from the teacher to the students. Hisham Dzalkiria and Rozhan Idrus (2003) reported that Malaysian adult distance learners needed continuous human contact and the presence of a teacher figure to guide their learning. This notion of teacher as the "expert" giving explanations and delivering the content was also noted by Daing Zaidah, Abu Daud, and Bahaman (2001). Daniel (2001) found adult online learners to perceive their instructor as stimulator, motivator, provider of guidance, disseminator of information, and navigator. This is again supported by Nor Aziah Alias, Ahmad Marzuki Zainudin, and Masitah Hashim (2003), who identified instructor's guidance and leadership as a vital component of the learner-instructor interaction.

Culture plays an eminent role in the learning approach, motivation, and perceptions of an adult learner. As illustrated by Adeoye and Wentling (2006) and Seufert (2002), culture affects the acceptance, use, and impact of technology-based learning systems at different levels and in various dimensions, including pedagogic philosophy, technology access, and student behaviors. Researchers such as McGee (2002) advocated the learning interface for high-power distance community to include structured and expert information presentation, strong use of cultural values, and emphasis on the leader and the expert rather than the user.

Furthermore, similar to learners from a Confucian-heritage culture, Malaysian learners are also achievement oriented and perceive grades as an indication of their competence. The competition to do better than others is very compelling among some school heads. A few express concerns regarding group work. They perceive some of their group members as not contributing and thus not deserving of the same grade. They prefer to be assessed individually as a means to differentiate them from their nonperforming peers. In addition, the pursuit of learning while working is almost always related to job enhancement or upgrade of skills and knowledge that would create better career opportunities. Being a few years away from retirement may dampen their enthusiasm to learn new technologies.

CONCLUSION

The task is to design an adult learning experience that will take into consideration the aforementioned multitude of factors. How best do we design a technology-based course where the older adults can learn about and with technology in a meaningful and less daunting way? There are various instructional design models and theories that have been developed and utilized in numerous circumstances. The onus is upon the designer to identify the essentials needed to design a technology-based learning experience for these nontraditional learners.

DISCUSSION QUESTIONS

1. What are the barriers to professional development in ICT for adult learners like the Malaysian school heads?
2. What issues arise when thinking about an adult learner-centered approach to the learning design of this curriculum?
3. How will the design of this course differ from the normal face-to-face university-level technology course? What alternative approaches to delivering the curriculum for vocational learners such as these school heads could you suggest?
4. What should be the expected learning outcomes of the technology-based course? How should each outcome be assessed?
5. What strategies should be employed in the design of the technology-based course for the adult learners?
    a. How do we bridge the gaps between the existing and required technology skills?
    b. How can learning elements identified as necessary for the adult learners pursuing a technology course be integrated into the learning environment?
    c. What motivational strategies should be employed in the design?

REFERENCES

Alias, N. A., Zainudin, A. M., & Hashim, M. (2003). Learner-instructor online interaction in an e-learning course. *Malaysian Journal of Distance Education, 5*(1) 31–51.

Adeoye, B., & Wentling, R. M. (2007). The relationship between national culture and the usability of an e-learning system. *International Journal on E-Learning, 6*(1), 119–146.

Cave, J., LaMaster, C., & White, S. (1998). *Staff development: Adult characteristics.* LinC Online. Retrieved April 13, 2004, from http://ed.fnal.gov/lincon/staff_adult.shtml

Chan, F. M. (2002). *ICT in Malaysian schools: Policy and strategies.* Retrieved January 28, 2008, from http://unpan1.un.org/intradoc/groups/public/documents/apcity/unpan011288.pdf

Conner, M., Wright, E., Curry, K., DeVries, L., Zeider, C., Wilmsmeyer, D. et al. (1996). *Learning: The critical technology* (2nd ed.). St. Louis, MO: Wave Technologies International.

Daniel, E. G. S. (2001). Participant interaction models and roles in a computer supported collaborative learning (CSCL) environment: A Malaysian case study. *World Conference on Educational Multimedia, Hypermedia and Telecommunications 2001*(1), 355–360.

Dzakiria, H., & Idrus, R. (2003). Teacher-learner interactions in distance education: A case of two Malaysian universities. *Turkish Online Journal of Distance Education, 4*(3) Retrieved March 5, 2004, from http://tojde.anadolu.edu.tr/tojde11/abs/idrus_abs.htm

Ibrahim, D. Z., Silong, A. D., & Abu Samah, B. (2001, October 24–25). *Practices that facilitate learner control in an online environment.* Paper presented at the Workshop on Developing Effective Online Delivery System for Institutions of Higher Learning, Shah Alam, Malaysia.

Imel, S. (1998). *Technology and adult learning.* ERIC Digest No. 197. (ERIC Document Reproduction Service No. ED 421639)

Knowles, M. S. (1990). *The adult learner: A neglected species* (4th ed.). Houston, TX: Gulf Publishing.

McGee, P. (2002). Web-based learning design: Planning for diversity. *USDLA Journal, 16*(3) Retrieved August 14, 2005, from http://www.usdla.org/html/journal/MAR02_Issue/article03.html

Selwyn, N., Gorard, S., & Furlong, J. (2006). *Adult learning in the digital age: Information technology and learning Society.* London: Routledge.

Seufert, S. (2002). Cultural perspectives. In H. H. Adelsberger, B. Collis, & J. M. Pawlowski, (Eds.), *Handbook on information technologies for education and training.* Berlin: Springer-Verlag.

Strother, J. (2003). Cross-cultural issues for Asian e-learners: An analysis based on Hofstede's cultural dimensions. *World Conference on E-Learning in Corporate, Government, Health & Higher Education, (1),* 1978–1984.

Tan, P. L., & Pillay, H. (2007). Understanding the learning behaviour of Malaysian adult learners: A cross cultural sensitive framework. *Education Research for Policy and Practice, 6*(2). Retrieved April 15, 2008, from http://dx.doi.org/10.1007/s10671-007-9039-5

Ziguras, C. (2001). Educational technology in transnational higher education in South East Asia: The cultural politics of flexible learning. *Educational Technology & Society, 4*(4) 8–18.

CHAPTER 3

COPYCATS OF THE CENTRAL HIMALAYAS

Learning in the Age of Information

Payal Arora
Erasmus University Rotterdam, The Netherlands

CASE DESCRIPTION

Background

Uttarakhand (previously called Uttaranchal), Central Himalayas, has become synonymous with spiritual exploration and learning, of *sadhus* and *swamis* for disciples here and abroad. While thousands of pilgrims flock yearly to this area in search of spiritual learning, another wave of pilgrims has been coming here for its more institutionalized learning—that of its schools and universities. In recent years however, there has been a migration of youth to the neighboring cities such as Delhi (Sati & Sati, 2000) for higher education. This has been primarily attributed to the dearth of high-end technologies within Uttarakhand's higher institutions, seen as failing to meet the needs of the current generation for relevant IT skills. In the last 3 years, the new state of Uttarakhand has sought to reinvent itself through

Cases 'n' Places: Global Cases in Educational and Performance Technology, pages 49–30

high-end technologies, putting itself on the fast track to e-readiness (Uttarakhand E-Gov). In particular, it has launched an ambitious project of disseminating computers to all intercolleges in its state (11th and 12th standard) as a means to reclaim its reputation by leading India in e-learning. With 45% of its population below 25 years of age, a critical need is felt to reshape its schooling in order to equip the students with skills appropriate for this new information and global age.

Some investigation has been done on problems arising from such digital initiatives including, but not limited to, issues of connectivity, teacher training, electricity, software and hardware access and design, maintenance, and more (Arora, 2006; Warschauer, 2003). Rather than follow the path of institutional and technical limitations on learning, this case study takes the approach of exploring how students *do* learn with computers and the Internet in its current capacity, in particular at cybercafés around these institutions. The rationale is that by looking at their interactivity with the Internet *outside* school settings, much can be learned about how youth actually engage with human and online resources to fulfill academic needs. Particularly, this case study highlights the sociocultural scenario within which acts that are deemed as plagiarism come about. This compels a resituating of computers from being an inherently positive intervention to being another technical tool with which a range of learning takes place. In doing so, we take this opportunity to address how we can capitalize on such practices to bring about genuine learning. Further, the range and type of online content being utilized becomes explicit as well as ways in which students go about instructing each other and themselves on such resources for academic projects.

Through an ethnographic investigation of such practices, the researcher brings to light the ingenuities of learning in the act of plagiarism within such novel afterschool spaces, particularly in information access and usage for schooling endeavors. Through action-research, participant observations and interviews, the researcher has been able to unearth prime issues of plagiarism beyond the morality aspect: gender usage of the Internet, social learning, and information-seeking as students navigate, cut, and paste online material and make it their own. Through interviews with teachers and students in their school settings, much is revealed in the juxtaposition of institutional expectations and perceptions of plagiarism and originality in academic endeavors.

Educational Institutions and ICT: Overarching Issues

Computers have arrived in all higher educational institutions in Almora. However, on average, the ratio is 2–3 students per computer with access to computers for 45 minutes per week on average in government schools, while in private schools it is per day. In spite of that, both government and private institutions emphasize the gaining of computer skills, particularly the Microsoft package of Word, Excel, and PowerPoint, as well as the usage of Encarta, an offline Encyclopedia CD-ROM for educational use given the offline status of most schools in the region. All computer classes are in English, and instruction in higher education is typically in English, even though the main languages of the region are Hindi and Pahadi. Further, while some homes in Almora town have computers, the absence of broadband facility coupled with lack of privacy drives students to cybercafés.

Having held focus groups with teachers in both government and private schools, it is clear that most teachers are aware of the plagiarism that goes on with the Internet, with some perceiving it to be a problem and others not necessarily seeing it as an issue to contend with. Even among those who are concerned, this does not evoke urgency for change and may even be seen as a necessity to get through the educational system. This is attributed to a combination of factors, namely the following:

1. State exam syllabus requires rote memorization and reproduction of enormous amounts of material with a focus on multiple choice questions over essay format for standardization on evaluation.
2. The dearth of quality and updated library resources available for students, particularly in English, compelling students to seek elsewhere for academic material.
3. Overburdened and often underqualified faculty at the universities. With higher education instruction in English, and the local and first language of students *and* teachers being either Pahadi or Hindi, desperation sets in to succeed in getting these projects right for higher marks. This leads to the seeking of material and assistance to complete projects the correct way, grammatically, stylistically, and the like, while teachers either turn a blind eye or become accomplices in this process.
4. Students often collaborate on their individual assignments given the limited computer resources available. This results in the sharing of material and ideas for academic projects. (Satyanarayana & Babu, 2008; Tiffin & Rajasingham, 1995)

Hayes, Whitley, and Introna (2006) sum up succinctly the prime issues regarding plagiarism within the Indian Higher Education System:

> The standardized syllabus taught to large numbers of students over large numbers of years also means that it becomes worthwhile for entrepreneurial students and teachers to write and publish "guide books," which cover all the topics for a particular course. These books are frequently available from university copy shops or markets and are, essentially, the key ideas from the

> course and its texts, presented in a simplified format and frequently (though not always) without attribution of where the original concepts came from. In addition, as the intention is to provide students from any college with the knowledge that they require in order to be able to answer the examination, they often focus on a conservative, uncritical approach to the subject (p. 1731).

A focus-group interview conducted by the researcher (R) with the principle (P) and her staff (T1 and T2) of an intercollege in the Almora area reflects the general understanding of those concerned with the intervention of computers in education and plagiarism in academia in particular.

> **P:** The computer has invaded our life . . . What I am concerned about is the impact . . . how they waste away their time on the Internet and do nothing useful educationally.
>
> **R:** Do you monitor them?
>
> **T1:** They are not doing it here [school] . . . it's all happening in these cybercafés. They stay there for hours and god knows what they do.
>
> **T2:** Sincerely, they use computers when they have to do projects.
>
> **T2:** As an information device, they are using it very well, but as far as integrating it into their studies, I don't think they are using it well at all . . . what they are basically doing is getting the information, getting the printout, compiling it, and of course, sometimes they have to get some sampling.
>
> **R:** Do you think they are creating any original work?
>
> **T1:** No, no, no . . . they are compiling it, they are editing it, they are doing some work of their own but that is very, very rare. They are producing the information that is already there.
>
> **T2:** It is not possible the way they are working . . . they are not producing anything new.
>
> **P:** They have become very good *copycats* [emphasis added] . . . that they do very well, but if you say do something on your own, they do not know what to do . . . original work is missing.
>
> **T2:** Say if our assignment is the use of various plants in Kumaon and its medicinal uses . . . they will take something from here and something from there and then here and then they just print and attach it and give it to us
>
> **R:** So how do you change this?
>
> **T1:** If we chose something rare then they will give us something of their own because they can't get it from the Internet.
>
> **T2:** Use of computers is not there except for typing purposes—they just put some visuals and text and then give it to us.

P: One day they will be in the global place in the world and they will have to learn the hard way... we will not be there to tell them to get curious and be original; it has to come from them... they need to be motivated to do something creative.

Cybercafés: The New Afterschool?

This case study takes place in Almora, a relatively recently developed area partly attributed to the strong infusion of local computer-based services and government initiatives to digitally connect this district. In the last year alone, broadband entered this area, stimulating the growth of cybercafés from around 4 to 20 and growing, students being their prime clientele besides tourists. For less than a dollar per hour, students come here to work, ranging from accessing information/visuals for school projects, getting their thesis typed (primarily in English), and discussing their projects, to applying for further education online. In interviews with cybercafé owners and managers, it is apparent that students are one of their prime sources of income, but it comes at a price. Students take over cybercafés, ask question, and demand constant and continued assistance, disrupting all other activity within these cafés that barely have standing room but for the space for two to three computers and a printer/fax machine.

Further, students come in pairs or groups but rarely alone. So at any given point in time, each computer is used by 2–3 students, often seen dictating their needs to one among them or a cybercafé staff sitting at the keyboard. The researcher herself volunteered to work as staff, given the space constraints, and for the opportunity to be *instructed* on the range of learning that takes place within such computer-mediated spaces. Interestingly, given that cybercafés are a relatively recent phenomenon, the owners themselves are facing a learning curve with the Internet, discovering its potential and usage from a range of actors, including IT crash courses, foreign tourists, friends, and the students themselves.

Discovering the Internet for Academia

Given the intense competition among the cybercafés, the owners become highly attuned to the needs of their clients, particularly students, and share online sites with them that can enable their projects. They gain favor with students by providing a package of services, including typing of their theses and other academic assignments, searching for information for their projects, organizing disparate information to form a cohesive thesis, formulating cover pages, searching for appropriate visuals to go in tandem with the text, and providing advice on the fonts, layouts, and print quality of the assignments. This is at little extra cost to the students as the staff labor comes practically for free with Internet time.

Surveying the past history of Web links over a month, alongside observations and informal interviews with students and cybercafé owners, reveals Google, Wikipedia, and Orkut (by far the most popular site among students) as the most frequented sites among students. Curiosity and entertainment are the chief reasons that draw students to these sites, and over time such sites are used for academic purposes.

As one student puts it, "with broadband, it is fun to browse... we can see what a tiger looks like on the computer like say, you type tiger and then the photos of a tiger appear; then you type Chicago and then photos of Chicago appear." Even the reluctant users come there to do their assignments because "nowadays everything is on the Internet, there is no choice."

The Instructed and the Instructing

The researcher, by becoming a temporary staff for a period of a month, was exposed to a range of projects accomplished in this space that adhered to school requirements and the range of strategies employed to fulfill these tasks. Assignments started from as simple as getting a cybercafé staff person to type a student's thesis directly from a printed textbook with no paraphrasing but citations included in the bibliography, to the more complex orchestration of multiple texts from multiple sources. Here, both print and online resources are used with entire paragraphs and pages highlighted, marked, with subheadings created to ease transitions from texts of one source to another with no acknowledgement of the authors.

There was never an instance during this period where a student chose to type directly the assignment given. Instead, they took on the role of supervisor and manager, overseeing the execution of the tasks by the cybercafé staff. Further, there was no discussion on whether these acts of plagiarism were permissible for school projects as they went about eliminating traces of the authored sources deliberately and efficiently. In fact, some acts of plagiarism were performed openly and collaboratively as a joint effort among the staff and students to successfully complete the assignment given.

Below are three distinct plagiarism cases where students along with the cybercafé staff harness the resources at hand to create and complete their projects. Rather than preoccupy oneself with these cases through the lens of academic dishonesty, one should pay attention to the actual process of accomplishing such acts of copying "patchwriting" (Howard, 1993) and tailoring—the relationship between the actors involved in this process, the discourse that shapes such acts, and the kinds of content and resources employed. In doing so, one should simultaneously center one's own perceptions of what constitutes plagiarism to gain a deeper understanding of such practices across sociocultural terrains.

Case 1

A girl (G) looms over a male staff (S) from the cybercafé as he gets instructed by her to copy the printed text highlighted from the *Great British Poets* onto Word for her assignment on "The Critique of Poetry." She stands while he sits and types at the keyboard. Her friend is talking on the cell phone by her side.

G: These words are not right, correct it... here, now separate this, these words are joint see [she remarks as he types onto Word]
S: Yes, but I will do that later
G: No, no, do it now or you will forget... god why are you making this so big?... ooh why are you... nothing... okay continue [exasperated about the font]
S: I'll go ahead then?
S: Ah, okay fine... array, I'll beat you... stop showing me the same photos for this... okay the one you showed me earlier will do... don't waste time now. [She finalizes on an English countryside image from Google to compliment her text]

Case 2

Two girls (G1 & G2) are at the computer trying to figure out how to access some "good Western artists" from the Internet for their midterm art history project. At this point, their art history teacher (T) enters the cybercafé. The girls wave him over.

G1: I couldn't find good Western artists, sir.
T: What is Van Gogh do you know?
G2: He's a painter
T: Of? Oh, I mean which village he is from?
G2: I don't know... from Europe?
T: So put both his name and his village in Google and search then you'll find something more.

Having stated this, the teacher heads to the printer to make copies for the next class assignment.

Case 3

Take the second-year biology student with a project to document animals of the region, their behavior patterns, and their habitats. He comes in and informs the owner of his assignment. The owner instructs his assistant to get to work. The student sits next to the staff member and quietly watches him as he opens the browser and gets onto the English version of the Wikipedia site. He enters "elephant" in the search section. He highlights the results by selecting all the data, then copies and pastes it onto a Word document. He proceeds to another animal. The cybercafé owner comes by and asks the student if he has any restrictions on page printouts and the number of documented animals. The student shares more details of the assignment, stipulating the limits as well as his budget on printing. Based on the given information, the owner (O) instructs the assistant (A) in front of the student (S):

> **O:** Just copy the text, not the visuals and just the first paragraph of each section of these animals from Wikipedia... you should pay more attention when copying.
>
> **O:** Save some time by not copying all the text—just copy what he [S] asks for.
>
> **A:** But sir, I was going to get rid of it anyway afterwards.
>
> **O:** What's the point... unnecessarily wasting time. Do Control C... why are you going to "Edit"?
>
> **S:** I want different... some new animals for my project... not the same one as the others.
>
> **O (to A):** Er... and make sure that you erase all signs of Wikipedia from the document... understood?

The staff member asks the student what other animals he wants besides "elephant" and "monkey" in his project sheet, but the biology student doesn't seem to come up with any names at the spur of the moment in English. Even the assistant appears to not know but is not fazed by the fact. He goes to Google and types "animals," and from that scrolls all the way down to "animal list" and clicks on that. The list however appears to be too difficult and exotic to understand as they both read through the list and struggle with "parma wallaby" and "coyote" as potential candidates. He goes back to the Google search and selects the next choice, ironically from Wikipedia itself, under "list of animal names." He clicks on that link. The student approves of the list and from that the assistant chooses "panda" and "squirrel" to enter into the Wikipedia search for further copying and pasting.

Moral Hazard or Strategies for the 21st Century?

Plagiarism as an issue has been written and discussed about extensively, particularly in the West. The dominant lens through which this is looked upon is through that of morality: that of "academic dishonesty," the "moral hazard" in education, an "epidemic" of sweeping proportion that needs to be "combated" (Gerhardt, 2006; Miall, 2005). Some go beyond condemnation to that of cultural understanding. The argument here is that diverse cultures, be it Indian to Chinese, come with ancient schooling practices that uses repetition as a pedagogic style to deepen understanding. Further, Asian cultures are seen as often being unaware of their actions when it comes to what is seen as plagiaristic acts (Introna, Hayes, Blair, & Wood, 2003). There is also an economic angle given where the opportunity cost of attending higher education, particularly in developing countries, creates tremendous pressure for students to perform and excel, even at the cost of their academic integrity (Pennycook, 1996).

However, in this frenzy to situate, condemn, or rationalize what constitutes plagiarism, the enormous accomplishment of computer and Internet usage by a relatively nascent group of IT users in a small town in a developing world gets overlooked. The sophistication and strategizing of such practices come in to play as students learn to draw upon the multiple resources available to them—technical, human, and sociocultural—and thereby exercise their authority over the authored. While this is not to romanticize such acts of copying, this case study provides a forum to unearth some key assumptions and common relationships of ideas moving beyond the act of plagiarism itself:

1. Plagiarism as more than just an issue of academic integrity and morality;
2. Gender marginalization and computer usage;
3. Direct versus indirect usage of computers and online learning;
4. Information seeking and knowledge through new technologies;
5. Formal versus nonformal computer-mediated spaces and online learning.

DISCUSSION QUESTIONS

This case is designed to compel the reader to reexamine the kinds of learning that emerge in such settings as demonstrated in the three cases and how it figures into the kinds of skills seen as necessary to succeed in this information age. Therefore, key guiding questions for this case study center around one prime question: What kinds of learning take place through the act of plagiarism and how can this be harnessed for academic purposes?

REFERENCES

Arora, P. (2006). The ICT laboratory: An analysis of computers in public high schools in rural India. *Association of Advancement in Computing in Education, 15*, 57–72.

Gerhardt, D. R. (2006). Plagiarism in cyberspace: Learning the rules of recycling content with a view towards nurturing academic trust in an electronic world. *Richmond Journal of Law & Technology, 12*(3).

Hayes, N., Whitley, E. A., & Introna, L. D. (2006). *Power, knowledge and management information systems education. The case of the Indian Learner.* Conference Paper, Twenty-Seventh International Conference on Information Systems, Milwaukee. Retrieved on September 29, 2009 from Website: http://personal.lse.ac.uk/whitley/allpubs/ICIS2006.pdf

Howard, R. M. (1993). A plagiarism pentimento. *Journal of Teaching Writing, 11*, 233–246.

Miall, C. (2005). Combating 'cut n paste' culture: The impact of new media technologies on plagiarism. In P. Kommers & G. Richards (Eds.), *Proceedings of World Conference on Educational Multimedia, Hypermedia and Telecommunications 2005* (pp. 2918–2923). Montreal, Canada.

Pennycook, A. (1996). Borrowing others' words: Text, ownership, memory, and plagiarism. *TESOL quarterly, 30*(2), 201–230.

Sati, M. C., & Sati, S. P. (2000). *Uttarakhand statehood: Dimensions of development,* New Delhi: Indus Publishing Company.

Satyanarayana, K. V., & Babu, R. B. (2008). Trends in the development of e-theses in India: Issues, constraints, and solutions. *Tata Research Development & Design Centre, Tata Consultancy Services Ltd.* In Proceedings of Tenth International Symposium on Electronic Theses and Dissertations, Uppsala, Sweden.

Tiffin, J., & Rajasingham, L. (1995). *In search of the virtual class: Education in an information society.* London and New York: Routledge.

Warschauer, M. (2003). *Technology and social inclusion: Rethinking the digital divide.* Cambridge: MIT Press.

CHAPTER 4

HEALTH SCIENCES CASE STUDY

Judi Baron and Lesley Steele
The University of Adelaide, Australia

Sausan Al Kawas
University of Sharjah, United Arab Emirates

INTRODUCTION

As an educational technology student, one of your learning objectives is to consider the learning design issues of an online role-play simulation, also referred to as a Web-based electronic simulation (e-Sim). The following Health Sciences Case Study illustrates how an online learning management system (LMS)—Blackboard, Moodle, Vista, Desire2Learn—can be used to deliver a role play within education. The methodology is constructivist, experiential, and authentic.

DISCUSSION QUESTIONS

In Table 4.1, the LMS design framework is provided to allow you to consider some of the educational technology aspects of the online role-play simula-

Cases 'n' Places: Global Cases in Educational and Performance Technology, pages 59–46

TABLE 4.1 Online Role-Play LMS Design Framework for Educational Technology Students

Features to be activated	Stage	Comments
Content, e.g., Briefing Pack, Role Profiles, Resources, including external links	1	Subject Matter Experts (SMEs) are critical to the development of a role play in order for ET to design and build the online environment. This is best achieved using project management principles under the guidance of a project manager. SMEs can collaborate on the content development via a wiki. The wiki can document both the content development, i.e., Briefing Pack and the process. The Health Sciences Case Study is an example of the type of content in an online Briefing Pack.
Multimedia, e.g., audio and video resources, persona photographs, course banners, logos, graphics, and icons	1	Copyright issues, e.g., photographs, need to be addressed and where necessary permissions in writing granted. Accessibility issues need to be considered with regard to audio and video downloads and options provided, e.g., mp3, 56K modem, broadband. Course banners need to be tested on multiple browsers and various desktop settings.
Persona logins and e-mail	2	There may be Lightweight Directory Access Protocol (LDAP) issues. ET may need to liaise with Information Technology (IT) with regard to the creation of persona logins to the LMS, i.e., usernames, passwords, and e-mail accounts. Each persona will have its own discrete login and e-mail account, even when/if there are multiple users allocated to one persona, e.g., username GovtDent01, GovtDent02, GovtDent03, with different passwords and e-mail accounts. This is important in order to keep the real identity of each person anonymous and to more effectively immerse the individual in their role.
User Tracking and Course Statistics	2	Most features of an LMS allow for user tracking of logins and access to content. This can include date and time of access and allows the teacher to track progress and evaluate the role play activities.
Adaptive Release	2	Each persona has a role profile. This is usually a public profile, which other personas can also view. In some role plays there is also a private profile only viewable by the persona concerned. Adaptive release is required to ensure that the private profile is kept private. In other cases, participants may be required to undertake a start-up quiz before certain information is released. It is possible to have multiple public inquiries occurring using the

Features to be activated	Stage	Comments
		adaptive release feature where there are large class sizes, e.g., discrete discussion-board forums for each public inquiry via the adaptive release feature.
Announcements, News Releases	3	Regular announcements or news items are common in online role plays. Some LMS allow for announcements that link to specific parts of the online course as well as automatic e-mail simultaneously.
Groups	3	The group feature of an LMS allows for multiple users of each persona to have their own private area with discussion boards, e-mail, and file transfer. This allows for multiple users of the one persona to work together and formulate one response only to the various class-level activities, e.g., public inquiry submission.
Discussion Board forums	3	Class-level forums and threads need to be created, ideally by the decision-making persona (e.g. the Dental Board), who is usually the teacher or facilitator of the online role play. Some LMS allow for grading of DB threads. Forums can be set up ahead of time and made available and unavailable on predetermined dates. Forums have the ability to collect threads and sort and search on keywords. Some LMS allow for grading of threads with an automatic entry into gradebook.
Assessment and Survey Tools	3	Computer-generated feedback on online quizzes is a useful feature of online role plays. Quizzes can be incorporated to test a user's understanding of the case study before the interaction stage commences. Adaptive release can be used to ensure that users obtain a minimum mark before being allowed to proceed. Online surveys or evaluation tools provide a vehicle for debriefing, which is an important feature of online role plays. Assignments, such as debrief reports, can be submitted electronically. These submissions can be viewed and downloaded, or electronic qualitative feedback provided via a gradebook feature of the LMS.

tion. As you read through the simulation, keep the following in mind: How can the online role-play simulation be improved? How can Web 2.0 tools be used?

The following pages contain a set of instructions given to one role player in the simulation.

SCENARIO

One of the materials for repairing various damaged or diseased teeth is dental amalgam (Figure 4.1), which comprises an alloy of metals and mercury.

The use of dental amalgam is a controversial topic at present, both in the Middle East and worldwide. Dental professionals, public health and environmental experts are presented with developing policies to meet industry and public health standards. There are multiple perspectives to this issue, including the effects of the constituents of amalgam on the human body and the impact of amalgam disposal and waste by-products on the environment.

The Ministry of Health in the United Arab Emirates (UAE) has requested the Dental Board to provide an evidence-based opinion on the use of dental amalgam. The Dental Board in turn decides to make this a public inquiry and invites opinions from various people, including government and private dentists, dental specialists, lawyers, public health officials, government officials, pharmaceutical representatives, consumer representatives, as well as patients and parents of child patients. Members of the press are also invited to inform the scenario participants about the latest developments and reports from media sources in the area of dental amalgam.

Your role is to consider the issues from one of these perspectives (not necessarily your own). Importantly, you will also need to consider other perspectives that may influence your position. You will have an opportunity at the end of the case study to reflect on your role perspective and how it does or does not mirror your personal views.

Although dental amalgam is used extensively in most countries as a routine part of restorative dentistry, its use is increasingly being prohibited. However, dental amalgam's longevity as a restorative material and the global migration of people with amalgam fillings make this a long-term issue for

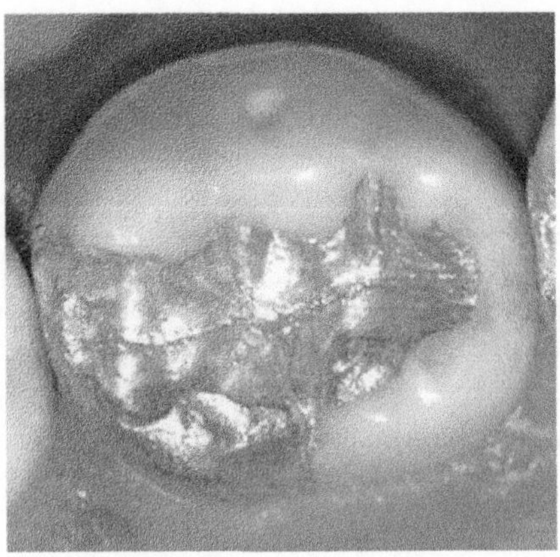

Figure 4.1 Amalgam as tooth filling.

today's dental practitioners in any country. In order to make an informed decision on whether or not amalgam should be used for restorative purposes, you first need to have an understanding of what amalgam is, its mechanical properties, and its suitability as a restorative material. You will then be in a better position to consider the advantages and disadvantages of the use of amalgam in the dental clinic environment.

YOUR ROLE: GOVERNMENT DENTIST

You have been allocated the role of a [Government Dentist]. You are an Ajman 2005 graduate with a Bachelor of Dental Surgery. You have a strong interest in community dentistry, fluoride, and caries levels in the public-sector population. Your experience is with primary dental care and complex treatment plans.

OTHER ROLES

There are 10 other roles: Private Dentist, Restorative Specialist, Adult Patient, Parent of Child Patient, Lawyer, Journalist, Government Official, Consumer Representative, Public Health Official, and Dental Representative. You need to consider whether you want to form a potential alliance with any of these other roles, which are described in detail below.

Private Dentist

The Private Dentist is an Ajman graduate with a Doctor of Dental Surgery (DDS) degree in 2001. This person works part-time in a busy practice at Corniche Road. Most of the patients are highly aesthetically orientated, with an interest in white fillings. The Private Dentist is also a part-time lecturer at the College of Dentistry, University of Sharjah, and requires current knowledge of dental materials and evidence-based practice.

Restorative Specialist

The Restorative Specialist is a United Kingdom graduate from Kings College, London, with a MDS degree in Prosthodontics, completed in 1986, and a PhD in amalgam dental materials in 1990. This person has a particular interest in aesthetic dentistry and has vast clinical experience and knowledge in dental materials. The Restorative Specialist has a professorial appointment at the Department of Restorative Dentistry, Louisville, Kentucky. In addition, the Restorative Specialist is co-editor of the British Dental Journal, an active member of the British Society for the Study of Dental Materials, and a Fellow of the Royal College of Dental Surgeons.

Adult Patient

The Adult Patient was born in 1975 in Sharjah, UAE. The Adult Patient finished studies in Marketing at the American University of Sharjah in 2003 and is currently working as a Sales Manager at BMW car sales in Sharjah. The Adult Patient's position on the use of amalgam is influenced by the informed recommendations of his dentist.

Parent of Child Patient

This person is the parent of a five-year-old child. The child has particular problems with cleaning her teeth and has a regular intake of sweets. The parent has attended a dental clinic and is particularly concerned about the filling material used on the child. The Parent's position on the use of amalgam is influenced by the informed recommendations of the child's dentist.

Lawyer

The Lawyer is a graduate of the University of Sharjah, School of Law 2001, and is currently completing a PhD at the University of Sharjah. The title of the thesis is *Human Rights and the Impact on Public Health.* The Lawyer currently works with the Municipality of Sharjah on policy development and public health strategy.

Journalist

The Journalist is a Health opinion writer for Sharjah News, a weekly newspaper that has a special section once a month called *What's New in Health in Sharjah.* The Journalist graduated from Damascus University, School of Journalism in 1993, and in 2005 received an award from the UAE Ministry of Health for excellence in journalism.

Government Official

The Government Official is convenor of the last review into public health safety and dentistry in UAE in 2000. The Government Official has written guidelines for the use of hazardous materials in the health area. The Government Official advises the Ministry of Health on international trends in health and is a very influential person, with many colleagues who hold important positions in the government.

Consumer Representative

The Consumer Representative is a retired person who lives in the Aged Care Facility, University City, at Sharjah. This person is a very astute and respected member of the UAE community.

Public Health Official

The Public Health Official is currently employed as a Senior Policy Writer for the Ministry of Health, Sharjah. This person is an advocate for environmental health issues in the dental industry. The Public Health Official has been involved in developing strict guidelines for public health waste management and is often called on to present at forums with scientists and academics. They also address queries from other officials in public health as well as the public and are required to defend public policy to the community and other departments.

Dental Representative

The Dental Representative currently works for Dentoworld, a global company that specializes in selling dental materials and products called Easyfix Dental. Dentoworld has developed its own amalgam, glass ionomer cement, and composite-resin range of materials. The company is the leading dental seller to private practice in the Gulf region. The Dental Representative is often required to answer concerns and queries from dentists about the safety of Dentoworld's products, the current materials available, and their comparability.

You will need to use your communication skills to interact with these representative groups with an interest in oral health, as well as your research skills and strategies to enable well-informed dental decisions. You will do this via an online role play.

ONLINE ROLE PLAY: THE DENTAL AMALGAM E-SIM

The Public Inquiry into the use of amalgam takes place in an online environment called The Dental Amalgam e-Sim. (e-Sim stands for electronic simulation). All resources and communications and final submissions to the Dental Board from each of the 10 roles take place within an online learning management system (LMS). You are provided with your own unique login username and password, and once you commence the online role play, you leave your own identity behind and assume the role of the persona of a [Government Dentist]. There are various elements to the online role play as outlined in Figure 4.2.

There are four main stages to the online role play: (a) Briefing, (b) Interaction, (c) Public Inquiry, and (d) Debriefing, as outlined in Figure 4.3.

You are given 3 weeks to complete the online role play, with an average of 3 to 5 hours per week, 9 to 15 hours in total. There are no scheduled times that you need to take part in the role play interactions, although there will be various submission deadlines. Resources, including journal articles and audio interviews with a dental specialist, will be released on a week-by-week basis. You are advised to log in and check the online role play for announcements and postings regularly, at least every second day. Communication with other roles and with the Dental Board is via discussion-board forums. There is a forum dedicated to the Sharjah News' health section, where letters to the editor can be posted and where news releases will be added. You can also communicate privately with other roles via e-mail. Anonymity is important. Do not reveal your true identity to other participants!

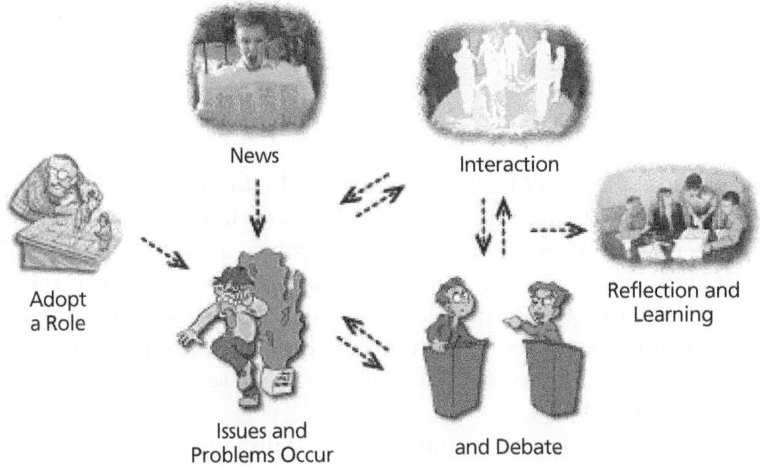

Figure 4.2 What happens in online role play. *Source:* Adapted from an illustration by Allan Carrington © 2004 University of Adelaide.

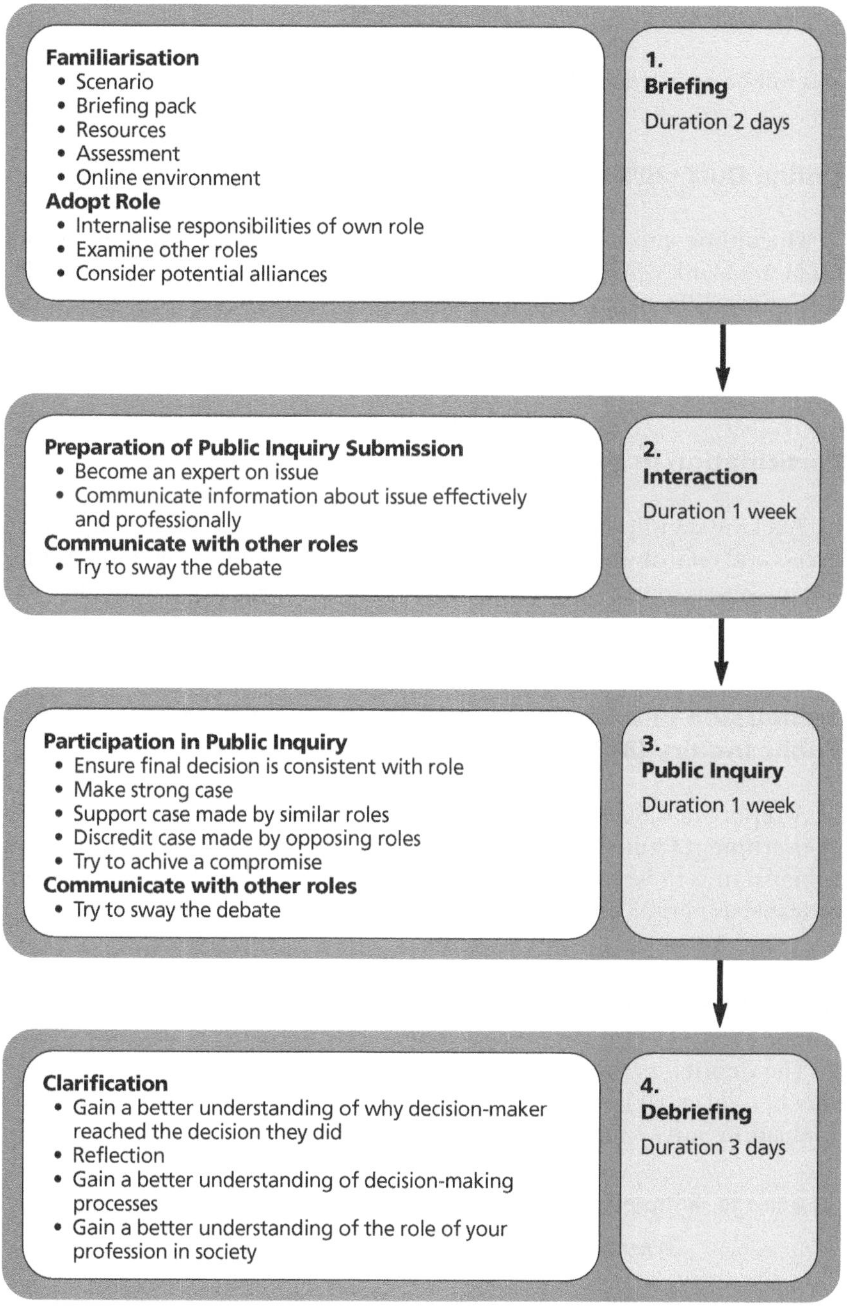

Figure 4.3 Stages of Online Role play. *Source:* Adaption of schema, Holger Maier ©2004 University of Adelaide.

ASSESSMENT

You will be assessed as follows:

Online Quiz (20%)

The online quiz will include multiple choice, true/false, matching, and fill-in-the-blank type questions. Your score will be generated automatically. The quiz will incorporate theoretical questions about amalgam and its use for restorative purposes, including the advantages and disadvantages. An example of the type of question is shown in Figure 4.4.

Participation in Discussion Board Forums (30%)

Tracking statistics enable the online facilitator to monitor your individual access and contributions to the discussion-board forums. More importantly, the quality of your contributions will also be assessed. Remember that you are to assume the role of a [Government Dentist].

Submission of a Final Report to the Dental Board Public Inquiry (30%)

A report of 1,500 to 2,000 words from the viewpoint of your role as a [Government Dentist] must be uploaded to the Public Inquiry Forum. This submission is to be in report format. Assessment criteria for the report are available as part of your Resources.

Submission of a Debrief Evaluation (20%)

The debrief is from your own personal perspective after the final decision of the Dental Board is released. The debrief is in the form of an online Evaluation Survey and is private between you and your lecturer.

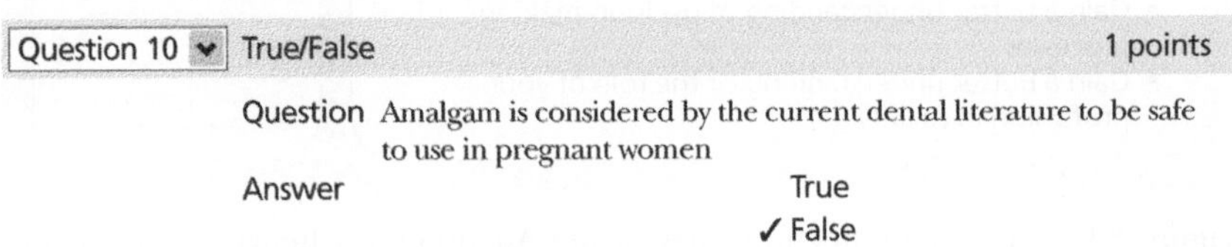
Question 10 True/False 1 points

Question Amalgam is considered by the current dental literature to be safe to use in pregnant women

Answer True

✓ False

Figure 4.4 Example of an online quiz question.

STEPPING THROUGH WEEKS 1–3

Week 1

Step 1

Log in to the Dental Amalgam e-Sim using your unique username and password provided to you. You will see the following Welcome page (Figure 4.5).

Browse through the various features, including Announcements, Briefing Pack, Role Profiles, Resources, and Discussion Board forums. The Quiz and the Evaluation will not be active until later in the role play. Resources will be released weekly. The features will be similar to those in Figure 4.6.

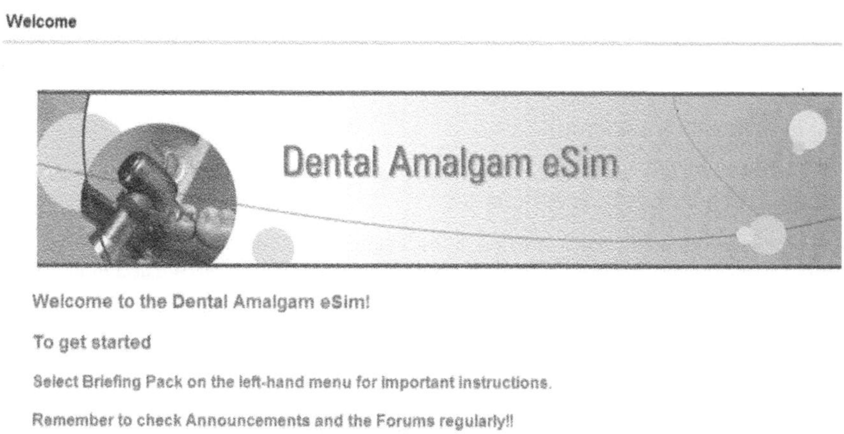

Figure 4.5 Example of a Welcome screen.

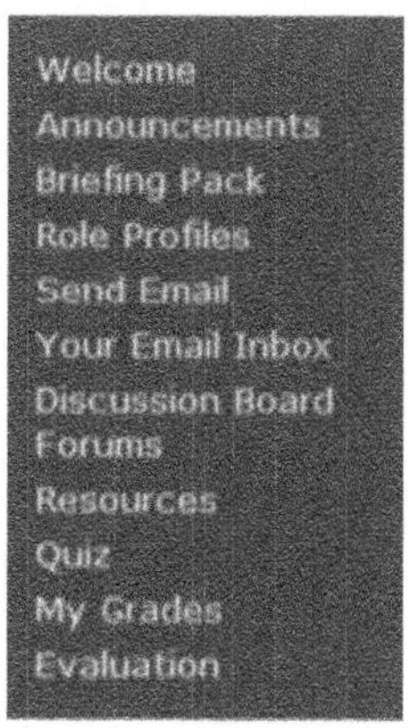

Figure 4.6 Example of Dental Amalgam e-Sim features.

Step 2

The next step is to choose your role and clarify your required input into the Dental Amalgam e-Sim.

Step 3

Introduce yourself as a [Government Dentist] to other role players by making a posting on the Class forum. Figure 4.7 is an example.

Step 4

So that you can develop an understanding of amalgam, its mechanical properties, and suitability as a restorative material, Week 1 Resources are provided. However, you are strongly encouraged to research other information via the Internet and other resources such as journal articles and periodicals. Check out the Press forum for news articles by the Journalist and Letters to the Editor. You can also send letters to the editor for consideration via e-mail. You can request anonymity if you wish.

Resources include audio interviews and transcripts with a Dental Specialist. Figure 4.8 is an example.

Subject: Hi from the Government Dentist   Reply | Modify | Remove

Hi I am a Government Dentist working at the Sharjah Dental Hospital. I have a strong interest in community dentistry. Most of my work is with basic dental care and treatment plans. This includes the use of amalgam for restorative purposes. My clients are both adults and children. I am looking forward to contributing to the Public Inquiry and to the interactions with the other roles in order to help me become better informed on the multiple perspectives of this important issue.

Figure 4.7 Example of an introductory discussion board posting.

Interview 1 - Listen to Associate Professor John Abbott speak about amalgam

01 Mechanical Properties (421.136 Kb)
02 How has composition changed over recent years (1.999 Mb)
03 What has been the rationale for modifications (831.34 Kb)
04 What are the clinical indications for amalgam to be used... (608.892 Kb)
05 In what circumstances would you never use amalgam (527.386 Kb)
06 What is the best practice in the management of safe use... (2.171 Mb)
07 Is amalgam cost-effective compared to other materials (631.213 Kb)
08 What are the main clinical impediments... (690.203 Kb)
09 What are the considerations when placing liners and bases... (973.305 Kb)
10 What is precipitation hardening and how... (232.615 Kb)
11 What is gallium and how has it been used (315.651 Kb)
12 What is amalgam bonding; is it effective; and could you describe... (1.193 Mb)
13 When would you use amalgam bonding... (225.346 Kb)
14 What is creep of amalgam and how... (374.197 Kb)
15 What are the dimensional changes that occur... (618.458 Kb)
16 What is micro-leakage and how does... (941.417 Kb)

Q01 to Q16 ***Transcript*** *(12 pages)* (434 Kb)

Figure 4.8 An example of audio interviews and transcripts within resources.

An excerpt from the audio transcript is as follows:

Q: What are the mechanical properties of dental amalgam that lead to clinical longevity?

Prof. Abbott: Generally, we would be looking at properties such as strength, and the main one would be compressive strength. That's because, obviously, in occlusion, the amalgam may come under functional loads. The other mechanical property would be tensile strength, and may be in lateral movements—chewing actions—this would also come into play. Another mechanical property would be that of creep. Creep is what happens to a material when it's placed under load. It tends to basically deform. The material starts to move out of the cavity, and where it moves away from the walls of the cavity, fractures can occur. Another property of amalgam, which is not necessarily a mechanical property, is one of corrosion. In the mouth, which is a very good environment for corrosion, we find that the amalgam can start to develop stress corrosion cracking, so that as the material is corroding, fine margins tend to break off.

Step 5

From the perspective of your role, begin to develop an informed opinion on the use of dental amalgam for clinical purposes.

If you have any comments to make, do so on the Press Forum, or send a letter to the editor to be published.

Step 6

Write the first draft of your submission to the Dental Board Public Inquiry and post your initial thoughts on the class forum.

After your first post, view other role players' submissions and consider developing an affiliation with one or more roles. You can liaise privately via the e-mail feature. Consider interacting with other roles by commenting on their initial submissions, querying their position, asking for further clarification, supporting their position, and so on.

Step 7

Consider the following questions:

1. Do other roles support your initial position?
2. Are other roles supporting opposition to your initial position?
3. Do you require clarification from either supporting or opposing roles?
4. Would forming an alliance with other roles assist you in your Public Inquiry submission?

Week 2

Step 1

Check to see if there are any new announcements that may have been posted by the Dental Board. See Figure 4.9 for an example of an announcement.

You should also check for newsworthy articles that may have been posted onto the Press forum.

View Week 2 Resources that have been released.

Undertake further research of your own.

Step 2

Reflect on any new information made available to you through affiliation with other roles and include consideration of alternative perspectives. This should be considered in relation to advantages and disadvantages in the use of dental amalgam.

Step 3

Decide if your initial position on the use of amalgam for restorative purposes has altered.

Post your reflections as well as any new understanding and information on the class forum.

View other postings and make comments or seek further clarification etc as relevant.

Mon, Mar 03, 2008 -- *LATEST UPDATE ON MERCURY*

Associate Professor John Abbott has alerted us to the following findings of Prof. Derek Jones, Dalhousie University, Canada and Chair of ISO/TC 106. He has estimated:

1. That at least 50% of environmental mercury pollution comes from natural sources eg volcanoes.

2. Some 42% of environmental mercury comes from burning fossil fuels.

3. No valid scientific studies have ever shown that dental amalgam poses a health hazard to patients, to dentists or the environment.

4. A patient with 10 amalgam surfaces in their mouth would have a mercury intake into their blood which would be only 2% of the WHO's Acceptable Daily intake (WHO ADI 40 micrograms per day) for mercury with no adverse health effects.

5. It has been estimated that the environmental impact of mercury from 800,000 dental surgeries worldwide represents between 0.04% to 0.2% of the worldwide environmental mercury pollution from all sources(would be reduced further with amalgam separators).

6. The worldwide environmental impact into the sewer from 20 billion amalgam surfaces in people's mouth's represents between 0.01 to 0.07% of the total environmental mercury pollution. (Jone's own calculations).

7. It has been reported that each year close to 8 tons of mercury from fluorescent lamps end up in landfill and incinerator plants in North America alone.

8. The pollution from dental mercury procedures is insignificant compared to that of industrial use and natural sources.

9. From the above the "banning of dental amalgam" would not have any impact whatsoever on total worldwide mercury pollution.

Figure 4.9 Example of an Announcement.

Week 3

Step 1

Check to see if any new announcements have been posted by the Dental Board and whether any newsworthy articles have been posted onto the Press forum.

View Week 3 Resources, which have now been released.

Undertake further research of your own.

Step 2

You are now in a position to prepare your final submission to the Dental Board's public inquiry. Your submission needs to be posted to the discrete Public Inquiry forum.

Step 3

On completion of your submission, you will be given access to an online quiz. The quiz is a test of your knowledge of amalgam, its mechanical properties and its suitability as a restorative material. You will be allowed only one attempt at the quiz.

The Dental Board is now in a position to view all final submissions that have been made to the public inquiry. Final submissions are from 10 different role perspectives, including your role.

The Dental Board will make a final decision and submit a recommendation to the Ministry of Health. A copy of this recommendation will also be released for all participants on the Dental Amalgam e-Sim. You will be given an opportunity to comment on the final decision on the Public Inquiry discussion-board forum.

Step 4

As a last step, you will be given an opportunity to debrief from your role and to provide feedback on the value of this learning approach via an online survey. The survey will include questions that align with the objectives of this Dental Amalgam e-Sim. For example:

> After taking part in the Dental Amalgam eSim, do you have a better understanding of:
>
> 1. amalgam, its mechanical properties, and suitability as a restorative material;
> 2. the advantages and disadvantages of amalgam in the dental environment;
> 3. the multiple perspectives on amalgam use in the dental environment;

4 the range of communication skills required to interact with diverse oral health groups; and
5. emergent technologies that enable research skills and strategies for the evaluation of new dental technologies?

Finally, you will be able to view your final assessment results for the Case Study from the online Dental Amalgam e-Sim.

Here is an example (Figure 4.10):

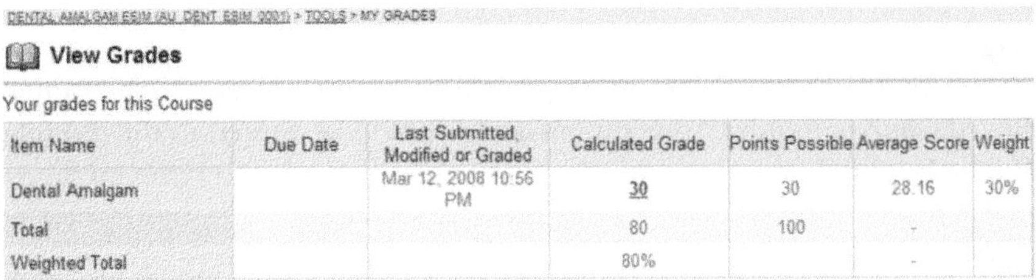
DENTAL AMALGAM ESIM (AU_DENT_ESIM_0001) > TOOLS > MY GRADES

View Grades

Your grades for this Course

Item Name	Due Date	Last Submitted, Modified or Graded	Calculated Grade	Points Possible	Average Score	Weight
Dental Amalgam		Mar 12, 2008 10:56 PM	30	30	28.16	30%
Total			80	100	-	
Weighted Total			80%		-	

Figure 4.10 Example of student view of grades.

SECTION 2

PROGRAM DEVELOPMENT

CHAPTER 5

THE PERILS OF PAULINE

The Initiation of a Novice Instructional Designer in an Industrial Setting

Wanjira Kinuthia
Georgia State University, USA

Grady Mclean
DiMac Educational Consultants, USA

Pauline waited impatiently on the other side of the train tracks as the train took its sweet time rolling through the shipyard. "Hurry along already! I'm going to be late for my interview," she thought. Finally the train made its way past the training department and she quickly jumped over the tracks, straightened her power suit and hair. Confidently, yet nervously, she walked into Mr. Peterson's office with her portfolio under one arm. Despite having read up on all the do's and don'ts of interviews and having attended many before, the interview was unlike any other she had attended. "Listen," said Mr. Peterson, "you won't need that suit here, and I can't pay you even close to what you were making at your other job, but here you'll get one heck of a good work experience." "Does that mean I get the job?" she asked. His

Cases 'n' Places: Global Cases in Educational and Performance Technology, pages 77–57

response, "Just be sure to be here bright and early and get you some good steel-toe boots on the way home. You'll need them here. The hard hats on that shelf are a little big, so pick the smallest one you can find. Be sure to wear your steel toes and hard hat any time you go out into the yard, otherwise the safety inspectors will write you up, and if they do, you'll be in trouble with me."

This was her introduction to the world of shipbuilding! What did she know about ships? As a midpoint graduate student, the opportunity to work as an instructional design intern had come up at just the right time. Time to put all the theories she had learned about cognitive psychology, adult education, and instructional development into practice. "Where to start?" she thought. The training department, which became Pauline's new home for the next two-and-a-half years, was constantly busy. The department was part of the personnel department but was also an operating unit of both the support and production departments. The company prioritized safety and training, thus the need for continuous training. The training department was continually tasked with designing and delivering instruction for management, leadership, and skilled crafts in these departments. This is where Pauline came in.

STEEL-TOE BOOTS OR COMPUTER? SO HARD TO CHOOSE!

At the time Pauline joined the department, the training was mainly instructor-led, but Mr. Peterson had been working on incorporating video and text-based instruction for several years. One reason he hired Pauline, the new instructional designer, was to help convert existing training and to develop new training into electronic formats.

The training department was part of the Personnel department, but it was under the operations of two other units: support and production. Peterson was in charge of delivering training and instruction to Management, Leadership, and Skilled Crafts in both the departments. This made for some interesting times!

By the time Pauline joined the company, the private shipyard had been in business for more than 70 years, working on all types of vessels in ship repair and new construction, including crabbers, offshore supply vessels, push boats, and shrimp boats. The company also engaged in research, design, development, manufacture, and integration of advanced repairs and new developments for government and commercial customers. At any given time, the shipyard employed between 600 and 1,000 temporary and permanent staff. Many of these staff members came through the training department, either for new or continuous training. The number of training classes or modules, especially the master craftsman skills, depended on the current needs and the amount of work available. Either way, all employees had to be fully skilled and trained to work on the ships.

The company offered a shipbuilding-craft training program to local residents for entry level positions. The goal of the program was for an employee to become a skilled craftsman while still earning income. This was achieved through the *Earn As You Learn* training program. The company would advertise locally when there were openings available, and the trainees would go through the program—which consisted of both academic and hands-on training—for about seven weeks.

At the time when Pauline joined the training department, Mr. Peterson had recently set up a new networked computer lab with about 20 machines. The trainees and other company employees would use the lab for training purposes during their work breaks and after their shift. When continuing education credits were required, the students could take tests set up in Trainersoft and the scores were automatically saved into a database.

One feature of the training program was that the trainees selected a field of interest or expertise. They were then further trained and mentored in the particular trade with a goal of becoming first class craftsmen within 12 months. Another main feature of the program was that the training department offered continuous education opportunities. For First Class craftsmen who excelled and chose to train in a second craft, they were reclassified as a Master Craftsman, and they received additional pay for being experts in the area. At this level of training, employees who excelled were encouraged to continue with their training in preparation for being evaluated for a future supervisory role such as a foreman. *Foreman Indoctrination* was Pauline's first big project. And was a learning experience!

HOW MANY COMPUTERS LANGUAGES DO YOU SPEAK?

Pauline's job required her to work two or three days a week during the semester and more days during the school breaks. Mr. Peterson was flexible with her schedule "as long as stuff got done." One day, Mr. Peterson dropped a pile of dusty, old, yellow typewritten papers and folders on her desk and said, "Here you go kid! See what you can do with those. I need for you to develop the Foreman Training program, and we need it soon." When she was done sneezing from all the dust, she asked him, "How soon do you need these?" He replied, "Yesterday!"

Pauline embarked on deciphering the content of the files before she could even contemplate how to use them in instruction. Was it even possible to have these in electronic format? "I hope you know how to use Trainersoft, because that's what I have here to design e-learning," added Mr. Peterson. Two daunting tasks early in her new job. Such was the life of an instructional designer she came to learn. "OK. What should I learn first: all about being a foreman or how to use the new software?" she thought to herself. Soon enough she came to learn that the Foreman Indoctrination course was a 10-part course, and that she would have to have a global understanding of the whole process before she could proceed.

HOW MANY SMEs DOES IT TAKE TO DESIGN A COURSE?

Pauline reviewed the text-based manuals on foreman training and realized that she had to devise ways to work with the materials in electronic format. She started out with the module on Shipyard Terminology, as she determined that both she and the foremen needed it equally. She also determined early in the game that she would be developing instruction in an area that she had no experience or knowledge in. "I suppose this is where Subject Matter Experts (SMEs) will come in handy," she thought. As it turned out it, this was not going to be as easy as working with SMEs.

Mostly Pauline tried to ensure as much as possible that she did not take up too much of the SMEs' time, since they were always on very strict time budgets. It was, however, a tricky situation to be in, because she needed accurate information due to the precise nature of the shipbuilding industry. One wrong measurement could cost lost time and money for reconstruction, not to mention the risk of vessels not meeting safety standards.

In one particular incident, Pauline had a foreman look over some shipfitting measurements, which he signed off as accurate. It, however, turned out to be incorrect, because he was going by previous standards. That meant revising a major portion of the e-learning, as well as some reconstruction of a vessel under construction. There was enough blame to go around, whether it was the training department or the SMEs who were at fault. Something else that Pauline had to contend with was the fact that when the SMEs were busy, she could not get ahead with her own work. It was pointless to design or develop any training materials and then have to go back to the drawing board. That meant that she too would fall behind the planned work schedule and consequently rolling out the training.

ARE THERE ANY QUESTIONS? DESIGNING FOR LEARNERS

Pauline and Mr. Peterson wanted to make sure that they had comprehensive ways of presenting the information for learners who have different learning styles. Every month, Mr. Peterson administered the Test of Adult Basic Education or TABE test to new entrants of the training program to analyze their reading and mathematics levels. Next, Pauline would ensure that the reading level of the instruction was appropriate. They did this using various techniques, including Microsoft Word's Readability features. Mr. Peterson and Pauline discussed the kind of training they were developing and conducting, and found it important to use lots of graphics, visual aids, and audio aids. Why go through all the trouble when it was expensive and time consuming? They had to come up with alternative solutions.

Pauline became an expert in photography and editing, but first she had to overcome several challenges. Mr. Peterson also bought voice recognition software. Pauline would first develop the scripts and save them as text files, which were then converted to audio files.

WILL ADAPTIVE PROJECT MANAGEMENT WORK?

Interestingly, Pauline learned about the final size of the project when it gained a life of its own. Mr. Peterson would reveal bits of the project one at a time, and it kept growing. "When is this project going to stop growing?" she asked him. "When we are done," he replied.

Pauline quickly learned to work on additional assignments that Mr. Peterson always seemed to drop on her desk without warning. "This was not in the project plan, Mr. Peterson," she often retorted. "It is now" was his standard response. What did they call it in her project management class? Scope creep? That's it! In one of her particularly large projects that she worked on for months, the Foreman Indoctrination training, she was feeling rather proud of her accomplishments and placed the finished packaged executable files on CD ROMs (or so she thought) on Mr. Peterson's desk. "Where is the rest of it? Where are the printed accompanying books?" Mr. Peterson asked. "What printed materials?" she responded. "You know we need those. You know some of the guys don't have computers at home. And you also know that some of them don't like to work on the computer." Back to the drawing board she went.

A SMALL BUSINESS MODEL OF CURRICULUM DEVELOPMENT

Since Mr. Peterson joined the company, the shipyard had been involved in a major restructuring of the training program for about 6 years. Much of the instructional material used before 1996 was developed in the 1940s. Since 1996, the company had invested an inordinate amount of effort in updating not only training material, but also the training programs.

Mr. Peterson, Pauline, and the rest of the training department learned many valuable lessons from their experiences, but the most important was that current curriculum models do not always fit in the "real world of business." To say that they actually developed a curriculum model and used it to develop their curriculum would be a sham. What they actually did was to develop the curriculum and then, through trial and error, discovered whether what they were doing was a true curriculum or instructional design model. They then edited, tuned, and refined the model based on fundamental business principles.

In the small-business community, every work process is driven by one single goal: make money. Resources are limited. Major corporations have the luxury of formal training departments with graphic artists, instructional designers, and educators, whose sole purpose is to develop the best training programs and courses that money can buy. Research, development, testing, and training is an expense that is well-budgeted, but small businesses see those same issues as luxuries that do not meet the bottom line of the company: making a profit.

The shipbuilding company invested in a small training department with the focus on updating the skills of its current craftsmen and new people entering the shipbuilding industry. They soon discovered a circular model of curriculum design much like the face of a clock. Nine distinct areas of development followed each other, but the center of the clock face was the important function: revise and update. The hands of the clock were independent. While one hand moved clockwise, in a progressive manner, the other moved counterclockwise. The midnight position was the first area of curriculum development. Identify business goals. This is the key element for any training function in any business.

MR. PETERSON'S BUSINESS CURRICULUM MODEL

Mr. Peterson taught Pauline many things about working with a limited budget and a time crunch without compromising quality. He designed a curriculum model whose lessons she took with her. He broke it down into the 9 aspects and phases below:

Business Goals

The CEO/upper management, and even lower levels of the company, may find areas where training is not meeting company standards. In some cases, it is meeting International Standards Organization (ISO) standards; in other cases it may stem from poor workmanship. No matter what area is selected for training, a clear case must be made to identify the objectives that the training is to meet.

Audience

This key element of the training picture is often neglected. In this particular training department, Mr. Peterson dealt with a wide range of educational levels. Cultural differences and social factors must also be included in identifying the audience. Skill levels, language barriers, and generational differences are also important elements in the training picture.

Gather Resources

Gathering resources is important to the development of any course. Often overlooked is the Subject Matter Expert and the person to be taught. Other items needs are company procedures, production records, observation, and don't forget a trip to the local library.

Chunk Information

The design team and the SMEs on a part-time basis divide the information into categories according to skill level or priorities.

Design and Development

The design team is involved in the crucial decisions of course development with help from upper management and SMEs. The most critical issue is cost. Once the budget is determined, the design team must make many key decisions before and during production. Since the training department had redesigned most of its training for e-learning, certain decisions had to be made, such as what software programs to use, graphics, and audio tools. During the course design phase, many designers pull out the important questions from the course objectives for later use in the testing section of the course.

Edit/Test

This phase is distinctly different. The design team edits each other's part of the program and tests it before going to the formative evaluation phase. Grammar, flow, and technical errors are the primary concern.

Formative Evaluation

This critical element is late in the development of the new course. In most companies, the loss of the SME for any period of time is detrimental to the efficiency and performance of the company. By putting the formative stage at this point, the SME still has an input into the finished product. Many times, the SME's patience fails them in the earlier stages, since this is usually seen as an extra burden beyond their normal job.

Implementation

Once the revised product is completed, it is immediately placed in service. Often, the minor technical glitches are not sufficient to delay the course from implementation. Experience showed Mr. Peterson and Pauline that they often had little time to produce a perfect product, but must settle for one with minor imperfections to get the product to the selected audience as quickly as possible.

Periodic summative evaluation

It is extremely difficult to do a comprehensive summative evaluation in the standard manner. In the business model, a periodic summative evaluation is performed to see if the course still meets the company goals.

PAULINE COMES FULL CIRCLE

One thing that Pauline reflected on was how much revising she had to do on all the training. As she developed glossary lists and word indexes, she realized that the process of course development is a continuous review and evaluation process! In addition, she researched current and relevant content and determined its organization.

Pauline learned about the important resources required in order to make instruction successful in a teaching or training environment. In her case, she surmised that the main ingredients were people, materials, technology, and time. She also came to realize that each successful training environment must also have at least one output in order to survive. The output was the final product, a service to its employees. As she compared that with the business curriculum development model, the product and services would aid or enhance the organization in its goal to produce a more efficient staff of employees.

Years later she would recall her interview, the hard hat, her steel-toe boots, and how that was truly the beginning of the makings on an instructional designer. Mr. Peterson, tough as he came across, taught her how instructional design and conducting business come together.

DISCUSSION QUESTIONS

1. What are the main instructional design themes that emerge from this case?
2. What do you suppose was the importance and challenges of developing and using graphics in the instructional design?
3, Outline some strategies for Pauline to get better results when working with SMEs and to alleviate the blame going around?
4. What do you suppose are the reasons that Mr. Peterson chose to use audio and graphics in the instruction? Discuss the implications for instructional design.
5. Pauline spent a lot of time taking photographs to use in the instruction. What implications does this have for both designing training and for copyright issues?

CHAPTER 6

DANCE OF CHANGE

Print-Based Distance Education to Creative Networked Learning

Cherry Stewart and Rachael Adlington
University of New England, Australia

SECTION A: BACKGROUND

"We've worked damn hard to overcome the initial resistance and inertia," said Darcy. She was furious. "Management is pulling the rug out from under us. The original committee set up to run this has been abandoned. I'm running around like a mad woman, trying to make decisions and find money. It's ridiculous."

Kirsi was no less angry. Computer hardware and infrastructure support were causing problems and now their Sakai programmer, who had been invaluable in getting the project to implementation stage, had taken a job overseas and management did not seem willing to find an appropriate replacement.

"How can we run a successful and fair trial of this system with this kind of support? They are replacing Brendon with two part-time help-desk personnel!" a frustrated Kirsi muttered.

Cases 'n' Places: Global Cases in Educational and Performance Technology, pages 87–70

Wattlegrove University was in a change process, moving from traditional distance delivery to online learning strategies, and like many institutions attempting radical change, it was finding that many obstacles lay in the way.

Wattlegrove University

Wattlegrove was the first university in Australia to provide off-campus programs to rural and remote students. The Wattlegrove Model was considered radically different from other first-generation implementations of the correspondence model of learning. Unlike other universities, all academics were required to teach internal *and* external students. The Learning Support Centre emphasized a systemic approach to creating effective learning systems, implementing strategies for staff/student contact and regular student group activities. The cornerstone of this model held high regard for *learners learning* rather than *teachers teaching*, aiming for didactic conversation and two-way communication between tutor and learner.

As differing technologies became available, Wattlegrove integrated many of these into its distance education programs, which grew rapidly. By 1979, Wattlegrove had over 5000 external enrollments, the largest in Australia. Progressively, the university became a leader in the use of interactive videoconferencing, talkback radio, and broadcast television, supplementing print materials with audio, video, and eventually the WebCT learning management system (LMS) for online delivery.

However, as other universities took these technologies onboard, didactic distance education at Wattlegrove diminished. By 2005, Wattlegrove had lost its leadership position to two other rural universities. Management became alarmed by this situation and undertook a comprehensive review of distance education provision at the university.

Wattlegrove's recent Distance Education (DE) Review highlighted the "need to develop an institution-wide strategic and academic direction" relevant to contemporary practices across the entire university. "Wattlegrove must implement modern, efficient administrative and customer support service practices." The review highlighted the serious gap between its technological capabilities and those of its competitors. "There has been insufficient re-investment in distance education to maintain Wattlegrove's leading position," it stated.

In a report for university staff, the DE Review Committee stated, "The approach to funding needs to be revised to overcome this problem. Residential schools have been a key feature of the DE model, but their role has now declined. There are many unfulfilled opportunities to achieve synergies between distance education and other Wattlegrove activities, not least on-campus teaching."

THE PROJECT

Arising out of this flurry of activity came a call across the university for faculty-based initiatives. "Most of our academics are experienced distance educators. You will find that they are quite proud of our reputation for serving students all over the world," Darcy Southall informed Kirsi Larnia, who had recently been employed as a half-time Educational Designer.

"Responding to a 'call to arms' by the university, our Faculty of Education submitted a proposal for a three-year project to redesign the off-campus Bachelor of Teaching for online learning. We started with focus-group discussions, and many members of the faculty agreed in principle that changes to our teaching practices were necessary. After all, in these times of a productivity and tight economic focus, personalized distance education had become a thing of the past, and our off-campus students had noticed."

While the university had encouraged the use of the WebCT LMS for over 10 years, few Education Faculty lecturers used the system, continuing to send out print-based study guides. Course evaluations showed that students were critical of the outmoded teaching materials, the level of contact and engagement with university staff, and more so, insufficient and tardy feedback on assignments.

"The university's DE Review Committee agreed to fund the project, a collaborative initiative between our faculty, the Information Technology Department and the Learning Support Centre. Several staff were encouraging us to trial an open-source Learning Management System (Sakai), so we planned redesign of twenty-four units of study using an action research cycle," Darcy continued.

The Project Manager

One of the youngest faculty members in the Faculty of Education, Darcy is a vibrant young mother and committed graduate student. After 8 years of teaching in elementary schools, she has returned to the university environment to gain a PhD. Besides teaching computer technology studies to undergraduates, she has been employed by the Faculty to coordinate the Distance Education Project. The BTeach, as it is nicknamed, is a fully external program servicing about 2,000 students. The Faculty wanted to move its print-based provision to an Internet environment.

"This project is of utmost importance, and we can't allow it to fail at such an early point," continued Darcy. "It has taken almost a year to get to this stage. Finally, after a protracted recruitment process, we've got all key personnel in place; and now the DE Review Committee has been dissolved! Well, at least the money has been allocated."

Darcy paused to reconsider. "We'll press on though, even though it seems as if the left hand is not talking to the right. I think our project design will help us overcome external issues. We used an action-research approach to project planning. The project is divided into four discrete stages, starting with a Reconnaissance Stage, in which data has been collected to inform the professional learning process and content. The experiences of the participants in one stage are to be shared with, and inform the learning of the next stage of participants," explained Darcy, as she shared a graphic representation of the cycle with Kirsi.

Reconnaissance Stage	**Action Research Cycle**				
Semester 1 Year A	Stage 1 Semester 2 Year A	Stage 2 Semester 1 Year B	Stage 3 Semester 2 Year B	Stage 4 Semester 1 Year C	Stage 5 Semester 2 Year C
	Redesign Stage 1 units	Implement Stage 1 units	Evaluate Stage 1 units		
		Redesign Stage 2 units	Implement Stage 2 units	Evaluate Stage 2 units	
			Redesign Stage 3 units	Implement Stage 3 units	Evaluate Stage 3 units

"The Reconnaissance Stage started with a focus-group workshop. Both teaching and administration staff contributed to discussions. This workshop showcased a range of technologies and tools available to use with online learning, discussed pedagogical approaches to online learning, identified issues that staff were concerned about regarding moving to an online environment, and established a shared vision of the redesigned BTeach. We also identified the steps we would take to actualize it. Although some lecturers are quite ambivalent and cite lack of time as a barrier, others like Rod Murray are keen to move ahead."

Faculty Commitment

Walking back to the education building with Darcy, after the project's focus group workshop, Rod Murray spoke excitedly. "I have so many ideas about how we could deliver this course in Sakai. It will be the first time we are able to really practice what we preach and test our constructivist philosophies." Generally, Rod, a reserved Indigenous Australian, keeps his thoughts to himself. He is one of a group of lecturers who provides the basic course in theory and practice of teaching.

"I've been reading about this new system," he continued. "We have seven-hundred students enrolled in our introductory teaching theory course, and could really get into group strategies. We could ask the students to blog their reflections and perhaps collaborate using the wiki tool. But the professor in charge of this course doesn't know much about technology and isn't really in favor of this project. His view is that there are just too many students for us to manage in an online environment. Old Sam doesn't think he'll be able to assure quality for so many students," worried Rod. "Not that he does much QA now!"

"I'm not very good with computers, but I think we could do it, if we got the right kind of support. There's some really good stuff on the Internet. We would need to set clear guidelines for the students, but we could ask them to find resources." Rod quieted his voice, and Darcy moved forward to listen. "Ours are so out-of-date now, it would save us a lot of time searching for readings, which I don't think the students actually read anyway."

Thoughtfully, Rod continued, "I don't know anything about creating multimedia resources, but I'd like to use some case-study videos for analysis in group work. I was chatting with Meredith in Criminology. Have you seen their problem-based learning stuff? And the Nursing Faculty showcased their online use of case-studies at a university seminar last week."

Darcy saw the enthusiasm Rod was sharing, but was also aware of the strong control that Sam Spring, the professor of Learning and Teaching, had over the content and format of the course. Sam was nearing retirement and had not kept abreast of the changes in learning technologies. He is a prolific writer, with many publications in constructivist theory. These are acknowledged as being substantive texts, and used in many education degree programs.

"What do you think the way ahead might be, Rod?" Darcy asked.

SECTION B: MOVING FORWARD

"Phew, we got through that!" Darcy reflected as she spoke with Educational Designer, Kirsi. The support that was removed from the DE project had been replaced, and communication channels were better established. "But I am still concerned about those techno-resistors who don't see the value of online learning. What do we do about them? We've given them time and support, but we can't force them to change."

The Sakai Project funding included a commitment to release course coordinators/designers from other duties by accessing a support teacher or research assistant for 45 hours. "We have to make sure they access their release, though. Sometimes they try to do everything themselves," explained Darcy.

Kirsi looked at the list of courses that she had been reviewing with coordinators, "I've heard some say they can't find a replacement. Others have told me it takes so much time to explain to someone else what they want done, they might as well do it themselves."

"We need to monitor the expenditure closely," replied Darcy.

"Don't worry, Darcy. The dance of change is like a long, slow waltz. It takes time, but as the dancers find their own rhythm, a thing of beauty emerges," Kirsi assured Darcy.

"I had a very interesting conversation with Rose yesterday. She absolutely refuses to be part of the project. It isn't that she doesn't like technology; she worries that students don't have the skills needed to use it, and it isn't right for her subject anyway,...or the way she likes to interact with students." Kirsi glanced down at her list of courses to be redesigned in each stage of the cycle. "How about we replace Rose in Stage 1 with Mathew from Stage 2? I think it is better to create an atmosphere where Rose can't help but become curious as her peers join in the action. Student expectation that she 'be like the other lecturers' can also work wonders on motivation."

"I wish I had your conviction," murmured Darcy, as she rushed off to attend to the ever-increasing administrative tasks generated by the project.

The Educational Designer

Since 1990, Kirsi had taken an interest in using technology to support learning for both children and adults. She considered herself a practical educator and well-read in both the philosophies and practical applications of using technology for learning. She had a 12-month contract to ensure the conversion of 10 of the 24 courses from print-based delivery to the Sakai Learning Management System.

Kirsi had been an elementary school teacher for 13 years. Then, after a short period as a housewife and young mother, she had returned to full-time employment as a tertiary technical college teacher. She rose rapidly in the ranks to Faculty Manager, responsible for the quality of learning across diverse programs from business and agriculture, to computing and hospitality.

A robust, good-humored woman, she was a perennial student herself; enrolling in courses to challenge her perspective on learning and educational management. She had had a stint as an education consultant providing advice to business and government departments about the design and development of staff training programs.

During her first two weeks at Wattlegrove University, Kirsi interviewed each course coordinator about course redesign ideas. She discovered that assignments were generally essays requiring students to use the provided materials to argue a theoretical question or submit a series of lessons or units of work to be taught in a primary classroom. Kirsi was absolutely amazed when one coordinator confessed it wasn't until halfway through a yearlong course, when the first assignment was due, that students first made contact with him. It highlighted the lack of real communication and engagement between leturers and distance students.

"It seems quite common that lecturers view their responsibilities in external studies as providing information for students to read and reflect on, and then to return students' analysis and understandings in a 'corrected' form, although this is not true of everyone."

"Where do I start?" Kirsi asked herself when staring at the results of her initial interviews. "How are we to provide effective online environments for students? With few technology skills, and little understanding of the Sakai tools and how they might relate to various pedagogies, how do we shift their mental models of teaching and learning?" she thought as she considered her next strategy.

Learning Designer 1: Mathematics

Kirsi leafed through some of her favorite texts and dug out models of learning that had been shared during her own postgraduate study. "It seems as though I am going to have to do a lot of one-on-one here," she decided. "Now that each lecturer has shared their view of what they do, I might just share a few of my own thoughts," she reflected as she headed for the photocopier to reproduce the teaching and learning models of Rod Sims, George Siemens, and Gilly Salmon.

"I haven't had any experience with distance education, although I am very keen to interact with students in the Sakai environment," Mathew Bloom had told Kirsi at their first meeting. "I haven't used computers for much more than word processing and research while I was doing my studies. I worked in an inner-city school in London, and there really wasn't much money for computers in classrooms. I got the students involved in group work though," he continued. "I think it is important for students to work with one another, and I would like to set up peer-support groups in this online environment. Can that be done?"

After completing his education studies in primary education, Mathew Bloom took a teaching position in metropolitan London. He remained in the UK environment for 8 years studying part-time to complete a PhD. Last year Mathew returned to Australia to take up a lecturer's position at Wattlegrove. He has taken over the provision of a mathematics unit developed by a colleague in his new department. "I don't want to make big changes just yet because I am not sure of how students will use the LMS. I know that David used the WebCT discussion board, but only for answering individual questions about the course. He also told me that there are a lot of personal e-mails that take up time," worried Mathew, who is a very strong proponent of constructivist pedagogy.

When preparing for his interview for this appointment, Mathew had investigated the distance education strategies used at Wattlegrove. He had also taken an online learning program in e-moderating provided by Gilly Salmon. He was impressed with how authentic learning could be supported in an online environment, and he wanted his students to engage with their peers as well as the content, and reflect on their own learning processes. "It seems too late to get approval for changes to the assessment. I guess I will have to keep things pretty much as they are. What do you think Kirsi? I really don't know enough about multimedia and how to make enhanced podcasts and things like that. Can I get some assistance? I've been told that there will be about 300 students in this course, but I have a research project going on and don't want to spend hours and hours managing the group. David told me that print materials have been sent out and I don't need to do anything until assignments come in. I think students deserve more than that, don't you?!"

Learning Designer 2: Creative Arts

Kirsi Larnia reflected on comments made at the sharing session by the Creative Arts coordinator: "How can I teach drama online? What a waste of time this whole process is," artistic and forthright Toni Carter challenged. "I want the students involved. I want them to understand that drama is not Christmas plays and poetry readings, but a tool for children's active learning. We DO things! We don't just sit around and type on a computer or write assignments!"

Kirsi had experienced this concern in several of her initial design interviews. She recognized the strong commitment of lecturers to encouraging a deep understanding of content, as well as each lecturer's need to be directly involved with student learning.

Most of these lecturers had emphasized the need for face-to-face contact and how residential schools were to impress the hands-on nature of their discipline. "Its hard enough trying to get students to commit to action in the few hours we get with them. How can we expect teachers to use drama effectively in a primary classroom if they don't experience it and practice it in a *real* situation with *real* people and things?"

Calmly, Kirsi had asked about the activities Toni planned. "What is it that your students achieve during such a short and intensive face-to-face session?"

"Well, they have to submit their first assignment when they come to the school. I ask them to prepare an action lesson, where their primary students will learn a concept from the curriculum through dramatic activity. When they come to the residential school, they are in groups of 12, and have to teach that lesson to their peers. I usually assign the grade levels so that they all end up with a variety of lessons to take home with them. We can't replace this with a computer. My students tell me it is the most valuable experience in the whole course."

"I am involved in a research program about active learning in the classroom. I need to complete this research, and I don't have time to get involved in any rich-media stuff. I don't even have enough time to rewrite courses to meet the teaching standards criteria, so I can't go to any workshops on this new system."

Learning Designer 3: Information Technology

"I can't wait to get out of this place. Why can't things be more coordinated? I've just about had enough of this. All these last minute decisions cause extra work for me!" was Diane's comment as she slumped into a seat in the common room after the sharing session. "You would think that communication could be more coordinated. Here we were, a few short months before the new semester, and those upstairs said that we have to use their electronic system for submitting assignments. And they couldn't even tell us how it works. Just who do they think they are?"

Diane Grassmin has been a lecturer at Wattlegrove University for almost 20 years. She began when the School of Education first started teaching about the use of computers in the classroom. She is skilled with technology, but has not taken a deep interest in pedagogy. The use of software and technical aspects of software integration are the focus of the introductory-level computer course, rather than the computer as a teaching tool.

"I've been having students submit their written assignments online for years using the WebCT drop box, and marking them online too. They've deleted the assignment tool in the Sakai system without even telling us! My students also create multimedia assignments. Their fancy little program can't accept multimedia, so I'm asking the students to submit their CD by post, as usual. Who's going to tell the students how to use Sakai, anyway? They don't come to the university with this knowledge, you know!"

Although Diane is officially part of a discipline team, she prefers to work alone. She often suggests that there should be increased avenues for sharing good practice and principles of course design. But she seldom participates in professional learning except as a presenter, demonstrating the latest technology and declaring the best ways to use it in teaching. "Our students don't have broadband, so it is important to provide them with all their materials on CD. Although, next semester I want to use a blog to present information to students. But it seems the Sakai blog tool isn't very good, so I'm using a commercial product. I'm not impressed with what I hear about this new LMS. It's not what I thought it would be when I agreed to be involved with the project," declared Diane at the sharing session.

SECTION C: LEARNING TOOLS

Brendon Lang, like many young programmers, was dedicated to setting up the Sakai LMS and linking it to other university administration systems. He was a graduate of the Wattlegove Science Faculty. He had earned a chemistry degree, but had been interested in computers and programming from an early age. He secured his full-time programmer position in the Learning Support Centre when he replaced two other full-time staff, redeployed to the Information Technology Division. He had worked with the WebCT environment for a number of years, when the opportunity to become involved in the Sakai trial came up. Brendon, a keen investigator, found Sakai to be a great environment to program in. He liked being able to modify things and see the results himself, unlike the proprietary system negotiations that resulted in little improvement. Being part of the Sakai development community was stimulating, and it was now a joy to come to work.

While Brendon had been working with Sakai for a few months, the IT Division was slow in making a development server available, hindering progress on readying the system for the Education Project. Resources were promised, but weren't made available by management. Even after the release of the first units in the project, ITD still believed that this was not part of "core business." There appeared to be little understanding of what was involved in setting up a highly interactive learning management system like Sakai.

Brendon had written new integration programs for the system and was recognized as "knowing Sakai inside out." He had become quite popular with the open-source community. "While we were still trying to set up Sakai and test the tools, management decided that we had to integrate a new plagiarism-detection system. We were taken off Sakai development and put onto other things without due consideration for project management and planning," Brendon shared with a few colleagues in the Sakai community. Communication with the Sakai community was far easier than within his own workteam. Information and decisions concerning the project were seldom shared and often made without any of his involvement.

"Project management is considered important, but not by this organization," confided Kirsi to Darcy on the first day of the release of the newly redesigned courses in the Sakai system. "We only had a few months to learn how to use the tools and enter our design strategies into the system before the release date. I've been telling the lecturers of all the wonderful things we could do with students, and now Brendon has had to remove half its capabilities because we haven't enough firepower behind us! I don't think that management really want us to succeed. They don't have any idea how much system traffic interactive learning creates. How can lecturers implement what we've planned? How will it impact on Wattlegrove's reputation?"

Embarking On Stage 2

"That sharing session was . . . interesting," Darcy commented as she walked into her office. In keeping with the action-research strategy, at the culmination of Stage 1, the process and products of redesign for this first group of units were shared with staff members involved in Stage 2. "Well, we have had our fair share of issues this semester," reflected Kirsi, "but I think we have won the hearts and minds of many. We have certainly come a long way, and people are beginning to change their mental models."

Darcy frowned. "I agree, Kirsi, but student feedback isn't so rosy, and Diane and Toni's comments really dampened the spirit." While many of the Education faculty had come around to the idea that an online learning environment could facilitate constructivist learning and provide guided learning experiences, Kirsi couldn't help but focus on the nagging doubts of a few. Sakai's "teething problems" had also added to the feelings of resistance. These problems had impeded the successful implementation of pedagogy and overshadowed the sharing session.

While most Stage 1 lecturers had given the trial of Sakai a fair chance, Stage 2 lecturers had learned of difficulties encountered and were wary about embarking on the redesign journey if their efforts proved fruitless due to ongoing issues with the learning environment.

Darcy flopped into her old faithful chair and groaned as she ran her fingers through her hair in mock despair. "On top of all of the problems with Sakai, management decides to demand that all courses offered at Wattlegrove are to have an online presence, students must have access to a computer and the Internet; and online electronic submission of assessment tasks has been mandated to enable student submissions to be screened by plagiarism-detection software. What more can they ask of us?"

"If you're feeling this way about change, just think of those people who aren't overjoyed by using technology, Darcy," replied Kirsi. "Still, some of these changes will actually help; lecturers can't just opt out of using technology anymore, nor can our students."

"I guess you're right Kirsi, but management might have thought a bit more about implications on teaching and given us some more guidelines. What good is an online presence if teaching delivery doesn't change? And what good is a fantastic learning design and a keen teacher if the technology infrastructure isn't robust enough? Do you think our present professional development and design strategies should be adjusted?"

CHAPTER 7

REUSING, REWORKING, AND REMIXING OPEN EDUCATIONAL RESOURCES

Andy Lane, Teresa Connolly, Giselle Ferreira, Patrick McAndrew, and Tina Wilson
The Open University, United Kingdom

BACKGROUND OF THE CASE

The Open University (OU) in the United Kingdom has made a significant amount of educational material freely available through its OpenLearn Web site (www.open.ac.uk/openlearn). The OpenLearn material has been published in a Moodle-based learning environment (www.moodle.org) so that the material can be studied online as is. In addition, all the published material is available in a variety of formats for downloading or taking away to be used elsewhere, either online or offline. This open learning environment also facilitates networking among users with several tools, giving users the ability to comment and communicate to, and with, other users. The OU has made this material available under a Creative Commons license (creativecommons.org), which allows people to freely download, use, or repurpose the content as long as they attribute the OU as original authors, use it for noncommercial purposes, and make their version available under the same

Cases 'n' Places: Global Cases in Educational and Performance Technology, pages 99–84

license. Licensing itself raises many issues, as discussed by the Commonwealth of Learning (http://www.col.org/colWeb/site/pid/3977), however in this chapter we will focus on other issues that affect the development or redevelopment of open educational resources.

The processes supporting the development and publication of open educational resources (OERs) have raised issues within the Open University and beyond it. Since releasing the material as OERs, we have evidence that a significant number of other people have been able to use them in a variety of ways, but we are also aware that there have been barriers, both real and perceived, to some people making use of this rich opportunity. The experience gained in OpenLearn has enabled identification of some emerging principles and practices to aid all users to gain benefits from the OERs on OpenLearn. These are presented as models and guidelines, and also as three activities that can be carried out using OpenLearn and other freely available resources.

CASE OBJECTIVES

Readers of this case study will be able to:

- Describe the basic features and potential benefits of OERs to course developers;
- Discuss the impact of the OUs course-development policies and practices on OER development and publication on OpenLearn;
- Describe and discuss the ways in which course developers might create, or are creating, OERs and also the main issues influencing their use.

THE CASE

Introduction

The concept of open content was first considered by David Wiley in 1998 (Wiley, 2006). Although Wiley's original concept was a development of his interests in Learning Objects as a means of enabling easier construction of educational materials from a repository of such objects, it refers to all types of content, not just that content originally claimed to be educational. When MIT decided in 2001 that it was going to make much of the content, used or produced by its faculty to support their teaching, freely available on the Web under an open license, it chose the term Open CourseWare for that content (MIT-OCW, 2007). In 2002, the term Open Educational Resources

(OERs) was adopted at a UNESCO Forum (UNESCO, 2002) and is becoming the most-used term for this concept.

Despite some terminological differences (OECD, 2007), open educational resources are largely digital assets (music, images, words, animations) put together into a logical structure by a course developer who has attached an open license to it. In other words, the content is openly available (it can readily be found or discovered), is openly accessible (in that it is in a form that others can take away) and openly reusable (in that the user can easily modify it and is allowed under the license to do certain things with it without having to ask the creator's permission first). This is in contrast to full-rights-reserved copyright, where the last aspect mentioned is always closed to users unless they seek and are granted permission, and where rights holders normally restrict the content's availability and accessibility in many different ways to avoid illegal use of the material. You can find more on these sometimes tricky issues of openness, including licensing, in relation to OERs in Schaffert and Geser (2008). In essence, though, creating an open educational resource is similar to creating any educational resource; what is different are the affordances offered to course developers and instructional designers by having a ready source of other people's material to draw upon for their own needs.

It may help to quote directly from David Wiley on what he calls the four Rs of open content (Wiley, 2007):

> When I began promoting the idea of open content almost 10 years ago, there were four main types of activity I was interested in promoting (although it took me some time to get to the point where I could articulate them clearly). The four main types of activity enabled by open content can be summarized as the "four Rs":
>
> - Reuse—Use the work verbatim, just exactly as you found it
> - Rework—Alter or transform the work so that it better meets your needs
> - Remix—Combine the (verbatim or altered) work with other works to better meet your needs
> - Redistribute—Share the verbatim work, the reworked work, or the remixed work with others
>
> Notice how each of the first three Rs encompasses those that came before it. Reusing involves copying, displaying, performing, and making other uses of a work just as you found it. Reworking involves altering or transforming content, which one would only do if afterward they would be able to use the derivative work. Remixing involves creating a mash-up of several works—some of which will be reworked as part of the remixing process—which one would only do if afterward they would be able to reuse the remix. (A "remix" in which no reworking is done is an anthology [a collection of simple reuses] and not particularly interesting for the purposes of this discussion).

OpenLearn was devised as a large Institutional action research project. The project was designed to address some fundamental questions about the potential role and impact of free educational content and an open, Web-based, learning environment on the work of the OU in particular and systems of education in general.

With substantial grant support from the William and Flora Hewlett Foundation, the 2-year start-up phase of the project began in April 2006. Following a few months of intensive work, the Web site was launched in October 2006 using Moodle (www.moodle.org) as the basis of the learning environment and with 900 hours of current content being published. By the end of April 2008, 5,400 hours of current OU content had been published in a LearningSpace, mainly aimed at learners; a further 8,100 hours of archived OU content published in a LabSpace, mainly for educators; as well as creating an enhanced learning environment with various tools and technologies to support users of the site. The Web site "entrances" to each area are shown in Figure 1 below. The units of material can be accessed through the LearningSpace block; the LabSpace block; or by "Browse Topics," the tab near the top of the screen in Figure 7.1.

A significant strand of OpenLearn was to make some of the OU's existing educational materials freely available on the Web as open educational resources. However, the existing educational material was written for one purpose: mainly as one part of a larger course with formal tuition, support,

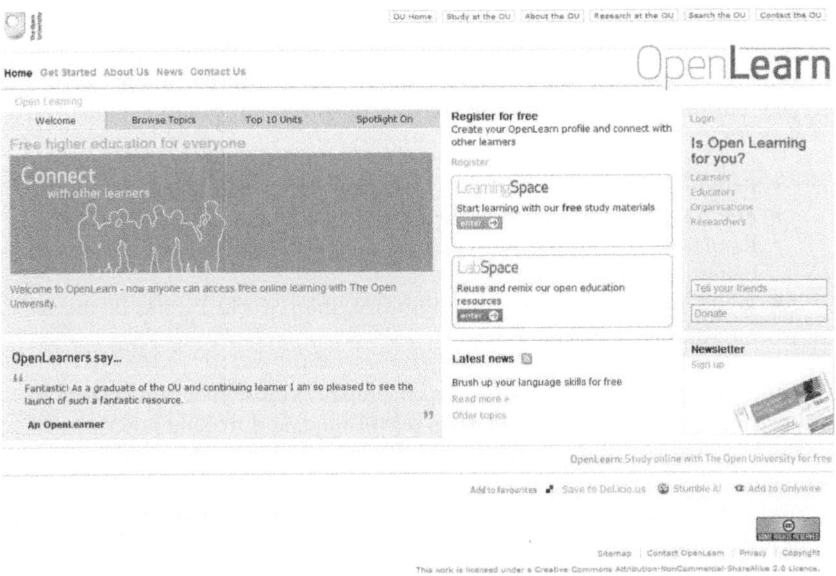

Figure 7.1 The OpenLearn home page, showing the entrance to the LearningSpace and the LabSpace.

and assessment services integrated, using a particular style of delivery and media formats. The content was now to be used for an entirely different purpose: as free-standing samples of OU educational materials with no formal support (but hoped-for informal support by other users) and where the style of delivery and media formats are also often different.

The first emphasis in this chapter is reflecting upon the *repurposing* of existing educational material for publication on OpenLearn and not the authoring of totally new material for publication.[1]

The second emphasis is on the issues facing other course developers wanting to use the open educational materials we made available in this way. In other words, this case exemplifies one approach to publishing open educational resources and the resulting implications arising from some of the decisions taken by the project team for both the OU and for other users.

Various terms and phrases can be, and are being, used to describe all of or parts of this act of repurposing, as we have seen already. For now we want to look at the act of *transformation,* since that was the term that had been most used when the project started. However, there was much confusion over what this actually meant in practice at the time, and even subsequently, and so this chapter unpacks what can seem to be a very complex process.[2] This complexity was created by the source material being in different media and formats, being written as part of a larger offering, having a variety of authoring and pedagogic styles, and by the media and formats that it was designed to be served up as on the two Web sites. If this mixture of technical and academic aspects were not enough, there were also continuing refinements of the specifications for the study units of the educational material to be housed on the two Web sites and who would be responsible for doing what.[3]

To more clearly define the nature and scope of the transformation process or processes we used, we first set out what were our views on the nature of the source material; followed by what it is that might, and could be, transformed; and finally described three broad categories or models for the transformation process that we expected to use during the start-up phase of the project. The start-up phase occurred over several months; the following section provides historical background to identify some of the issues raised.

The Source Materials

We, like many others before and after us, were faced with significant tension at the beginning of the project between making existing educational materials freely available on the Web, on the one hand, and believing that materials on the Web should (ideally in many peoples' views) utilize the capabilities of the Web and how people use it. Thus it was (and still is) believed there should be fewer words, more graphics, and much more dynamism or interactivity in a highly structured, more resource-based style of pedagogy when authoring courses for the Web. Therefore, one aspect of OpenLearn was to explore, review, and possibly to redefine what it means to author open and distance learning materials.

At one extreme, the OU has industrialized the development of open and distance learning courses, producing integrated sets of resources, each with a strong pedagogic structure, but heavily reliant on text. Early forays into online courses retained a strong (often linear) narrative structure and still used lots of text, albeit Web based. In both cases, the supporting of groups of students through batches of tutors that have acted as guides to this rich set of resources, has enabled large numbers of students to simultaneously study the same course. At the other extreme, most Virtual Learning Environments (VLEs), including Moodle, are based on a classroom model, with fewer structured resources; many more activities; and facilitated by a single tutor, who is often the sole course author. The number of learners is limited by the capacity of the single tutor. We expect that somewhere in between, there lies a model that retains the collective development of well-structured resources in a more flexible format, but that is also scalable in delivery to large numbers at the same time.

We believed that the task of transforming existing educational material would vary in part depending on the nature of the source material. An empirical review of some early source material at a workshop within the OU suggested that it fell into three broad categories,[4] based upon high-level teaching approaches and founded on the medium of instruction. For instance:

- Material that was authored for the Web and so is largely structured for online study but might have a different technical treatment and design look from that which would be possible in Moodle;
- More heavily structured multiple media materials designed for resource-based learning that needed reconfiguring for Web delivery within Moodle;
- Large, discursive, narrative-style printed pedagogic texts, which would require more effort to repurpose.[5]

Next, we turned our attention to the expected features of the OERs.

THE SPECIFICATION FOR STUDY UNITS

The samples of educational materials taken from OU courses that were to be included on OpenLearn were called (study) units. Early in 2006 we set out some ideal specifications for the major structural features of OERs for the LearningSpace at three levels: the units themselves, groups of units, and features within an individual unit.[6] The units and features within units are detailed and slightly expanded below; the issue of groups of units is beyond the scope of this chapter.

Units

We decided that the major characteristics of a unit should

- be 3 to15 hours of study time in size, ranging from roughly an evening's worth of study to a week's worth of study part-time;
- be labeled as being at a particular HE level (1, 2, 3, or M) as known within the UK Quality Assurance Agency's Framework for Higher Education Qualifications and articulated in an OU levels framework document;[7]
- be self-contained, with no references within them to other units and limited references to external URLs;
- possibly be subdivided into smaller sections or bits of 3 hours length;[8]
- normally have no more than one learning outcome or competency per 3-hour bit;
- Involve a mix of media, but will use more activities[9] than is traditional in a pedagogic text;
- comprise both material study time and learner thinking time.[10]

Features within Units

A variety of media resources can be incorporated within a unit, but they needed to conform to the following rules:

- On-screen text and static graphics (pictures, diagrams) representing a Web page, with normally no more than two screens to read at any one time to stop excessive scrolling;
- Web pages should be joined by hot links in the simplest manner possible, with no more than two levels of hierarchy;
- Text as PDFs for reading on-screen or printing off, with each document usually no more than 5 standard A4 page sides for each;[11]
- Total text components, whether Web pages or PDFs not to exceed 1,000 words per study hour;[12]

- Animations, audio clips, and video clips can be used but kept to a minimum, unless already available. They must also be pertinent to the topic and not seen as infill;
- Similarly, software applications can be included if already available and suitable for open content use on the Web;[13]
- In a few cases, it should be possible to base a unit around a readily available printed document or book(let), which users can get for free or at very low cost.

In addition to these resources, there would be other features within a unit:

- Self-assessment tasks should be included that cover each learning outcome.[14] These may be either an interactive quiz or a reflective activity in which the learner writes down notes for them to refer back to if they ever have to undertake formal assessment on that topic;
- An acknowledgements section that details the authors and possible sources of material included, including copyright status;
- A discussion space (a forum) where different learners can post comments,[15] including evaluations of the unit.

Remember that these were an early "ideal" specification, before we had published anything! Our initial experiences of transforming material raised several issues, which we address in the following sections; further experience will no doubt throw up yet more for years to come.

MODELS FOR TRANSFORMATION

Soon after this specification was set down, we held workshops with both potential internal (academic staff from faculties) and external transformers (people who had expressed an interest in reworking materials from seeing publicity about the project). We asked the participants to look at samples of source material in paper format and reviewed these responses to see what type of transformation they thought was required to make these resources suitable for presentation in the LearningSpace. The discussions that followed highlighted a fundamental higher-level issue to the detail provided in the "ideal" specification: the balance between (a) keeping faith with the source material and retaining most of it, albeit with some presentational changes and (b) with undertaking substantive reworking of the material to fit the currently assumed ideal characteristics of Web-based learning materials—notably, limited text and plenty of interactivity.

This led us to identify three models for transformation to aid our work:

- The *Integrity* model, where all the material in the unit would be recognizably very similar to the original material and as complete as possible, with the ability to study it in exactly the same order as the original. In practice, this would mean slicing existing text into smaller units, each of which would be delivered as a text page or PDF, with activities translated into an interactive form and other resources such as audio clips added to it rather than being delivered separately;
- The *Essence* model, where the source material would be cut back to the essential features, with text heavily edited into shorter blocks fitting a single page (or two), new activities being added to increase interactivity, and other resources changed or added, such as images or short animations. In practice, this would mean keeping the key elements of the original but making it more suited to Web-based interaction;
- The *Remix* model, where the source material would be used as a starting point or early draft of what needs to be taught, but where the unit would be designed from the outset for ideal Web-based delivery. This was seen as akin to writing the screenplay of the novel, where the source is a good starting point but the finished article is an almost complete reworking.

Then we got down to the serious business of actually doing the work rather than discussing it, such that we established the site and published 900 hours within 4 months. What follows is an update on these models (and the specifications), written some months after the first units had been published on the live site and where pragmatism overrode idealism in the case of some of the units.

The Integrity Model

To a large degree, the Integrity model involved the best possible translation of content from one medium of delivery and use to another within an existing structure and implied pedagogy. In some cases, we changed or added to the user experience using the scope of dynamism and interactivity in a Web-based environment. One example is the "click and reveal" of activity answers compared with having to look them up in the back of the book. Another example is having the audio-visual clip integrated on the page and immediately accessible rather than having to hunt around for the separate CD/DVD, then having to put it into a computer or CD/DVD player. In other cases, the current (print) medium allowed for some interactivity between learner and content (filling in missing word quizzes on the page) that cannot yet be replicated online using the Moodle quiz functionality (which although present, was not fully functional on OpenLearn until early 2008).

Something that could be added, where appropriate, was the replacement of a static diagram with a Flash animation of that diagram (for example, look for the Water Cycle diagram from *T210_1 Potable water treatment* at http://openlearn.open.ac.uk/course/view.php?id=2457 and which has been reused in other units).

However, the process was still one of replacing parts of a unit by an equivalent, usually more dynamic or interactive, part. And it was still the case that Integrity units were mainly a vertical slice or segment of study taken out of the original course, which does not disturb the linear flow of the original material.

Nevertheless, in a small number of cases, we did publish units that we sometimes referred to as "tasters" (for example, *T206_1 Why sustainable energy matters* at http://openlearn.open.ac.uk/course/view.php?id=1697 and *Y156_1 Understanding children—taster materials* at http://openlearn.open.ac.uk/course/view.php?id=2294) that were more of a horizontal slice from the whole course, with lots of very small vertical slices having been linked together by the course team to create a new linear flow different to the original course (although this may not be apparent to learners in the case of T206_1 because of how it was put together). They were tasters for a whole course rather than a single sample taken from the course. On reflection, we felt that these tasters might be more appropriately labeled as an Essence or Course essence model, where they do try to capture the essence of the content for the whole course.

Lastly, to be complete, we thought there was one further variant on the Integrity model whereby the unit provides a simple guide and (additional) activities to complement some educational materials held on another OU or OU-related site, for example, www.Open2.net (although it could be argued that this is actually a remix variant). We did not have precise examples of this model (the Tour Guide model?) at the time, although the series of units about Finding Information In "a topic" (for example, *Lib_1 Finding Information in arts and History* at http://openlearn.open.ac.uk/course/view.php?id=2227 and Lib_2 Finding Information in Business and Management at http://openlearn.open.ac.uk/course/view.php?id=2503, and so on) appeared to come close.

The Nonintegrity (Remix) Model

Remixing should normally involve much greater changes to the ordering/learning design of the assets within a unit, types of interactivity, and the substance of the content, not merely its medium/format. Thus, many of the things we previously put into the Essence model specifications were changes to pedagogy, if not learning design, and the way content was to be covered, for instance, editing down or switching from text to animation, the use of Moodle quizzes, links out to external resources, and so on.

Of course, there were fine lines between some variants of the Integrity model and possible variants in the Remix model, such as the Tour Guide model mentioned above, but one way to distinguish them was on the basis of the amount of new academic authoring of content, especially text, being required prehandover as opposed to just editorial reworking of preexisting text.[16]

However, at this stage in the project's development, we could only distinguish clearly between the remixing of the order and type of assets through the use of the Compendium knowledge mapping tool available on the site (the Mapping model?) until we had worked through some actual Remix examples that involved considerable rewriting of the content (by this time in the project, nearly everything was following the Integrity model so as to maintain publication rates needed to meet our agreed-upon targets). One example of remixing assets was the unit DSE212_1 EPOCH Psychology history timeline— http://openlearn.open.ac.uk/course/view.php?id=2850&ONEML=OLNL06&MEDIA=OLN619—where Compendium acts as an interface to a wealth of bibliographic style resources to be explored (but could this just be considered the Tour Guide model again?).

Terminology can have a significant impact on how a process is viewed. From the outset, the term *Remix* had been generally used to talk about the significant repurposing of materials by any user, within or without the OU. This was because this was a term with greater currency in the open content and open educational resource fields. However, in relating the process to usual OU processes, it had become clear that it was the same as the process of *remaking* a taught course covering basically the same subject matter; that is, it occupies the same space in the curriculum, but where new and updated material would be added to some of the original material as appropriate. Accordingly, for internal purposes, we began referring to units that require substantive repurposing as Remake Units, but externally still talk about the remixing of units. Does this matter? It certainly helps clarify matters internally, but whether Remix as a term is also off-putting to external users is as yet unknown. It does highlight that discussions of this matter can be fraught with misconceptions or misunderstandings and the degree of transferability of our experiences to others.

DISCUSSION

This chapter has given you some historical background to the early thinking that went into the creation of open educational resources for publishing through OpenLearn. There is much more we could say and have said elsewhere on this subject and on the various uses others are making of what we have done, but we want to leave you to discover for yourself what has happened rather than rely on what we have to say here.

Below are three interrelated activities for you to explore the issues in reusing, reworking, and remixing OERs:

1. Find some examples of non-Web-based educational materials and try to determine what you might need to do to reuse, rework, or remix them for Web-based delivery and use;
2. Explore the LearningSpace and see how many of the aspects of the detailed specification have or have not been followed and try to determine or imagine why;
3. Search OpenLearn or the Web for as many different uses of open educational resources as possible and think in more detail than set out here about what is being transformed when you transform or repurpose educational resources.

REFERENCES

MIT OCW. (2007). MIT Open CourseWare—Our history. Retrieved October 7, 2008, from http://ocw.mit.edu/OcwWeb/Web/about/history/index.htm

OECD. (2007). *Giving knowledge for free. The emergence of open educational resources.* Paris. Retrieved October 7, 2008, from http://213.253.134.43/oecd/pdfs/browseit/9607041E.PDF

Schaffert, S., & Geser, G. (2008). Open educational resources and practices: e-learning papers, No 7. ISSN 1887-1542. Retrieved October 7, 2008, from www.elearningpapers.eu

UNESCO. (2002, July 1–3). *Final report.* Forum on the Impact of Open CourseWare for Higher Education in Developing Countries, Paris. Retrieved October 7, 2008, from http://portal.unesco.org/ci/en/ev.php-URL_ID=5304&URL_DO=DO_TOPIC&URL_SECTION=201.html

Wiley, D. (2006). The current state of open educational resources. Retrieved October 7, 2008, from http://opencontent.org/blog/archives/247

Wiley, D. (2007). *Open education license.* In proceedings of the 2007 Open Education Conference, pp. 221–227, Utah State University.

NOTES

1. However, if you are also interested in the pedagogical issues behind creating new Web-based open educational resources, you could always study the unit we have published on OpenLearn for that purpose, which you can find at http://openlearn.open.ac.uk/course/view.php?id=3636. Indeed, you may

find that helpful, if you have never authored such material yourself, to better understand the issues surrounding repurposing.

2. As OpenLearn was run as an Action Research project, most of the many reports and research papers we authored during this start-up phase have been made openly available at http://kn.open.ac.uk/public/workspace.cfm?wpid=6087, with some informing this very case study. A selected number of these relevant publications are listed in the Bibliography. In addition, we held a conference in 2007, at which many interesting papers and presentations were made and which can be found at http://www.open.ac.uk/openlearn/openlearn2007/conference.php.
3. The OpenLearn team consisted of editors, media developers, graphic designers, and various academic staff with different subject backgrounds and technical skills in authoring educational materials. The division of the work activities needed to complete transformation between these different staff categories and the detailed technical specifications are interesting issues as well, but are not ones covered in this chapter.
4. There is a fourth category, which is of material that cannot easily be re-presented on the Web without significant resources to accomplish , including many proprietary software packages, but these were discarded as un-doable for the time being.
5. Of course, printed texts can be simply delivered as PDF documents that are a facsimile of the original. However such a format is very restricting for the user in many ways, including onscreen reading and reworking; an early decision was made not to use large PDFs (although PDFs of small documents were to be used in specific circumstances).
6. Archived material for placing in the LabSpace was not so tightly constrained in terms of size and media content, as it was there primarily for others to rework and repurpose rather than simply study.
7. This framework is UK based and so not always directly applicable in other countries. Further, the level of material can change in context, as it is the learning outcomes and their assessment that are major determinants of level of achievement in the FHEQ, not level of skill and knowledge needed to engage with the material, although that is a desirable prerequisite. If nothing else, a progressive system of classification (e.g., introductory, intermediate, advanced, and masters) would be needed to indicate to users what to expect, plus some indication of desirable prior knowledge, skills, and understanding.
8. This was advocating that all open content in the LearningSpace should be devised around 3 hours as the basic unit for structuring material.
9. By activities, we meant something the learner is asked to do other than just reading what is on the screen. So it could, for example, involve reading a PDF off line, listening to an audio clip, or doing an interactive quiz. It is more a recognition that Web-based material can be studied in a much more nonlinear fashion than an integrated textbook.
10. This is directly equivalent to the idea of course-directed study and student-directed study time within the OU's own course-models framework. Direct engagement time with materials and directed activities should be no more than 80% of any unit.

11. The emphasis is on not having too much material as PDFs; but some units may be based heavily on prior texts (e.g., a chapter or block), in which case a lengthy PDF needs to be broken up into smaller PDFs on a section by section basis.
12. This means there will be trade-offs between different text items as two screens amounts to about 150–200 words, while one side of an A4 page is equivalent to 200–300 words.
13. It is preferable for any software application not to have to be downloaded by the learner but usable online.
14. These are found in all OU course texts as a matter of course, so the question became more one of whether the self-assessment matched up to the Learning Outcomes or not, or whether units with few self-assessment tasks should have more added using the quiz facility in Moodle.
15. In terms of unit design, this was to be automatically included; but if used by learners, it could grow into a significant element that some would want to read through as part of the course. It also raised issues about how such a space is adequately (self) managed, and it might have had to be tightly structured to make it useful when comments could be so wide ranging.
16. In the OU's production processes, the authors of educational materials hand them over to the media specialists when they have finished the main authoring process.

CHAPTER 8

RETOOLING FOR NEW OPPORTUNITIES

Faculty Development, Technology and Change

Danilo M. Baylen
University of West Georgia, USA

Joan Glacken
Florida Gulf Coast University, USA

CASE CONTENT AND NARRATIVE

This case is situated in one of the public universities of a southeast Asian country. This public university considers itself a premier institution of higher learning in the southern region. Its charter dictates the advancement of knowledge through instruction, research, extension, and production. It enjoys a well-established academic recognition and reputation among other universities and colleges in the country and in the region.

The College of Education, as the flagship college of this university, states in its mission that it "continues to move onward as it aims to produce glob-

Cases 'n' Places: Global Cases in Educational and Performance Technology, pages 113–96

ally competitive life-long learners by providing instruction that is responsive and relevant, initiating and undertaking research in teacher education and allied fields, collaborating and sharing expertise with local and international entities and continuously exhibiting and nurturing a culture of excellence."

Two major changes are happening at the college in the coming year. First, the National Accrediting Agency (NAA) team will be visiting the college for its fifth year review at the end of the academic year. The year before, a self-study report was submitted to the NAA in preparation for the accreditation visit. Feedback from the NAA team identified areas that the college needs to work on prior to the visit.

Second, a new dean was appointed to lead the college in the coming academic year. The incoming dean was a former faculty in the laboratory high school but currently had been teaching master's and doctoral level courses at the graduate school.

The Faculty Meeting, End of Second Semester

It is a hot summer afternoon in early March at the southeast Asian Country National University. Room 101 is full of people as they await the administrators to join them for the last faculty meeting of the academic year. Excitement seems to be in the air, given that in a couple of weeks school will be over. Everybody seems to be looking forward to a break before summer school starts, especially Mr. Tolentino, a Social Studies Education faculty member. This year he is thinking of reviewing new texts for his undergraduate classes as well as exploring new materials on the Internet.

Dr. Villavicencio, the new dean for the College of Education, and Ms. Agora, the college secretary, walk into the room with serious looks on their faces. The chatter in the room quietly fades. It is a quarter past 3 o'clock.

Alumni Connection

Around 11:50 a.m. in the Education dean's office:

Ring. Ring. Ring.

"Hello. Good morning, Office of the Dean. May I help you?

"Hi! This is Dr. Pineda in the Arts and Sciences. Is Dr. Villavicencio available?

"Alma, this is Maria. The staff is out for an early lunch."

"Hi, Maria. I was wondering if you will be at Main Hall later today. I'm hoping you are because I need to talk to you."

"Sure, but it will be late in the afternoon. Is this something you can talk about over the phone?"

"Of course. Not sure if you know this former student of mine, but I got an e-mail yesterday that he's coming home for a visit. Based on the information he shared, he's an education faculty at one of the American universities. He was asking if he can visit my classes and talk to my students, but I don't teach undergraduates this coming summer semester. So I thought that maybe a member of your faculty would be available and interested in having him speak to his or her to class."

"Have any idea what his area of expertise is and when he is coming?" asked Dr. Villavicencio.

Hallway Conversations

The following day, Ms. Reyes, the English Education coordinator, ran into Mr. Tolentino in the hallway on her way to a program meeting.

"Mornin' Tony! How did the meeting go yesterday?"

"Well, it was the usual end-of-the year reminders. Then the dean, for most of the hour, talked about the accreditation visit report. It looks like we were strong in some areas but need to improve in others. I was just thinking, there goes my summer vacation."

"No kidding? Is it really that bad? I thought we did better and ranked highly in our content areas and methods. Remember that they praised us for the academic credentials of our faculty, given that at least 90% have graduate degrees and 20% have doctorates?"

"I do, and it is reflected in the report. If I heard correctly, the report mentioned more use of technology in our teaching. If they ask me, I would say that a globe and a blackboard would be enough to teach my freshmen courses."

"That's interesting, because last month I was in the capital city for our annual conference and there were not many sessions focused on using technology."

"Oops, I'm already five minute late for my next class."

"Okay. Catch you later."

Phone Conversation with Dean of Arts and Sciences

Around 3:30 p.m. in the Arts and Sciences Dean's office: One can hear the phone ringing in the background.

"Hello, Dr. Pineda please. This is Dean Villavicencio calling."

"Hi Maria! How can I help you?"

"Alma, I have a couple of questions about the accreditation visit. I know that you've been involved with last year's self-study and the preaccreditation visit. I'm new to this, so I'm asking for help wherever I can get some. Hope you have a couple of minutes to chat."

"No problem. Is there anything in particular that you want to talk about?"

"Well, the preaccreditation visit report identified areas for improvement, especially in the use of technology. Can you help me understand what they were looking for when they were here last year?"

"If I remember correctly, they were interested in our facilities. So we showed them our state-of-the-art computer classrooms. But that show-and-tell opened a lot of questions. Who is using them? What courses are supported by the computer classrooms? What kind of training do faculty members get as part of their professional development?"

"Interesting questions. Anything else?" asked Dr. Villavicencio.

"Then they started asking about what applications are being learned by our students. Who chooses these applications to be learned; what is the rationale for these selections; how do faculty integrate these applications in supporting their curriculum; how do we know that these technology-based tools are really impacting student learning?"

"That sounds like a lot, doesn't it? Who was there aside from you to answer these questions?"

"Your predecessor was there during these question-and-answer sessions with the visiting team. A couple of your coordinators, Ms. Reyes and Dr. Bautista. Then several faculty members—I remember Mr. Tolentino."

"That's good to know. Any suggestions on how to respond to these questions as we prepare for our next accreditation visit?"

"Not sure if you're familiar with a couple of UNESCO reports on use of technology among Asian countries. I believe there is a country report for us. Most of the data were collected from schools in the capital city, but some of the recommendations might be applicable to our context."

"Thanks Alma. I'll keep that in mind. How about lunch sometime?"

The Summer Workshop Announcement

Two junior faculty members and a senior faculty were having a conversation as they looked over the summer workshop announcement.

"Who is this Dr. Bernal?" asked a junior faculty.

"From what I heard, he was a former student years ago. He has been living in the United States as a faculty member in one of the universities. I believe he graduated the year I came in as a faculty member."

"So how come I will end up in his workshop instead of enjoying the last days of my summer vacation?" quipped another junior faculty.

"Who said you'll be enjoying your summer vacation? With our summer salary stipend per course, I don't think I can afford to take a vacation. But to make a long story short, I heard that the dean of Arts and Sciences asked our dean if we are interested in him coming to our college and conducting this workshop. Our dean agreed, thinking that it will be good for our accreditation visit at the end of the year," replied a junior faculty.

"I understand the idea of grabbing an opportunity, but what does he know about our issues. If he's been living in the states, then he has no idea of our needs and how to address them," stated a senior faculty.

"I believe he will show us how to use technology to support our teaching."

"That's great, but when are they going to replace my antique computer with a green monitor," asked another junior faculty.

"Ha! Ha! That's funny, Rick. But we are not talking here about your office computer. Remember those computer classrooms in the Main Hall."

"Yeah, those computer classrooms! Have you used them in the past?" asked a senior faculty.

"No, because I can't fit them into my schedule. It takes more effort to schedule one from what I was told."

Hallway Conversation, Early Summer Semester

Around 2:15 p.m., Education Annex hallway:

"Hi Tina! How did your year go?"

"Good morning, Dean Villavicencio! Busy as usual! My freshmen are keeping me on my toes this year. Quite a different bunch."

"How so?"

"We had the usual group from the local town comprehensive high schools—cream of the crop I would say. Then we had those from the private high schools—very competitive and energetic. Then finally, the students from the city high schools were just phenomenal. In the past, I tended to see some differences between these three groups on college readiness—writing skills, reading comprehension, et cetera. Much more variances in social skills."

"That's pretty much what I observed, too. So what's the difference this year?"

"Well, that's what I'm trying to identify, but I'm not sure yet. But I can tell you that they know more technology than I do."

"That's an interesting observation. Would you care to elaborate more?"

Cafeteria Conversation

It is lunchtime at the university cafeteria at the beginning of a work week: Five faculty members are seated in a roundtable having lunch.

"So what do you think of the workshop?

"Well, I really enjoyed the digital storytelling section of it. I thought it was creative and would really engage my freshmen and sophomores," replied an English Education faculty.

"I feel the same way, but I wish we had more time for the other sections. I'd like to see how PowerPoint can be used for an interactive quiz. I think it has potential to help me work with math problems. It was a good overview, but I would have preferred a more hands-on experience," answered a Math Education faculty member.

"I'm not sure I am ready to do those things in my classroom."

"How come?" asked a Science Education faculty member.

"Well, I don't think it is possible to do these things given our resources."

"But we have those computer classrooms. Isn't that the reason why we held the workshop in one of those classrooms?" replied an English Education faculty member.

"Did you see the waiting list last semester? Also, when I use it and encounter some technical problems, I feel really stupid in front of my class."

"Well, then maybe we need more training on how to work in these computer classrooms."

"Yes, I like his ideas on Web 2.0 technologies. I hope that we can get more training in these areas," stated a Social Studies faculty member.

"I agree. I can't believe how easy it is to create a blog. I thought you had to learn computer programming, but the brief experience we had with Dr. Bernal proved me wrong."

"Let's bring this up in our next faculty meeting so we can ask the dean to provide more training support in these areas."

Dean's Council Meeting, End of Summer

"Thanks for your work this past year. Again, I look forward to working with all incoming and continuing-program coordinators. I know that this is early, but things can never start too early when you are preparing for an accreditation visit. The office of the vice president informed me that we are scheduled for a site visit in early December of this year. That gives us about five or six months to prepare and address those areas needing improvement as identified in our previsit report and self-study. Comments anyone?"

"Since I'm new to the Dean's Council, I'm wondering if we have a plan in place on how to address these areas for improvement," asked by Mrs. Andres, the Math Education program coordinator.

"I echo that question. But how many areas are we talking about here?" asked Dr. Bautista, the Science Education program coordinator.

"Dean Villavicencio, I'm not sure if you released the full previsit accreditation report to the faculty, but maybe that is one document we need to review before our next meeting. If I remember correctly, you brought it to our attention in our January council meeting," stated Ms. Reyes.

"Good point. Ms. Agora, did we ever do that?"

"Let me check the minutes from that meeting."

"The Plan"

The College of Education is facing another accreditation site visit at the end of the year and only has four to five months to prepare and address compliance issues. Administrators and faculty will have to work quickly to resolve these issues. So where do they start? Dean Villavicencio decides to convene all the program coordinators and review the previsit accreditation report. The report cites some of the following issues:

- What courses are taught in the computer classrooms?
- How many faculty members use the computer classrooms?
- What kind of training do faculty members receive as part of their professional development?
- How do the students utilize the technology in the classrooms?
- What applications do the students learn?
- What process and rationale is used to select these applications?
- How do faculty integrate these applications to support curriculum?
- What impact does technology have on student learning?

At the meeting, Dean Villavicencio informs the committee that she heard several faculty members commenting on the increased technological literacy of the incoming freshman class.

"I heard that the students appear to have more knowledge of technology than the faculty," Dr. Villavicencio pointed out to the committee.

"That's so true. I was amazed how much technology my students used during their class presentations last week," added Mr. Tolentino.

"How do you feel about that, Tony?" asked Ms. Reyes.

"To be honest, I'm impressed. But now I worry, because I know it took more time for those students to create their presentations. I wonder if they did learn the material. At times I think that some of the presentations contain less substance. More glitz and entertainment."

"You don't think that the students learned the material?" asked Mrs. Andres.

"I believe they did and enjoyed preparing for it. But..."

A Private Conversation

After the meeting, the dean asked Dr. Bautista to join her in the office. They discussed what must be done quickly for two reasons—address the issues cited in the previsit accreditation report and prepare faculty to teach to a new breed of technologically literate students. Both also knew that several of the faculty were quite satisfied with maintaining the status quo and were resistant to learning and acquiring new technology-literacy skills.

Dr. Bautista suggested that a small-scale needs assessment would be an effective tool to gather evidence to help convince both faculty and higher administration that a faculty development program in the area of instructional technology was necessary to meet accreditation standards, as well as to keep pace with educating technology-savvy students.

"We have the instructional technology in our classrooms, and our students have embraced it. Our accreditation body is requiring that we utilize the technology on campus. But many faculty do not know how to use it," explained Dr. Bautista.

"Yes, that's a good strategy to pursue. The needs assessment will provide information on what is lacking, especially on technology literacy among the faculty. This may help us find and identify potential solutions so we can offer activities and incentives that will encourage the use of technology in the classroom."

"That's a good point. The needs assessment will help us define the actual problem."

"I agree. The information collected will help determine why technology is underutilized in the classroom."

"Yes, it will provide supporting evidence—fear of technology, lack of skill or knowledge, or some other underlying problem such as motivation."

"Once we define the problem, we can brainstorm on potential solutions and plan to implement them. It will take some time and effort on everyone's part, but it will be worth it. We will be addressing the technology literacy needs of the students as well as complying with accreditation standards."

"So who do you think will be the best person to spearhead this?"

The Needs Assessment

Several faculty members volunteered to help the dean with the needs assessments, and Dr. Bautista agreed to lead and coordinate the project. The committee discussed and debated the purpose and value of conducting a needs assessment. Also, Dr. Bautista provided guidance in identifying various sources of information. Since the faculty are having problems using available technology, she suggested that the committee start interviewing a sampling of faculty members and staff to gain some insight into their personal views on using technology in the classroom. The committee brainstormed on what questions they might ask. The list generated by the committee members turned out to be similar to the questions asked in the previsit accreditation report:

- What courses are taught in the computer classrooms? If none, why not?
- How many faculty members use the computer classrooms?
- How do the students utilize the technology in the classrooms?
- What applications do the students learn?
- What process and rationale is used to select these applications?
- How do faculty integrate these applications to support curriculum?
- What impact does technology have on student learning?
- If you were trained to use the technology, would you use it more often in your classroom? Why or why not?

After several faculty and staff interviews, the committee met for a day off-campus and analyzed the initial data collected. They readily agreed that the main problem seemed to indicate a poor performance in using technology.

"Do you think this is really the root cause of this problem?"

"Well, the results of the data analysis point out that faculty are not knowledgeable nor do they possess the skills to utilize the technology in campus classrooms."

"This is causing a noncompliance problem with accreditation standards."

"Also, students are really more proficient with technology than the professors."

"Yes, we heard from several faculty and staff that all the new equipment is somewhat daunting to them."

Another Off-Campus Meeting

Once the report from initial data-gathering activity was read by Dean Villavicencio, the committee received a new charge. This time the dean asked them to expand their information-gathering activity. Another off-campus meeting was convened where the committee decided on what information they needed to gather as well as tools needed for collecting the information.

"Given our short timeline, how do you propose we collect this data?"

"Interviews!"

"I think that will take a lot of time. Remember that everybody's busy at the beginning of the academic year."

"How about surveys?

"That might be cumbersome. What happens if we get a low return rate?"

"You got a point there. So what do others think of focus groups?"

"Well, if we provide food, then most likely those invited will come."

"You're funny, but quite right."

"Everybody's in agreement with this strategy?"

The committee presented their recommendation to the dean. They argued that a short time frame gave them no alternative and conducting focus groups to collect the data was the most viable and effective strategy.

The focus groups were very successful, with 80% of faculty participating. The committee reconvened after all the focus groups were completed to analyze the data. The committee's investigation found the following:

- The majority of faculty (65%) realize that students are more knowledgeable than they are when it comes to technology.
- Only 25% of the faculty participating in the focus groups utilize the computer classrooms. The faculty who do not utilize these classrooms state they do not know how to use them.
- The computer classrooms are used mainly to teach accounting courses in business.
- The computer classroom is used quite often to teach courses not requiring technology.
- The majority of the students using the technology are very proficient. The students who are not proficient require a lot of help from the professor. This means the professor must be very knowledgeable.
- Students use Excel and Word only because not enough faculty members know how to use other technology applications.
- Students who attend classes that utilize technology appear to be more attentive and eager to learn.
- The majority of faculty (62%) would like to learn to use technology in the classroom. About 50% of the faculty expressed concerns that students need to be technologically literate to succeed professionally in the world today.

The Fork in the Road

After reviewing the information gathered from the focus groups, the committee makes some recommendations given the issues identified in the preaccreditation visit report. Again, the dean asks the committee to join her for lunch at an off-campus location to minimize any interruption. After lunch, the dean asks the committee several pointed questions.

"Given the things you learned by now, do you believe this problem can be resolved by teaching the faculty how to use the technology?"

"I believe so. But..."

"It is not a magic bullet. Others things should be done to complement the training activities."

"What other things should be added to the faculty development programs that would assist faculty in gaining the skills needed to use the technology in the classroom?"

"Have you considered providing some incentives?"

At end of the luncheon, the dean tells the committee, "I'm very proud of the work you have done. I will bring your recommendations to the president, and I'm quite certain he will approve them. He is anxiously waiting to see what he can do to help faculty overcome their fears of technology and gain the skills needed to implement more technology in the classroom."

"Maybe he can convince Dr. Bernal to come back and teach us more. Dr. Bautista can't help but think of new opportunities for learning."

DISCUSSION QUESTIONS

Needs Assessment

1. How critical is a needs assessment in this scenario?
2. If needs assessment is critical, what strategies will be used for implementation?
3. Who will be involved in the needs assessment as participants?

Faculty Training and Development

1. What areas are identified for training and development activities?
2. What resources are needed to support training and development activities?
3. What delivery strategies will be effective in meeting the training and development of participants?

Leadership Roles

1. What role should the incoming dean assume relevant to this scenario?
2. What decisions does the incoming dean need to make?
3. What actions does the incoming dean need to take?

REFERENCES TO ANCHOR THE CASE

Belawati, T. (2003). Philippines: ICT use in education. In G. Farrell & C. Wachholz (Eds.), *Meta-survey on the use of technologies in Education in Asia and the Pacific 2003–2004* (pp. 121–128). Bangkok: UNESCO Asia and Pacific Regional Bureau of Education. Retrieved March 20, 2008, from http://www.unescobkk.org/fileadmin/user_upload/ict/Metasurvey/COMPLETE.PDF

UNESCO Bangkok. (2006). *Using ICT to develop literacy*. Bangkok: UNESCO Bangkok. Retrieved March 20, 2008, from http://www.unescobkk.org/fileadmin/user_upload/ict/e-books/Literacy/Using_ICT_to_Develop_Literacy.pdf

CHAPTER 9

MANAGING THE DELIVERY OF COMPUTING PROJECTS IN HONG KONG FROM AUSTRALIA

Iwona Miliszewska
Victoria University, Australia

INTRODUCTION

Since 1992, Victoria University (VU) has offered a degree in computer science, both at home in Melbourne, Australia, and transnationally in Hong Kong (in partnership with an educational institution based in Hong Kong). Initially, all units of the degree were taught with the aid of part-time local teaching staff (Hong Kong lecturers). However, several years on, after an annual revision of the program, VU's External Programs Committee decided that a final-year unit, a Project, was to be taught and supervised entirely by VU lecturers; this decision necessitated the development of a new approach to the delivery and management of the Project unit. At a staff meeting that followed, John, the VU Director of the offshore degree program in Hong Kong, pondered the feasibility of this decision:

Cases 'n' Places: Global Cases in Educational and Performance Technology, pages 125–106

> I agree that the project is critical to the quality of the degree, and I understand why they recommended that it should be entirely our responsibility, but we are here in Melbourne and the students are in Hong Kong. How are we going to support the students? How are we going to find projects from local industry and business? Do any of you speak Cantonese? How much is this going to cost?

The case writer wondered what would have to happen in order to deliver the project successfully in Hong Kong.

THE TRANSNATIONAL DEGREE PROGRAM IN HONG KONG

Transnational education, often referred to as offshore education, describes all programs in which the learners are located in a country different from the one where the awarding institution is based (van der Vende, 2003). This definition includes education that is provided by collaborative arrangements, such as franchising, twinning, and joint degrees, where study programs are provided by another partner, as well as noncollaborative arrangements such as branch campuses, offshore institutions, and corporate universities. The number of Australian universities involved in the provision of transnational education, as well as the extent of their involvement has expanded considerably in recent years. Leask (2004) refers to this expansion as a transition from *cottage industry* to *core business.* Coupled with this expansion of the transnational education business has been an increase in the number of tertiary institutions in Australia that have started operating in transnational environments over recent years; each of the 38 universities in Australia provides transnational education programs (Harman, 2004).

Victoria University offers the same computing degree program in Melbourne, Australia, and offshore in Hong Kong. Regardless of location, the degree program leads to the same award upon its completion; thus, the university is required to deliver the same program to students in both locales. However, minor variations are allowed to accommodate the barriers of time and distance and logistical hurdles. The degree in Australia is a 3-year full-time program, and the majority of students enter the course as school-leavers. The degree in Hong Kong is an articulation program that is offered in part-time mode only for students who are normally in full-time employment and have previously approved tertiary qualifications. Depending on the type of the qualifications, students are required to complete between 10 and 12 units to graduate. The units are offered over three terms a year; students usually study two units per term—a total of six units per year.

The Hong Kong program is a twinning program; this means that the program is a fully taught program and it follows the same syllabus and timetable as the corresponding Melbourne program. The Hong Kong students follow the same study materials, assessment tasks, and examinations as VU students in Melbourne. VU lecturers are responsible for the design of curriculum, provision of detailed weekly teaching plans and study materials for each unit in the program, design and provision of continuous and final assessment tasks, as well as face-to-face delivery of 25% of the program. Part-time local (Hong Kong) lecturers, associated with the partner institution, teach the remaining part of the program following the teaching plans provided by the university lecturers. In addition to the face-to-face component, the program relies on the Internet for communication, for example, unit Web sites, bulletin boards, and e-mail. Classes are held at night, starting at 6:30 p.m. during the week, and in the afternoon on Saturdays; classes are held at a venue provided by the Hong Kong partner institution. Classes for a single unit are held once a week with the exception of times when Australian lecturers come to Hong Kong to teach; then, for logistical purposes, classes are held more often; for example, three classes might be delivered over a period of 10 days.

The program is registered with the Education and Manpower Bureau of Hong Kong in order to satisfy regulatory requirements of the Hong Kong government. Under Hong Kong legislation, all award-granting programs offered by transnational (nonlocal) institutions must be registered; the registration criteria include the following condition:

> In the case of a course leading to the award of non-local higher academic qualification, the course must be offered by a recognized institution and is itself recognized by its home country as being of a comparable standard to a similar course operated by the institution in the home country (Hong Kong Government, 1996, Section 10, p. A666).

IMPLEMENTING THE MANDATORY PROJECT UNIT

The degree includes a mandatory final-year project unit, in which students develop a real-life computer system. The aim of the project is to provide students with an opportunity to work on a real-life software development project; to appreciate the needs of the business client for whom they are expected to build the software system; to apply software engineering and database design methodologies to the design and implementation of a complete system; to confront issues developers face on a daily basis, such as liaison with clients, working in a team, documenting the project; to gain experience in translating their knowledge into practice; and to obtain feedback concerning their progress from intensive reviews of their work. The project is designed to consolidate existing knowledge, and to empower students through engagement with a genuine work environment. It is an integral part of the computer science degree and, as a consequence, an elaborate system of project supervision exists to support Melbourne students.

The Melbourne Project Model

Students are divided into groups; each group is allocated an industry project and an academic supervisor. The project is sourced, by the project coordinator, from local business and industry, and typically is an application of interest to the client. Over a period of an academic semester, approximately 4 months, students proceed with project work at a pace that enables them to gain maximum benefit from the experience and complete work that is of a high standard. The groups meet with their academic supervisor on a weekly basis and review progress, but major responsibility for project completion rests with the students. Assessment is based on project reports and two presentations—one midterm and one at the conclusion of the project—and, thanks to the frequent meetings with the project groups, the academic supervisor is able to assess the individual contributions of the group members to the overall project effort.

The Original Project Model in Hong Kong

Like in Melbourne, students in Hong Kong were divided into groups (usually of four members), and each group was allocated a local academic supervisor and a project sourced by the supervisor from local business and industry. The sourcing of projects was a bit problematic, as the local lecturers worked only part-time for the partner institution in Hong Kong, and their workloads had little provision for sourcing of projects; consequently, some project groups were given textbook case studies instead of real-life problems to work on. The project was conducted over a period of two academic terms—approximately 6 months. Melbourne lecturers provided students with comprehensive project guidelines that specified all project requirements, identified milestones and deadlines, and described assessment. In addition, at the beginning of the project, a Melbourne lecturer assessed project proposals submitted by each group and delivered a lecture in Hong Kong on project objectives, documentation requirements, project management, and time management, and conducted consultation sessions with individual project groups. Then the local lecturers took over and led the students to completion. Assessment was based on two reports and a final project demonstration, and each project received a single mark, making no distinction between the contributions of individual project group members.

THE PROBLEM

In 2001, the Hong Kong government provided the opportunity for nonlocal programs (such as the transnational degree program offered by VU) to seek official accreditation. In response to this offer, VU committees reviewed the program quality-control procedures to ensure that they satisfied both the university requirements and the Hong Kong accreditation criteria. During the meetings with the Hong Kong Accreditation Committee, the project became a point of contention. The academic members of the committee were concerned that the Hong Kong educational system may not have equipped students with the independent study skills required to complete this unit. The committee stopped short of recommending that the project be restricted to a laboratory exercise, but it suggested that the university should take a greater responsibility for the project and provide better support to students on a day-to-day basis. Following this recommendation, VU's External Programs Committee decided that the project was to be taught and supervised entirely by VU lecturers. A staff meeting was called to discuss the implications of this decision and develop a workable solution.

The Learning Experience

> Why not turn the project into an assignment? Maybe that is not such a bad idea. Students already work on software development assignments in the Software Engineering unit, so they could do the same in the project. (suggestion by Dan, a lecturer in software engineering)

Several colleagues agreed and suggested that online support through WebCT could be provided to address the requirement of better student assistance. Bay-ling, a lecturer of Chinese background, went on to say that an assignment would better suit Chinese learners for two reasons:

> Firstly, Chinese education is firmly based on knowledge transmission with a single curriculum, often a single textbook, so making the curriculum relevant to everyday life has low priority. I do not believe that the project's emphasis on real-life context is important to the Hong Kong students. Secondly, Chinese students are passive learners, used to a very teacher-centered learning, so they would prefer to reproduce what the teacher has taught.

Others objected to turning the project into an assignment, stating that, for one, it would challenge the equivalency requirement of the unit (too big a difference between its Melbourne and Hong Kong offering). And, in response to Bay-ling's statement about learning preferences of Chinese students, John pointed out that there was also evidence to suggest that many of the preferences of Chinese learners may depend on teaching practices, and that Chinese students could adapt quite easily to student-centered approaches if they were in learning environments that encouraged them to do so. John, an academic, had managed VU's Hong Kong program since its inception and had taught extensively in Hong Kong.

Finally, Iwona, a lecturer, presented a summary of her research study into Hong Kong students' perceptions of the project learning experience—refer to Table 9.1.

The study investigated attitudes of Hong Kong students toward the significance of the project experience. All students enrolled in the project subject were surveyed after its completion; participation in the survey was voluntary. The students were asked to complete a questionnaire: of the 160 students enrolled, 143 completed the survey. Students were asked to rate three aspects of the project, namely group context, project-based task,

TABLE 9.1 Student Perceptions of the Learning Experience (as percentage of students)

Group Context	Strongly Agree	Agree	Neither	Disagree	Strongly Disagree
Improved my communication, planning, and management skills	44%	53%	3%		
Forced me to clarify and describe problems, thereby facilitating solutions	42%	52%	6%		
Helped me understand and accept the perspectives of fellow group members	41%	53%	6%		
Project-based Task					
Made me apply my knowledge and ideas to a specific task	43%	54%	3%		
Was more interesting than working on tutorial exercises	41%	55%	4%		
Gave me a sense of control of my learning	44%	50%	6%		
Outside Focus					
Increased my motivation for work	26%	62%	11%	1%	
Taught me skills associated with client interaction and customer service	30%	64%	6%		
Was more satisfying than working on a textbook problem	30%	64%	6%		

Source: Miliszewska, Horwood, & McGill, 2003.

and outside focus. The results of the study indicated that the project is an important learning experience to the Hong Kong students. They regarded both "group context" and "project-based task" as equally important in terms of their contribution to the learning experience. In addition, students singled out the project's focus on communication, planning, and management skills, opportunity to apply knowledge and ideas to a specific task, as well as opportunity to control their own learning as most important characteristics.

Iwona also presented a comment included in one of the project reports and reflecting on lessons learned and benefits gained from the project:

> Very importantly, we experienced teamwork while developing the project. Developing the system was not an easy task. Time was short, while problems surfaced from time to time. Through cooperation, we solved the problems one by one and managed to complete the system within the time limit. Developing the system was a valuable experience for each of us, and we will apply what we have learned in our work.

Technology and Logistics

The discussion then turned toward the issue of possible fully online supervision of the project. Dan supported this idea; according to him, all Hong Kong students had a computer and Internet access at home, and online supervision of the project would allow them a greater flexibility in their learning. Others agreed, proposing that even the initial project lecture and consultations with students could be conducted via a videoconference. Ian, a lecturer specializing in user interface design, dismissed the idea of videoconference, citing his "disastrous" videoconferencing experience from a year before; his attempt at conducting a lecture from Melbourne to Hong Kong failed miserably, as students were reluctant to interact. Ian said, "I may as well have sent them a video of my lecture, or maybe just the overheads. They did not wish to ask any questions, or respond to any of mine. It was a useless exercise."

John expressed his reservations regarding a fully online provision of the project, citing statistics on declining popularity of transnational programs offered in this mode, as presented in Table 9.2.

Iwona referred to her recent study of Hong Kong students' learning preferences and commented on the importance of face-to-face communication (Miliszewska, 2007). Students participating in the study overwhelmingly preferred face-to-face to online communication (91% to 9%); they claimed that it offered instant feedback, afforded easier communication with fellow students and instructors, was better suited to the resolution of

TABLE 9.2 Declining Interest in Online Programs

Rank	Distance Online	Number	Growth
1	Malaysia	3,846	–29%
2	Singapore	2,952	–16%
3	Hong Kong	1,952	–25%
4	China	1,867	23%
5	Canada	807	–15%
	Total	**16,053**	**–15%**

Source: IDP Education Australia, 2004, p. 12

study problems, and gave better motivation to study. Some students were of the view that learning in front of the computer only was too "cold" and too difficult, while others were of the opinion that Hong Kong people had traditional attitudes toward education and therefore face-to-face communication was more suitable for Hong Kong students. Students did, however, acknowledge the usefulness of the Internet as a means for provision of course material and communication with instructors and fellow students.

"Online or face-to-face, how are we going to source the projects?" asked Dan and suggested that, perhaps, they should be sourced from businesses in Melbourne.

Some colleagues agreed, particularly those who were involved in the supervision of Melbourne projects. Others questioned the benefit to Hong Kong students of working on problems that might not be relevant to the Hong Kong context, but found it difficult to offer an alternative.

CONCLUSION

The discussion in the staff meeting continued for one more hour. Many more meetings and discussions followed, as several key issues continued to be debated including:

- Is it necessary that students meet face-to-face? If not, what alternatives can be suggested?
- What is the role of the supervisor? How involved should he or she be in the project conduct?
- What technologies could be used to foster group interaction and facilitate assessment?

Views varied and opinions were divided. What is your recommendation for ensuring appropriate design and implementation of the project unit in this course curriculum?

REFERENCES

Harman, G. (2004). New directions in internationalising higher education: Australia's development as an exporter of higher education services. *Higher Education Policy, 17*(1), 101–120.

Hong Kong Government. (1996). *Non-local higher and professional education* (Regulation) Ordinance. Hong Kong.

IDP Education Australia. (2004). *International students in Australian universities.* Report, semester 2, 2004, IDP: Canberra. Retrieved March 4, 2008, from http://www.idp.com/research/fastfacts/Semester%20Two%202004%20-%20Key%20Outcomes_Web.pdf

Leask, B. (2004). *Transnational education and intercultural learning—reconstructing the offshore teaching team to enhance internationalisation.* Refereed paper presented at the Australian Universities Quality Forum: Quality in a time of change, July 7–9, Adelaide, S.A. http://www.auqa.edu.au/auqf/2004/program/papers/Leask.pdf

Miliszewska, I. (2007). Is it fully on or partly off? The case of fully online provision of transnational education. *Journal of Information Technology Education, 6,* 499–514.

Miliszewska, I., Horwood J., & McGill, A. (2003). *Transnational education through engagement: Students' perspective* (pp. 165–173). Proceedings of the Informing Science and IT Education Conference InSITE. Pori, Finland.

van der Vende, M. C. (2003). Globalisation and access to higher education. *Journal of Studies in International Education,* 7(2), 193–206.

ADDITIONAL RESOURCES

Bower, M. (2006). *Virtual classroom pedagogy* (pp. 148–152). Proceedings of the 37th SIGCSE Technical Symposium on Computer Science Education, Houston, TX.

Bower, M. (2006). *A learning system engineering approach to developing online courses* (pp. 45–54) Proceedings of the 8th Australian Conference on Computing Education, Darlinghurst.

Lisewski, B., & Joyce, P. (2003). Examining the five stage e-moderating model: DeSIGned and emergent practice in the learning technology profession. *Association for Learning Technology Journal, 11*(1), 55–66.

Pullen, J. M. (2006). *Scaling up a distance education program in computer science* (pp. 33–37). Proceedings of the 11th Annual SIGCSE Conference on Innovation and Technology in Computer Science Education. Houston, TX.

Raisinghani, M. (2003). Web-based education in the 21st century: A transnational perspective. In A. K. Aggrawal (Ed.), *Web-based education: Learning from experience* (pp. 71–88). Hershey, PA.

Sabin, M., & Higgs, B. (2007). *Teaching and learning in live online classrooms* (pp. 41–48). Proceedings of the 8th ACM SIGITE Conference on Information Technology Education. Destin, Florida,

Sheard, J. (2004). *Electronic learning communities: Strategies for establishment and management* (pp. 37–41). Proceedings of the 9th Annual SIGCSE Conference on Innovation and Technology in Computer Science Education. Leeds, UK.

Wang, H. (2006). Teaching Asian students online: What matters and why? *PAACE Journal of Lifelong Learning, 15,* 69–84.

Whatley, J., & Bell, F. (2003). Discussion across borders: Benefits for collaborative learning. *Educational Media International, 40*(1&2), 139–152.

Wong, J. K. K. (2004). Are the learning styles of Asian international students culturally or contextually based? *International Educational Journal, 4*(4), 154–166.

SECTION 3

TEACHER EDUCATION AND DEVELOPMENT

CHAPTER 10

FRESHMAN SURVIVAL GUIDE

A Multimedia Case Study Approach for Exploring High School Writing Instruction in Teacher Education

Ewa McGrail
Georgia State University, USA

INTRODUCTION

Preservice teacher instruction traditionally relies on instructors' lectures, textbooks, and supplementary readings. While all of these resources are useful in providing much relevant content and information about instruction, many instructional practices often remain abstract to novice teachers (Kinzer & Risko, 1998). This is because these systems of knowledge transmission cannot always provide novice teachers with the opportunities of seeing instructional practices in authentic teaching contexts, analyzing decision making behind such practices, and learning on their own how to make such decisions for new instructional contexts. These skills are, however, critical for developing preservice teachers' pedagogical content knowledge (Shulman, 1987). As Shulman explains, pedagogical content knowledge "represents the blending of content and pedagogy into an understanding of how

---

Cases 'n' Places: Global Cases in Educational and Performance Technology, pages 137–122

particular topics, problems, or issues are organized, represented, adapted and represented for instruction" (p. 8). Like Shulman, Segall (2004) underscores the critical importance of understanding the link between content and pedagogy when he argues "that powerful teaching (and powerful means for learning to teach) are an outcome of recognizing that interrelationship" (p. 489).

Audio-visual (multimedia) case studies, situated in real classrooms, may provide preservice teachers with opportunities for inquiry-based learning focused on observational, analytical, and critical synthesis of the ways content knowledge and pedagogy are merged in specific educational contexts. In exploring the use of digital video in enhancing reflection of preservice teachers, Yerrick, Ross, and Molebash (2005) found that teachers changed their thinking about children's thinking, planning, and instruction, as well as their respective understanding of teaching expertise and requisite knowledge. Similarly, Masingila and Doerr (2002) argue that "a multimedia case study can be a site for investigation, analysis, and reflection by preservice teachers" (p. 235). In their own research on multimedia case studies in which preservice teachers practiced meaning-making in complex classroom experiences, they observed that these preservice teachers not only connected the issues in the case study teacher's practice to their own practice, but also reflected upon some of the sources of typical dilemmas and tensions involved in teaching their content area (math), and in doing so, mapped out strategies and approaches toward solutions.

This multimedia case study was designed to engage preservice teachers in this type of reflection, through inquiry and in-depth analysis of teacher decision-making about writing instruction in a high school setting. More specifically, the class that this case study investigates with preservice teachers is senior English, with an emphasis on the writing curriculum. Critical to this case analysis is deconstructing and evaluating the blending of the content knowledge and pedagogy, as applied to real classroom challenges when teaching writing to a group of students with diverse learning needs. Through social knowledge construction (Vygotsky, 1962) and active problem-solving analysis of the multimedia case study (Cognition & Technology Group at Vanderbilt, 1993), preservice teachers learn to transfer the pedagogy content knowledge about writing instruction acquired in lectures, textbooks, and additional course readings in methods courses to a new authentic teaching context, the macrocontext of the case study. This experience takes place under teacher-educator questioning and guidance that encourages theorizing about this inquiry-based learning. From a pedagogical standpoint, this method reflects the merging of constructivist and instructivist approaches (Clark, 1994; Kirschner, Sweller, & Clark, 2006). The constructivist view assigns to the student an active role in the process of knowledge generating (constructing) and processing, while the instructivist view positions students as receptacles of the knowledge and skills shared with them by someone in authority (the teacher).

WRITING INSTRUCTION AND HIGH SCHOOL STUDENTS

Writing continues to be an area of challenge for many high school students. Although a comparison of the results from the recent National Assessment of Educational Progress (NAEP) writing assessment with earlier years shows increases in percentages of 12th-grade students "performing at or above the *Basic* achievement level," no increases *were reported* at or above the *Proficient achievement level compared with 2002. There was only a 2% increase in performance compared with 1998* (Salahu-Din, Persky, & Miller, 2008, p. 2). Research offers some explanation for this situation. One such reason is shortage of time. As a result, students are asked to write few long-paper assignments, and they have less time during the school day to develop good writing skills. Similarly, their upper-level high school English teachers, who may face 120 to 200 students weekly or daily, struggle to teach and respond to writing in the time available to them during the school day (National Commission on Writing for America's Families, Schools, and Colleges, 2008).

Others argue that students are not fully taught the writing process (Scherff & Piazza, 2005). The current political climate, which emphasizes product over process, limits the opportunity to write for a real audience (Darling-Hammond, 1997). Such a climate further erodes process-based approaches to writing in the classroom, leading to an excessive focus on form versus content in teaching writing in the classroom. Hillocks (2005) finds the latter approach problematic when he argues that

> Writers do not decide to write an expository paragraph or an evaluative theme. If they decide to write prose at all, they decide to write about specific subject matter. Moreover, knowledge of form does not translate into the strategies and skills necessary to wrest from the subject matter the ideas that make up a piece of writing. (p. 238)

The answer Hillocks offers to this challenge is to return to a process-focused writing curriculum. Such a curriculum engages students in a writing process that emulates the way real writers write, and where elements of the writing craft (grammar, syntax, style) are being taught during revision, and in relationship to the authentic audience and their needs. To practice such a pedagogy, more time and resources need to be devoted to writing in the classroom. This agenda reflects the National Commission on Writing for America's Families, Schools, and Colleges (2008) report recommendations: "More attention must be paid to writing. More time must be found for it.

And teachers must be provided with the time and resources required if they are to perform their work professionally" (p. 59).

This case study asks preservice teachers to explore one teacher's use of a process-based approach in teaching writing to students from diverse learning backgrounds, and in doing so, to develop their own strategies and rationales for meaningful writing instruction, when working with struggling and disengaged high school writers (for more information about student learning backgrounds, see section "Students"). As such, the multimedia case study approach described in this chapter provides preservice teachers with the opportunity to reflect on their own epistemological beliefs about writing and writing instruction (Many, Howard, & Hoge, 2002). In order to be effective teachers, preservice teachers must develop teacher identities that will support continued success as writing teachers. Knowing their own epistemological stances with respect to the craft of writing, and understanding the origin of these stances, is a first step toward such identity development. Additionally, careful scaffolding of this reflection by the instructor through a case study method allows preservice teachers to learn from one another in a community of practice (Street, 2003; Wenger, 1998). A case study approach also helps preservice teachers to see the student perspective by asking them to think about the ways students think about writing and interpret writing activities, as evident in student work samples and interviews included in the study under review. The following statements summarize the overall objectives established to guide preservice teacher and teacher-educator readers of this chapter as they explore this multimedia case study:

1. To help preservice teachers gain pedagogical content knowledge about writing instruction; that is, the ability to make decisions about optimal instructional strategies for specific teaching contexts through problem solving and social learning;
2. To sensitize preservice teachers to situational and student factors when weighing options for instructional procedures for a particular student population and context;
3. To help preservice teachers to learn about effective ways to integrate technology into the writing curriculum;
4. To provide teacher educators with the necessary macrocontext for learning and teaching in general, and in particular for the learning and teaching of writing with technology.

THE MULTIMEDIA CASE STUDY

My colleagues from a graduate school of education (Liu Xiaoyan and Carol Kuria) and I designed and developed this multimedia case study for use with preservice teachers of English and English language arts. The purpose of this multimedia case study is not so much to show how to teach writing but rather to engage preservice teachers in developing their own theories (Many et al., 2002) of teaching writing through an examination of the approach adapted by a teacher in this multimedia case study. In other words, this case study allows preservice teachers to analyze how composition theory studied in the literature, textbooks, and lectures is translated into a specific educational context. It also helps them to realize that while theory provides content knowledge about specific concepts or classroom practices, it is often an idealized version of a concept or procedure (Kinzer & Risko, 1998). In the real writing classroom, as featured in this case study, pedagogical content knowledge (Shulman, 1987) is modified, augmented, and reinvented to fit the particular context realities and the students' needs within this context.

The case study materials that assist preservice teachers in the exploration of this study include the teachers' lesson plans, the classroom teacher's video reflections before and after the class, video of the class, as well as the assistant teacher's video interview, reflections, and notes. Additionally, student work samples and video interviews with select students are used to counterbalance the classroom and resource teachers' perspectives. References to the relevant literature provide further context for this case study.

Instructors and the preservice teachers are encouraged to access and process any information available in this multimedia case through multiple channels: audio, visual and print. Each of these channels has the potential to bring the perspective unique to them, often adding completeness to the picture of the case under investigation (O'Brien, 2004). For example, the audio-visual aspect of this case study allows preservice teachers to make their own interpretations of the facts observed, as opposed to the facts in the written report that tend to be presented to the reader primarily through the author's lens. Additionally, the audio-visual feature of the case provides many opportunities for inquiry-based assignments with the focus on observational, analytical, and critical synthesis skills (Masingila & Doerr, 2002) to be practiced by preservice teachers as part of the case analysis. These skills are critical for developing preservice teachers' conditional knowledge (Kinzer & Risko, 1998), the knowledge allowing teachers to assess the context by themselves and access the procedures relevant for that context.

The Setting

There were about 1,700 students at West Bank (WB-pseudonym), grades 9 through 12, at the beginning of our multimedia case study (year 2002). Shortly thereafter, the school was successively recognized as one of *Newsweek*'s

"Best High Schools in America" in 2003, 2005, 2006, and 2007. The school is located in a suburban residential area nearby a major private university that provides in-service and staff professional development in the teaching center housed on the school's premises. According to school district profile for the academic year of 2003–2004 (Office of Information and Reporting Services, 2003–2004), WB had 5% and 3% of the student body eligible for free lunch and reduced-price lunch respectively, with the following racial/ethnic breakout within student population: 98% white, 1% black/African American, and 1% Hispanic/Latino. The school ranked high in terms of highly qualified teachers, with 20% of teachers with a master's degree or higher.

The Students

The class selected for the case study reflects the complexities of teaching writing to students with low writing proficiency levels and with a range of learning disabilities (Swain, 2006). More specifically, the class was a senior writing class, including 8 female and 13 male students. Many students had writing disabilities, and as a result were assigned individualized education programs (IEPs). Other students were identified as having difficulty with staying focused, due to high levels of hyperactivity or a chronic lack of engagement and confidence in their writing abilities. Additionally, many of these students had attendance or behavioral problems. The decision to take the senior writing support class featured in this case study was often the students' or their counselors' choice.

The students also varied greatly in terms of computer skills. Some were comfortable with word processing, while others, the classroom teacher attested, "had little ability to even select font or page setup." Some students were fluent in a variety of technologies available in the school. The students did not receive any formal training on technology. Generally, the teacher explained, "a more knowledgeable student will help less knowledgeable students if they are struggling. If all students encounter a technical problem, a system operator might come and troubleshoot the problem." To help students with navigating the Internet sites in search for information, the teachers in this study guided them as they followed directions or they worked with a peer to assist them with Internet searches. In this case study, students used technology in the following manner: computers for word processing, journaling, note taking, and composing brief overview narratives for individual sections in a class project; drawing programs for designing art, headings, and covers; and a tape recorder for recording and transcribing the results from the interviews with students and teachers.

The class engaged in an authentic writing assignment intended for a school audience beyond the teachers. The assignment asked students to compose a survival guide for freshmen, hence the name of the case study, *Freshman Survival Guide.* The guide was presented to freshmen students and teachers in a reception at the beginning of the new school year. Copies of the guide were also made available from the library to prospective students and parents inquiring about the school and the senior program. The guide consisted of several sections. These were the following: poetry, art, advice, quotes, sports, and activity. The research part of the project required that students seek advice from former seniors and teachers. Students themselves developed the interview questions and questionnaires used for the project. The students interviewed both seniors and teachers in other classes. In terms of a workload policy, students were assigned sections for which they were responsible. The members from each section were also asked to keep progress notes in manila folders created for their individual sections. The members of the class who were present on a given day referred to the information from the manila folders to tell them what they needed to be working on next. Students worked on the Freshman Survival Guide project for about 5 weeks at the onset of the multimedia case study. They completed about 70% of the project, with all sections still needing editing, organizing, and proofing. There was also some additional artwork necessary and the finishing up of reporting from the questionnaires administered to former seniors and teachers.

The Teachers

Senior Writing in this multimedia case study was taught by two teachers: a classroom teacher and a resource teacher. The classroom teacher had been teaching for 31 years and had a master's degree in English education and a doctoral degree in cultural foundations of education. She had been teaching English at the case study site for 15 years. Her vision of teaching was constructivist (Fosnot, 1996; Vygotsky, 1978). The teacher explained in her own words what that meant to her: "I try to construct an environment that allows my students and myself to learn—to learn what perhaps they need to learn, given state requirements—what they want to learn." Within such a classroom environment, she saw herself as "authority, facilitator, friend, translator, and encourager," and described her teaching style as "focused, flexible, and constant." She also strove to ensure "student growth in whichever ways [she] can manage." She worked hard to push her students "to thinking and writing they have not done before." She utilized a great deal of technology in her writing class, because she believed that "the technology gives [her] students what they need to make writing less painful, less impossible than it has been in the past." The senior writing class was held in a computer lab. Her own computer skills lay in "basic word processing" and "the ability to search the Internet."

Because, as the teacher explained, senior writing class was not a traditional class, "its population comes with emotional and academic problems which must be never ignored." She developed certain strategies to help her teach this class. These were "patience, high energy and [being] calm at the same time." She gave students simple directions and assignments "geared to [student] interests and experiences." Also, because this senior writing class had a high absence rate, the classroom teacher looked out primarily for some degree of progress. "That is really all I can expect from this class," she argued. The overall assessment plan for these students was "to work towards a final product," which was a creation of the guide.

The resource teacher had been at the school site for 12 years. She had a master's degree in special education and a bachelor's degree is speech pathology. In her capacity as a resource teacher, she worked with students who had learning disabilities in the area of "reading, writing, math, sometimes behavior problems, or emotional situations." More specifically, the resource teacher helped the senior writing class "with organizational, writing, and reading strategies." Her technology expertise was limited. As she admits, "I am very good with word processing and e-mail, and that is about it." She let students take the lead in this area because she felt that "usually the students know more than I do. So I sort of depend on them or call our subs, who are our experts at the school."

The two teachers (a classroom teacher and a resource teacher) discussed the plans before the lesson, and "adjust[ed] accordingly to the population present that day and their mood." The process and responsibilities for each teacher "changed as the lessons changed." The classroom teacher explained in more depth the nature of this cooperation:

> I tend to do the overall weekly planning, but we designed the course together over the last summer. I take more authority in the class so that she can work with the specific needs of the IEP kids.

The resource teacher added to this description her own perspective in this excerpt:

> However, [the classroom teacher] builds on many of my ideas, and I build on her ideas; and it is a constant creating process that happens in a split second, at the end of class, beginning of class, during the day we ran into one another, "Here is an idea I had," and we go with it.

The resource teacher occasionally graded papers; however, most of the grading was done by the classroom teacher. The two teachers "shared the discipline and attention to the general needs of the kids."

DISCUSSION FOCI WITHIN MULTIMEDIA CASE STUDY

This multimedia case study stimulates thought and problem-solving around four broad categories within writing instruction: (a) management, (b) facilitation, (c) instruction, and (d) technology.

Management

Different groups of students (gifted, at-risk, or mixed ability), and different types of classes (writing, reading, or literature classes) created different managerial demands for teachers (Vaughn, Boss, & Schumm, 2000). Similarly, different lesson types and procedures contained in them influenced teachers' decisions about their lesson planning and management. The teacher in this multimedia case study dealt with what she called "never a traditional class, where anything and everything can happen, and does happen everyday." The discussion of the management strategies in this case study brought to preservice teachers' attention an array of issues and potential problems characteristic of different student groups and class types. The analysis of the potential causes for managerial problems, and the ways of dealing with them, prepared preservice teachers for a richer exploration of these issues, not only in this case study but, more importantly, in their future instructional practices.

Facilitation

The teacher in this multimedia case study used a variety of inquiry-oriented (Larkin, 2001) strategies to facilitate the students' work on the project. For example, she inquired about the students' work progress and resources used for their project. Based on this information, she typically offered suggestions for changes or additions to the project. This example of an interaction in the classroom would open up a discussion of other issues around teacher facilitation in the classroom such as questioning, ensuring all students' participation, matching students' learning preferences, peer conferencing, revision, and final editing. There were many other examples of facilitation and interaction in the classroom that not only provided different types of support but also engaged other members of the classroom, the assistant teacher, and the students. These examples can be further analyzed and critiqued by preservice teachers for their effectiveness in this particular case context.

Instruction

In this case study, the classroom teacher explained that she wanted to "give the students an opportunity to engage in an authentic writing assignment—one for a school audience beyond the teachers." Such an assignment is challenging, for it requires both the knowledge of the content and of the ways of teaching the content to students with differentiated learning abilities. An educator working with preservice students on this multimedia case might want to explore preservice students' background knowledge of writing and their teaching experiences with less proficient writers and use this insight to guide them how to plan for differentiated writing instruction (Kirby, Kirby, & Liner, 2004) that will be most meaningful and effective for all students at all levels of writing abilities.

Technology

Computer technology with Internet access is becoming commonplace in American public schools (Wells & Lewis, 2006). The teacher in this multimedia case study stressed the importance of computers for her students: "The technology allows me to create the environment in which my students can be authentic writers. They can be authentic work producers, which I don't think it would happen with pen and pencil." Although limited to word processing and Internet searches, the computer use in this multimedia case study raises important questions beyond this case about technology in teaching writing, particularly digital inquiry and writing (Beach, Anson, Bruech, & Swiss, 2008).

At the heart of the analysis of these four areas of focus in this case study are discussion questions. In creating the discussion questions for this case study, Christenbury's (1994) Questioning Circle framework was used. The framework distinguishes three circles or areas for potential questions: (a) the matter, (b) personal reality, and (c) external reality.

In this case study, the matter questions address the facts or the main concepts related to the subject of the study. Samples of questions from this circle are the following:

1. Who are the participants of this study?
2. What project are the students working on in this class?

The personal reality questions ask preservice teachers to filter the information that they access and analyze in the case study through the lenses of their personal experiences and value systems. Representative questions from that circle are the following:

1. How does the teacher's monitoring system compare with the techniques that you are familiar with?
2. If you were the teacher in this class, how would you structure instruction to make sure that all students stay on task most of the time?

The external reality questions ask preservice teachers to go beyond the world of personal experiences, since they encourage them to draw upon the knowledge of the world and concepts and perspectives of other researchers and educators. Sample questions from this circle are the following:

1. The teacher in this case study used informal ways of assessing students' progress on the project work, such as inquiry about the problems that they were facing or the materials they needed for the project. Can you think of additional assessment techniques described in the professional teacher literature?
2. What recommendations does research offer as to the questioning techniques in the classroom? Use one or two findings that you find most appealing.

As the areas of knowledge overlap, so do the questions in this case study, which may lead to questions that refer simultaneously to two or three areas of questioning identified by Christenbury (i.e., the matter, the personal and the external reality circles). Examples of questions with two and three areas intersecting are the following:

1. What type of instruction does the teacher in this class practice? Critique this instruction using the theoretical framework of sociocultural constructivism.
2. What did you learn about classroom management from watching this case study and reviewing the relevant literature? What are the issues that you would like to further explore for better understanding of the issues around classroom management in a writing classroom?

To conclude, the sample discussion questions presented in this case study are intended as suggestions that might be used in a variety of assignments in teacher education programs: written and oral narratives or critiques, or individual or group inquiry projects, with formal or informal documentation. Similarly, the four broad discussion foci (i.e., management, facilitation, instruction, and technology) are not the only areas of interest for exploration in this multimedia case study. Although presented as separate topics, they need not be seen as disconnected entities, as they can be brought together or grouped differently. As such, these discussion foci serve as starting points for the analysis and inquiry about the features in the case study: teacher's processed-oriented writing pedagogy, the instructional decision-making process in executing this pedagogy, and student learning experiences and outcomes.

Neither does this multimedia case study intend to offer a single approach for writing instruction. Rather, the case study method advocated in this chapter is meant to guide preservice teachers in developing their own pedagogical content knowledge (Shulman, 1987) about important aspects of writing instruction. Although acquiring such knowledge can be accomplished independently, a collective effort is recommended because it can lead to richer learning for all involved, than if the participants in it were asked to work alone. This is because of the multiple perspectives, experiences, and unique philosophical frameworks that the participants as individuals can bring to their teacher learning community of practice (Street, 2003). More information about the case study itself and the ways to explore it in the college classroom is provided in the instructor guide accompanying this chapter.

REFERENCES

Beach, R., Anson, C., Bruech, L. A., & Swiss, T. (Eds.). (2008). *Engaging students in digital writing.* Norwood, MA: Christopher Gordon Publishers.

Clark, R. E. (1994). Media will never influence learning. *Educational Technology Research and Development, 42*(2), 21–29.

Cognition and Technology Group at Vanderbilt. (1993, March). Anchored instruction and situated cognition revisited. *Educational Technology, 33*(3), 52–70.

Christenbury, L. (1994). *Making the journey: Being and becoming a teacher of English language arts.* Portsmouth, NH: Boyton/Cook Publishers Heinemann.

Darling-Hammond, L. (1997). *The right to learn: A blueprint for creating schools that work.* San Francisco: Jossey-Bass.

Fosnot, C. T. (1996). Teachers construct constructivism: The Center for Constructivist Teaching/Teacher Preparation Project. In C. T. Fosnot (Ed.), *Constructivism: Theory, perspectives and practice* (pp. 205–216). New York: Teachers College Press.

Hillocks, G. Jr. (2005). The focus on form vs. content in teaching writing. *Research in the Teaching of English, 40*(2), 238–248.

Kinzer, C. K., & Risko, V. J. (1998). Multimedia and enhanced learning: Transforming pre-service education. In D. Reinking, M. McKenna, L. D. Labbo, & R. Kieffer (Eds.), *Handbook of literacy and technology: Transformations in a post-typographic world* (pp. 185–202). Mahwah, NJ: Erlbaum.

Kirby, D., Kirby, D. L., & Liner, T. (2004). *Inside out: Strategies for teaching writing.* (3rd ed.). Portsmouth, NH: Heinemann.

Kirschner, P. A., Sweller, J., & Clark, R. E. (2006). Why minimal guidance during instruction does not work: An analysis of the failure of constructivist, discovery, problem-based, experiential, and inquiry-based teaching. *Educational Psychologist, 41*(2), 75–86.

Larkin, M. J. (2001). Providing support for student independence through scaffolded instruction. *Teaching Exceptional Children, 34*(1), 30–34.

Many, J. E., Howard, F., & Hoge, P. (2002). Epistemology and pre-service teacher education: How do beliefs about knowledge affect out students' experiences? *English Education, 34*(4), 302–322.

Masingila J. O., & Doerr, H. (2002). Understanding pre-service teachers' emerging practices through their analysis of a multimedia case study of practice. *Journal of Mathematics Teacher Education, 5*(3), 235–263.

Mooney, M. (1990). *Reading to, with, and by children.* Katonah, NY: Richard C. Owen.

O'Brien, D. G. (2004). *Using digital tools and the new media literacies to promote teacher reflection.* Paper presented at the annual meeting of the National Reading Conference, San Antonio, TX.

Office of Information and Reporting Services. (2003–2004). *New York State School Report Card.* Albany, NY. New York State Education Department. Retrieved April 12, 2008, from https://www.nystart.gov/publicweb-rc/2006/AOR-2006-420101060009.pdf

Segall, A. (2004). Revisiting pedagogical content knowledge: The pedagogy of content/the content pedagogy. *Teaching and Teacher Education, 20,* 489–504.

Salahu-Din, D., Persky, H., & Miller, J. (2008). *The nation's report card: Writing 2007* (NCES 2008–468). National Center for Education Statistics, Institute of Education Sciences, U.S. Department of Education, Washington, DC.

Scherff, L., & Piazza, C. (2005). The more things change, the more they stay the same: A survey of high-school students' writing experiences. *Research in the teaching of English, 39*(3), 271–304.

Shulman, L. S. (1987). Knowledge and teaching: Foundations of the new reform. *Harvard Educational Review, 57*(1), 1–22.

Street, C. (2003). Pre-service teachers' attitudes about writing and learning to teach writing: Implications for teacher educators. *Teacher Education Quarterly, 30*(3), 33–50.

Swain, K. D. (2006). Students with disabilities meeting the challenge of high-stakes writing assessments. *Education, 126*(4), 660–665.

Yerrick, R., Ross, D., & Molebash, P. (2005). Too close for comfort: Real time science teaching reflections via digital video editing. *Journal of Science Teacher Education, 16,* 351–375.

Vaughn, S., Boss, C. S., & Schumm, J. S. (2000). *Teaching exceptional, diverse, and at-risk students in the general education classroom* (2nd ed.). Needham Heights, MA: Allyn & Bacon.

Vygotsky, L. S. (1962). *Thought and Language.* Cambridge, MA: MIT Press.

Vygotsky, L. (1978). Interaction between learning and development. In M. Cole, (Trans.), *Mind in society* (pp. 79–91). Cambridge, MA: Harvard University Press.

Wells, J., & Lewis, L. (2006). *Internet access in U.S. public schools and classrooms: 1994–2005* (NCES 2007-020). U.S. Department of Education. Washington, DC: National Center for Education Statistics.

Wenger, E. (1998). *Communities of practice: Learning, meaning, and identity.* London: Cambridge University Press.

National Commission on Writing for America's Families, Schools, and Colleges. (2006). *Writing and School Reform, including The Neglected "R": The Need for a Writing Revolution.* Retrieved January 15, 2007, from http://www.writingcommission.org/prod_downloads/writingcom/writing-school-reform-natl-comm-writing.pdf

ADDITIONAL RESOURCES

Calandra, B., Dias, L. B., & Dias, M. (2006). Using digital video for professional development in urban schools: A pre-service teacher's experience with reflection. *Journal of Computing in Teacher Education, 22(*4), 125–133.

Hughes, J. E., Wai-Ling, B., & Pearson, P. D. (2000). Pre-service teachers' perceptions of using hypermedia and video to examine the nature of literacy instruction. *Journal of Literacy Research, 32*(4), 599–629.

Kolodner, J. L., Owensby, J. N., & Guizdial, M. (2004). Case-based learning aids. In D. H. Jonassen (Ed.), *Handbook of research on educational communications and technology* (pp. 829–861, 2nd ed.). Mahwah, NJ: Erlbaum.

Mishra, P., & Koehler, M. J. (2004). *Technological pedagogical content knowledge: A new framework for teacher knowledge.* Retrieved November 13, 2005, from http://punya.educ.msu.edu/PunyaWeb/publications/inpress/MishraKoehler_TPCK.pdf

Shrin, M. G., & van Es, E. A. (2005). Using video to support teachers' ability to notice classroom interactions. *Journal of Technology and Teacher Education, 13*(3), 475–491.

Young, C. A. & Bush, J. (2004). Teaching the English language arts with technology: A critical approach and pedagogical framework. *Contemporary Issues in Technology and Teacher Education, 4*(1). Retrieved March 15, 2009, from http://www.citejournal.org/vol4/iss1/languagearts/article1.cfm

Wold, L. S. (2003). An examination of teachers' "learning to act on reflection." *Reading Research and Instruction, 42*(3), 52–74.

ACKNOWLEDGEMENTS

I would like to thank Liu Xiaoyan and Carol Kuria, doctoral fellows, who contributed to the design and production of this multimedia case study. I would also like to thank the teachers in this case study who gave so graciously of their time and who shared openly their thoughts about teaching writing to students with differentiated learning needs. Thank you as well to the participating students for sharing some of their work and thoughts for this case study.

CHAPTER 11

DEVELOPING PROFESSIONAL COMPETENCIES OF TEACHER EDUCATORS IN THE USE OF EDUCATIONAL TECHNOLOGY, WITH SCENARIO-BASED LEARNING

Shironica Karunanayaka
The Open University of Sri Lanka, Sri Lanka

Som Naidu
Charles Sturt University, NSW, Australia

BACKGROUND

The Faculty of Education of the Open University of Sri Lanka (OUSL) offers several programs of study using open and distance learning (ODL) techniques, with the objective of expanding opportunities for higher studies for personnel in the field of education and enhancement of their professional competencies. Recently, the faculty developed a practitioner-oriented professional development program for teacher educators: the Master

Cases 'n' Places: Global Cases in Educational and Performance Technology, pages 151–132

of Arts in Teacher Education–International (MATE-I) program. A unique pedagogical design called Scenario-Based Learning (SBL) was adopted in this program, which was radically different from the pedagogical approach that is commonly used in such programs at OUSL.

Scenario-based learning seeks to focus learners' attention on critical reflection and problem-solving activities, promoting a more learning-centered focus, which represents a major shift away from traditional content-based approaches to learning and teaching. In this innovative approach, learning and teaching activities are orchestrated around authentic learning scenarios drawn from the field, seeking to make learning more meaningful for practicing teacher educators. Learners are presented with authentic situations (learning scenarios) that unfold in the form of a storyline. In this scenario, the learners are required to assume a key role that they might actually perform in real life in their profession as teacher educators, and engage in challenging activities leading to the achievement of desired learning outcomes. This SBL approach also allows building on the existing competencies of teacher educators (see also Karunanayaka, Gunawardena, Naidu, Lekamge, & Menon, 2007; Karunanayaka, Lekamge, Gunawardena, Naidu, & Menon, 2005; Karunanayaka, Lekamge,Gunawardena, Naidu, & Menon, 2007; Naidu, Menon, Gunawardena, Lekamge, & Karunanayaka, 2007).

TEACHER EDUCATOR AS AN EDUCATIONAL TECHNOLOGIST

Teacher Educator as an Educational Technologist is one of the courses in the MATE-I program that aimed at developing competencies of teacher educators in utilizing appropriate educational technologies in their profession. The course team undertook the challenging task of developing this course using a scenario-based learning approach.

Initially, the continuously evolving concept of educational technology was carefully studied by the course team. Educational Technology has been defined by the Association for Educational Communications and Technology (AECT) in 1977 as

> A complex, integrated process involving people, procedures, ideas, devices, and organization, for analyzing problems and devising, implementing, evaluating, and managing solutions to those problems, involved in all aspects of human learning.

A more recent definition of educational technology by AECT states that

> Educational technology is the study and ethical practice of facilitating learning and improving performance by creating, using and managing appropriate technological processes and resources. (AECT, 2004)

As indicated in these definitions, educational technology is more than just the use of equipment or tools to enhance the teaching-learning process. Along with its focus on tools, educational technology also includes the processes of applying these tools in the teaching-learning process, under the guidance from theories of learning. Thus, it was realized by the course team, that when new technologies become the focus of instruction in teaching and learning situations, it is equally important to pay attention to develop new instructional approaches that would complement the potential of new technologies to increase the quality of teaching and learning.

Accordingly, the goal of the Teacher Educator as an Educational Technologist course was determined to be the development among teacher educators competencies and practices in relation to the following areas:

- Designing and sequencing of learning experiences;
- Media selection, utilization, and integration of media into teaching and learning;
- Design and development of technology-enhanced learning materials; and
- Evaluation of technology-enhanced learning.

In the study of the course Teacher Educator as an Educational Technologist, the teacher educators are required to develop a rationale for using educational technology, design learning experiences, select and use appropriate media to develop technology-enhanced learning material, and evaluate its effectiveness with their student teachers. This is achieved through situating the teacher educators in a learning scenario in which they have to face several challenges in the form of learning and assessment activities. The specific learning outcomes of the course mentioned below indicate these.

- Develop a concept map of a selected topic and prepare the instructional objectives, learning outcomes, and the learning experiences;
- Select appropriate media and incorporate into the teaching and learning materials;
- Design and develop technology-enhanced teaching and learning material; and
- Evaluate the technology-enhanced teaching and learning material and prepare an evaluation report.

Further, the course team considered the fact that with the increasing presence of Information and Communication Technology (ICT) in schools and everyday life, there was a crucial need for continuing professional development of teachers as well as teacher educators who train teachers in the use of educational technology, including modern ICTs. Teacher professional development in the use of technology should be concentrating not only on training teachers on how to integrate technology into their teaching, but also on using technology as a means for offering their professional development (Carlson & Gadio, 2002). Innovative approaches such as collaborative, reflective practices and use of Open and Distance Learning (ODL) and ICTs are considered essential to replace the existing conventional approaches in professional development programs for educators (Menon, 2004). This emphasized the need for a carefully planned professional development program for these teacher educators, who were following the courses as distant learners, while being engaged in their profession, training teachers.

The major forms of learner support were composed of print materials and multimedia resources, including a Study Guide and a Resource Pack. A limited number of face-to-face contact sessions held with the instructors provided opportunities for closer interaction. In addition, local study-center support with library, computer, and Internet facilities, electronic media such as CD ROM, course Web site and online provision for instructor support and assignment submission, were also provided. Learners were encouraged to use a learning management system (LMS) designed to support their learning process. This facility enabled learners to receive notices, access resources, communicate with staff, collaborate with peers, submit their assignments, and obtain feedback.

This course carries a weight of one third credit, equivalent to 150 study hours, and the minimum course duration is 24 weeks. There is no final examination, while student performance is evaluated through continuous assessment based on marks obtained for four compulsory interrelated assignments. The pass mark for each assignment is 50%, and the cumulative marks will lead to the final assessment in the course (MATE–International Program Handbook, 2004).

COURSE IMPLEMENTATION

The implemetation of this course was a challenging experience for the course team (the instructors) as well as the teacher educators who were the learners of this course—Teacher Educator as an Educational Technologist. At the commencement of the course, an orientation session was conducted by the instructors in order to provide initial guidance to the learners on its unique pedagogical design, SBL, and also on the course-related activities, consisting of introducing the learning scenario, learning activities, and assessment tasks. A detailed study schedule provided in the Study Guide specify week-to-week activities that students needed to perform in order to achieve the specified learning outcomes of the course. It was very important to emphasize to learners that a considerable amount of interaction was expected between the learners and course materials, learners and instructors, as well as learners and learners, in addition to engagement in the weekly activities as specified in the detailed study schedule.

A limited number of interactive contact sessions were held, which required students to present their work and obtain instructor and peer feedback, resulting in group discussions facilitated by the instructors. These sessions also provided an opportunity for learners to have team discussions that enabled sharing their experiences with peers. Considering the practical nature of this course, skill-development workshops were also held to provide learners with hands-on experience on using new technologies such as in e-learning and multimedia development. These included a one-day orientation session to the LMS and e-learning, 2-day audio-video production workshop, and 4-day interactive multimedia development workshop. During these workshop sessions, learners received expert support and guidance in using and applying new technology.

A Web-based learning management system (LMS) called Manhattan, and later Moodle, was integrated with the course as a supplementary means to further support the teacher educators. Through this LMS, these distant learners were able to communicate with staff and their peers and engage in course-related discussions as well as social discussions. Five threaded discussions, one to familiarize the students, and four in relation to the four assignments, were initiated and moderated by the instructor. Each discussion started with a question with supportive Web links provided as resources, and students were given clear guidelines on their task. They were required to engage in each discussion by posting at least two meaningful contributions, and finally, considering everybody's views, agree upon a suitable answer for each question. Each discussion continued for about 2 weeks. By mutual agreement, 5% of assessment marks were allocated for engaging in the discussions.

A CHALLENGING EXPERIENCE

Feedback received from instructors as well as learners indicate that this approach has been very challenging to both groups. From extensive discussions with a range of staff associated with the program, it was abundantly clear that, as a result of this exercise, there had been a considerable amount of capacity building among academic staff in the faculty in relation to teaching and learning generally. However, their reflections clearly indicate how challenging and demanding the whole process had been for them during the design, development, and implementation of this program/course.

> The initial challenge was articulating the story. Situating the story—make it authentic. I think we are all used to traditional methods. Although we do use stories, case studies in some of our other courses, in SBL where the learner is placed in the story itself where he or she has to play a role is a new approach. I thought that was very interesting, but it was difficult also. I knew the value of self-regulated learning. Still, only when you are really engaged in developing the stories, placing the learner in a role, when you are actually going through the process, it was really interesting and challenging. It took us a long time to really come out with what we wanted. I thought it was a very good experience for me.
>
> At the inauguration, everybody was highly motivated and said that they found the program very interesting and challenging. However, after three months, we observed several problems. Some students had dropped out. The reasons given were inability to cope with the workload due to their other commitments.
>
> This needs the continuous engagement of the learners. We found out that some students had not understood exactly what was expected from the assignments. They faced problems with time. They had to think what to write, not just reproduce material.
>
> The problem they had, they were unable to relate theory into practice. That was the main difficulty they had. Even though we had asked them to think as the main actor in that scenario, they were trying to repeat what was given in the material.
>
> Delays in submission of assignments is another problem. We had been very flexible and had extended the deadlines. Despite several reminders, many students delayed submission of assignments on time. According to the rules, all assignments were compulsory, and if they didn't submit they would fail the course. This was a concern.
>
> In particular, in this course students need more help as it is a practical-oriented course. Coping with the technology will be new to most students and coping with SBL is also new.
>
> When there are some students who are unable to cope with the work themselves, how are we going to tackle them? That is my concern.

Learner reflections revealed that one of the main challenges faced was changing from the traditional teacher-directed approaches, which they were comfortable with, to this very learner- and learning-centered approach, in which they had to take the responsibility of their own learning. This resulted in time-management issues, as they were engaged in the learning process while being employed full-time. However, gradually they adapted to it and found the process interesting and very useful. There is general consensus among learners in the program around the view that scenario-based learning as an approach to teaching and learning is working well for those who are already practicing teacher educators. This is reflected in the following excerpts from selected learners.

> The scenario-based approach to learning was a new thing, which made me feel that I had done something new and useful and above all, directly related to my field of work. In fact the learning activities were directly related to my profession so that putting what I learned into immediate practice was immensely useful.
>
> The new method of teaching and learning in the MATE program (scenario-based learning) is really interesting and practical. Most of the learning activities in the courses are highly practical, and the learners are given many chances to learn by doing and not by only reading. The knowledge derived through these activities is concrete and creative.
>
> The guidance provided during the day schools made me happy and made me feel a bit relieved. Whenever I got feedback with a good grade (which I thought I deserved), I felt happy and motivated. Whenever the feedback was substantiated well with suggestions for improvement, I always felt encouraged.

However, as expected in a developing educational setting, the delivery technology was going to be a challenge. Not surprisingly, there were more than a few situations in which the technology left both the staff and students frustrated and disappointed, as indicated by the following excerpts:

> I think most of us need time management. We are involved in so many duties in our colleges the whole day.
>
> I missed both day schools, and I really got stuck in my assignment. We had submitted the first assignment before the first day school and then there were problems.
>
> Actually I was about to give up because it was too heavy for me. Because of the heavy workload. But because of the last day school, I got some confidence and I thought even though I don't get a good mark for this, I will just continue.
>
> Though I had no prior knowledge in working with the required software, the sheer thrill of working with new technology made me engaged with practical work. There were times I had to redo the same things over and over again. There were many last minute disappointments. There were technical failures as well as blunders from my side either due to my over enthusiasm or clumsiness. Anyway, with great difficulty, to my utmost satisfaction, I managed to hand over my completed multimedia package on CD.
>
> At times the excitement of online learning too was dampened by technical factors beyond my control. As can be expected in a country like Sri Lanka,

> technology failure (no electricity, computer breakdowns, difficulty in logging into an educational site, and in many occasions difficulty in connecting to the Internet) caused havoc and much anxiety. When unexpected events stood in my way of working according to the schedule and the way I wanted, I felt depressed and threatened. I was concerned that I might be penalized due to no fault of my own. These moments put me really under pressure. Such events occurred often and at a time when we expected them least.

Further, engagement in online learning in this course has been perceived as a highly challenging, yet motivating, experience by the learners. The opportunity to make use of this facility to communicate with academic staff and peers was viewed as particularly important because they were physically remote from each other as distant learners. However, as online learning was totally new to them, adapting to this was not so easy, as evidenced by the following reflections:

> At the beginning of the week one, it was like being in the middle of a dark, thick jungle. It was very confusing to click which buttons to visit a particular site, as there were so many links. The begining of the first week was trial and error for me.
>
> Actually in the first week I did not have a clear idea about how to follow the course as both "ET" and "Online learning" were new things for me. So I missed many activities that we were assigned to do during the first week. When I saw others' contributions and our teachers' guidelines and encouragements, I understood my role and started my work.
>
> Honestly, I found nowhere even after the inauguration. I left OUSL speaking to myself "nothing to worry. If I want to swim, I can't learn it by being in the ground. I must jump into the water and see." Our instructors gave enough guidelines on how we have to act when we jump into the water. So I had enough confidence to jump into the water.
>
> I couldn't draft the proper answer at once and didn't answer immediately. I need time to form the answer. Also it was not so much clear enough to me. Anyhow with a lot of disturbances it was delayed and I couldn't open the computer. At last! I followed the answers given by other members and I tried to draft my answer. BUT! I found the time given to it is over. Hard luck!

Several students faced certain challenges such as limited access to the Internet, coping with the technology, information and interaction overload, time constraints, increased workload and changing from conventional teacher-centered approaches to a more self-regulated and reflective learning approach. Yet, a sense of achievement was claimed by the learners, once they became confident in using this facility, and gained advantages through it.

Having obtained this feedback, the course team is now in the process of identifying suitable measures to further support learners to overcome challenges and successfully complete this course.

DISCUSSION QUESTIONS

Critically analyze the unique contribution of the pedagogical design of this course, scenario-based learning, in developing the competencies of teacher educators as educational technologists.

1. What are the key challenges faced by the course team, who were the instructors of this course?
2. What are the key challenges faced by the teacher educators, who were the learners of this course?
3. What issues do you consider as most critical and how could these be resolved?
4. Compare and contrast the challenges faced by Sri Lankan teacher educators in the learning process of their professional development in educational technology, with challenges that would be faced by teacher educators in your institution.
5. What other meaningful learning and teaching solutions could challenge teacher educators in your institution in relation to their professional development competencies in educational technology?

REFERENCES

Association for Educational Communications and Technology (AECT). (1977). *The definition of educational technology*. Washington, DC: AECT

Association for Educational Communications and Technology (AECT). (2004). *The definition of educational technology*. Washington, DC: AECT. Retrieved April 21, 2008, from www.indiana.edu/~molpage/Meanings%20of%20ET_4.0.pdf

Carlson, S., & Gadio, C.T. (2002). Teacher professional development in the use of technology. In W. D. Haddok & A. Draxler (Eds.), *Technologies for education: Potential, parameters and prospects*. UNESCO & Academy for Educational Developed. Retrieved January 20, 2004, from http://www.aed.org/publications/TechEdInfo.html

Karunanayaka, S., Gunawardena, C., Naidu, S., Lekamge D,. & Menon, M. (2007). Questioning best practices with an innovative pedagogical design for professional development of teacher educators. *INTI Journal Malaysia* Special Issue on International Conference on Teaching and Learning, 1–8.

Karunanayaka, S., Lekamge D., Gunawardena, C., Naidu, S., & Menon, M. (2005). *MATE (International) Programme: A novel approach to developing global partnerships in teacher education.* Paper presented at the Asian Roundtable on Open and

Distance Learning for Attainment of Millennium Development Goals. 20–22 May Colombo.

Karunanayaka, S., Lekamge, D., Gunawardena, C., Naidu, S., & Menon, M. (2007). Professional development of teacher educators with collaborative learning designs and networking in the OUSL – MATE (International) program. *Indian Journal of Open Learning, 16*(2), 101–112.

MATE – International: Program Handbook. (2004). *Master of Arts in Teacher Education (International).* The Open University of Sri Lanka: Department of Education, The Faculty of Education.

Menon, M. (2004). *Networking for quality assurance in alternative modes of teacher education.* Paper presented at NAAC-COL Roundtable on Innovations in Teacher Education, Bangalore, India, 2004. In K. Rama & M. Menon, (Eds.), *Innovations in teacher education: International practices for quality assurance* (pp. 205–212). Bangalore: NAAC.

Naidu, S., Menon, M., Gunawardena, C., Lekamge, D., & Karunanayaka, S. (2007). How scenario-based learning can engender reflective practice in distance education. In J. M. Spector (Ed.), *Finding your online voice: Stories told by experienced online educators* (pp. 98–130). Mahwah, NJ: Lawrence Erlbaum Associates.

CHAPTER 12

ONLINE HYBRID TEACHER EDUCATION PROGRAM CASE STUDY

Thanh T. Nguyen
Bridgewater State College, USA

INTRODUCTION

While developing online hybrid classes for a teacher's education program, a professor on tenure track is shocked to discover that her first group of students has filed a grievance against her. She finds, however, that the complaint is unjustified: though her students were unable to navigate the online aspect of the curriculum, the proper academic channels did not provide an appropriate organization for her to teach online hybrid classes.

THE LETTER (PART 1)

Jane soon wished she had not opened the letter on her desk.

"Dear Dr. Evermans," it began. "There is a grievance against you on my desk that needs to be addressed immediately. Please come see me as soon as you can."

Cases 'n' Places: Global Cases in Educational and Performance Technology, pages 161–140

After earning her doctorate from a well-known university in Boston 3 years ago, Jane could only get part-time adjunct teaching jobs at different colleges. As a single parent, she relied on her mother to take care of her two young children. Frustrated with the lack of full-time teaching positions with no chance of advancement, she considered moving to the West Coast. Through an alumni support network, she finally got a tenure-track position at a small state college. With her online teaching experiences as a teaching fellow in her doctoral program, Jane was expected to teach her full-load courses online. This new online program was to attract teachers who were working on fulfilling the Department of Education requirements for licensure, but did not want to drive to the college campus every week after work. Within the last few years, the college lost many teachers who preferred to pay more for weekend courses offered by another private university in which they could take courses through an off-campus program at a local school. In past years, the School of Education Dean, Dr. Johnson, saw many more colleges move courses online, so he decided that the Instructional Technology program would be an appropriate first program to move online. He assumed that these student-teachers would know more about technology, and taking online courses would not be too difficult.

Jane's first semester bore mixed results. In addition to her teaching responsibilities, she had to redesign all the courses in her department to fit an online hybrid format. Her department chair, Dr. Latham, though not opposed to the dean's suggestion, wanted to supervise Jane's teaching. He requested that she meet with students face-to-face once a month, or four times per semester. He also wanted Jane to use his syllabi and requested Jane to add his name to her BlackBoard courses so that he could oversee her online teaching. Although Jane did not like how these courses were designed, she did not want to offend her department chair. At the end of the semester, he would tell Jane how to grade these students instead of letting her, their instructor, evaluate them on their merits. For instance, he would send Jane an e-mail to instruct her on how to spell the world "minus" on a grade in case they mistook the grade as something different. Jane felt very uncomfortable but dared not say a word.

The second semester did not start out well either. The first two face-to-face meetings were canceled due to snowstorms. Jane received many furious e-mails from students demanding information on starting their classes, understandably worried about failing the courses. Jane contacted the scheduling office to reschedule her face-to-face classes and reassign her to another available classroom two weeks later. Many students demanded to move out of her courses because they were uncomfortable with online learning. They were enraged because they were not aware that they would have to take courses online. Her department chair had to reassign many of them to cross-departmental classes, where they would take equivalent courses with other professors or request the registrar's office refund their money. Her face-to-face classes finally met after the snowstorms had passed. Though her classes were far from full, she had enough students to run the class. Why did the provost want to see her?

Nervously, Jane called the provost's office and was asked to come to see the provost immediately. The provost greeted her with a stony face and informed her that the meeting was not a formal evaluation but a chance for discussion. The provost told her about complaints from students expressing their concern and confusion because they did not realize that the course they had registered for was online. They had no idea what to do once the face-to-face meetings were canceled. They were not sure if they would learn anything in an online learning environment and wanted to know why they had to take online courses. The provost asked Jane to come up with a plan to address these concerns. Jane walked out of the provost's office feeling distressed and hopeless. What could she do now?

THE CHALLENGES

Walking back to her office, Jane wondered what went wrong. For the next hour, Jane sat numbly in despair as she thought about her options: looking for another traditional teaching position, or facing the challenges without knowing how she would get tenure for her online course.

Although Jane was familiar with BlackBoard, an online course management system, she did not know how she could train students to use the system before starting her first lecture. In a traditional classroom, students came to class to get the syllabus and the first lesson in person. For Jane's hybrid online classroom, the first face-to-face meetings was mostly questions asking how to register for an e-mail or a BlackBoard account. Another problem that Jane had not prepared for was the time lag: after they signed up for college e-mail accounts, students had to wait 24 hours to begin using them. Without their BlackBoard accounts, Jane could not train students to maneuver around the online course management system. Although Jane asked her students to work with those who had BlackBoard accounts, she could not begin her first lesson because of all the troubleshooting issues. Once the course was moved online, her students kept sending Jane requests for basic how-to instructions: from technical problems they were having to course schedule and assignment. Jane felt that she had to work 24 hours a day in order to keep the courses going.

Another challenge Jane faced was the use of syllabi that were·given to her by her department chair. These courses were designed for a traditional classroom where students would come to class for lectures and discussions. When the course was moved online, these requirements did not work. For example, students had to write up and submit a midterm paper to the instructor. With an online course, students had to send their papers to a digital drop box, an equivalent of a mailbox. Students ended up sending their papers to Jane via e-mail or posting them on the online discussion boards instead of the digital drop box. Some students even drove to campus and put their papers in Jane's mailbox or gave them to her secretary. Despite her hard work, her students did not enjoy her online hybrid course and gave her low ratings in their evaluation. Jane desperately needed higher ratings for her tenure review.

After going through different options, Jane decided to call her mentor and former graduate school professor, Dr. Perrone, for advice. Fortunately, he had just returned from vacation and was in a good mood. He asked her to meet with him the next day in his office.

(Stop reading here and discuss Part 1 Questions)

PART 1 QUESTIONS

- Why was Jane's first face-to-face meeting so disorganized and confused?
- Why did Jane's students not understand how to submit their papers online?
- Should Jane look for another teaching job?
- Should Jane appreciate Dr. Latham's mentoring efforts in sharing his syllabi?
- Should the Department Chair be held responsible for forcing her to use his syllabi?
- Should the dean be held responsible for moving courses online?

FACING CHALLENGES (PART 2)

When they met, Dr. Perrone sympathetically listened to Jane's problems while taking notes. He asked Jane if students knew that the courses they registered were hybrid-online. If they did not know, the grievance against her was unjustified. This problem was bigger than Jane thought. This was a problem with the administration and governance. Although the School of Education Dean, Dr. Johnson, wanted to move more courses online, he did not propose any change to the college governance for approval. The registrar's office entered traditional classroom coding for Jane's online hybrid course.

Dr. Perrone suggested Jane find out if there was anyone in her college who would help advertise her courses as online, inform students in advance, and instruct them on proceeding. She ought to explore mediums to send students instructions weeks in advance, in the simple form of either a letter or a video. She realized that it was imperative that students should know how to sign up for their e-mail and BlackBoard accounts before the first meeting or take an online classroom tutorial.

If Jane received many e-mails from her students asking how to fix their technical problems, instead of the course content, she had to find out if there was someone in the college who could provide technical support for her students, Dr. Perrone suggested. When Jane asked him whether or not she should look for a new teaching job because she had not received any good evaluation from her students, Dr. Perrone leaned back in his seat, contemplating Jane's situation in silence. Jane thought he was thinking about some other openings that he knew, but instead he said it also was not fair for Jane to use the same form of evaluation for a traditional classroom. He suggested Jane find out to whom she should approach to request a different form of evaluation for her courses, and how to convince her department chair to let her redesign her syllabi. Who would be willing to support her quest? Jane began to feel overwhelmed with Dr. Perrone's questions.

(Stop reading here and discuss Part 2 Questions)

PART 2 QUESTIONS

- What are challenges that Jane discovers?
- Who should initiate the proposal for an online program through college governance?
- Why should any program change go through college governance for approval?
- What does Jane have to do to inform students that her courses are hybrid-online, not traditional classrooms, or how to contact her if there was another snowstorm?
- Who would help advertise her courses as online, inform students in advance, and instruct them on proceeding?
- Who could provide technical support for her students?
- Whom should Jane approach to request for a different form of evaluation for her courses?
- Why did Dr. Latham not want Jane to change his syllabi?
- Why should Dr. Latham let Jane redesign his syllabi?

SOLUTIONS

In order to inform students about her hybrid-online course, the registrar's office ought to have a different number coding in the schedule book. With help from her department, Jane wrote up a program change proposal. After receiving an approval from her department and the dean, she sent the proposal to the college governance for approval. Although her proposal was sent back for revision a few times, her proposal was finally approved. The committee sent its recommendation to the president who would usually seek advice from the provost. This complicated process took a whole year to change the course number and coding for the registrar's office. To move a program online, Jane learned how to work with the college system, governance, and policy. By going through the college governance, Jane's courses now were clearly stated in the catalog and schedule book as hybrid-online courses, with specific dates for meetings on campus.

To prepare her students for how to study online before the first face-to-face meeting, Jane established a diplomatic relationship with the Distance Learning Director, Dr. Fuller. Although the Distance Learning office was mostly supporting videoconferencing classrooms, online classrooms should be next on her list for supporting. She agreed to have her secretary send Jane's letters out to students. Jane could instruct students a couple of weeks before the class started how to sign up for an e-mail and BlackBoard account, how to get used to an online classroom by taking a BlackBoard tutorial course, and how to get reading materials in advance. Jane also instructed her students on how to work online without the first face-to-face meeting and how to contact her in case of another snow day. With the BlackBoard tutorial as her prerequisite, students were not able to tell her that they did not know how to maneuver through BlackBoard.

Dr. Perrone advised Jane to meet with the vice president of the college's Information Technology division, Mr. Smith, and ask for his support in establishing a helpdesk team that would provide technical support to her online students. Jane took his advice and made an appointment to meet with Mr. Smith. He enthusiastically supported her proposal to set up the college infrastructure in terms of supporting students and faculty once courses were moved online. This would require the college to set up a BlackBoard support team, which would offer workshops for students. When Jane mentioned her concerns for her tenure promotion in the future, Mr. Smith promised to discuss their plans for online programs with the provost, the dean and the president. Since the college was also planning to offer more online courses, a different form of faculty evaluation should be discussed. Jane left his office relieved, but knowing that she had more hurdles to overcome.

With Dr. Perrone's advice, Jane cautiously planned her approach to her department chair. In a few years, Jane would be up for promotion and did not want Dr. Latham to write a bad recommendation for her. One of her colleagues suggested Jane contact the union. Afterward, a union grievance officer suggested that Jane set up a meeting for the two of them plus the department chair. Jane decided not to pursue this path. Instead, Jane shared articles and books about online course design with Dr. Latham. Jane asked for his opinions about changing the design of the courses for the online classroom. After reading some of Jane's articles and books, he agreed to let Jane redesign all of her course syllabi.

With her department chair's agreement, Jane eliminated midterm and final exams. Instead, Jane used an incremental learning method in which students studied and worked on their assignment one week at a time with a clear and consistent deadline for every week. Students culminated their learning growth with a final project or paper. To help her students manage their time for weekly online assignments, Jane employed a learning contract, a form of agreement between Jane and the students based on methods and teaching techniques used to teach adult learners (Knowles, 1980, 1986). Jane spent a lot of time at the first face-to-face meeting discussing the reasons why students wanted to take her courses, as well as the course objectives and outcomes. Jane also made sure that students could contact the technical support team for technical problems. She helped students see how the role of a professor was different from a technical support staff by clearly stating problems and to whom they should contact for answers. Jane clearly stated that any late assignments due to technical problems must be accompanied by an e-mail from or a name of a technical-support staff member. This helped reduce a series of e-mails from students to Jane with requests about how to fix their computers.

After in-class discussions, Jane required students to respond to her list of objectives and outcomes in the form of questions, then post their questions on a discussion board forum. Jane also set up a feedback system in which students knew the due date for each assignment, to whom they must provide feedback, and from whom they should receive feedback. Students checked each other's learning contract in class and then posted their contract online for checking again. With her redesigned syllabi for online courses, students knew exactly what to expect, and in the end, they gave Jane higher evaluations. Through word of mouth, Jane's program has been expanding.

REFERENCES

Knowles, M. S. (1980). *The modern practice of adult education: From pedagogy to androgogy* (2nd ed.). Englewood Cliffs, NJ: Cambridge Adult Education; Chicago: Follet.

Knowles, M. S. (1986). *Using learning contracts: Practical approaches to individualizing and structuring learning.* San Francisco: Jossey-Bass

SUGGESTED RESOURCES

Bauer, B. A. (1985). Self-directed learning in a graduate adult education program. In S. Brookfield (Ed.), *Self-directed learning: From theory to practice* (New Directions for Continuing Education, Number 25, pp. 41–50). San Francisco: Jossey-Bass.

Brockett, R. G., & Hiemstra, R. (1985). Bridging the theory-practice gap in self-directed learning. In S. Brookfield (Ed.), *Self-directed learning: From theory to practice* (New Directions for Continuing Education, Number 25, pp. 31–40). San Francisco: Jossey-Bass.

Holmes, G., & Abington-Cooper, M. (2000). Pedagogy vs. andragogy: A false dichotomy? *The Journal of Technology Studies, XXVI*(2). Retrieved May 20, 2008, from http://scholar.lib.vt.edu/ejournals/JOTS/Summer-Fall-2000/holmes.html

CHAPTER 13

THE OUCH DIP

Teacher Education Technology Training at the Overland University of Central Hattiesburg

Jason G. Caudill
Carson-Newman College, USA

INTRODUCTION

The experiences of the graduate assistant in this case are based on the author's own actual experiences and observations from professional practice. The university and the course presented in this case, however, are fictionalized in order to guard the anonymity of actual persons involved.

This case takes place at the Overland University of Central Hattiesburg (OUCH). OUCH is a large research university of approximately 30,000 students offering programs from the undergraduate through the doctoral level and has numerous undergraduate classes taught by graduate assistants (GAs).

The OUCH Instruction for Education program (OUCHIE) houses both the undergraduate and master's level degree programs for K–12 teacher education. The undergraduate program does not possess the appropriate accreditation to license teachers, so OUCHIE students wishing to teach in

Cases 'n' Places: Global Cases in Educational and Performance Technology, pages 169–149

the public school system are required to complete the master's program, including a full year of student teaching. All teacher education majors are required to complete one 3-hour instructional-technology class during their senior year. At OUCH, and within the OUCHIE program, this is the only required technology class for education students.

THE CLASS

The class, OUCHIE 415, is designed as an instructional-technology survey course for students in the teacher education undergraduate program. The goal of the class is to provide aspiring teachers with the tools that they need to utilize technology in their courses as practicing teachers. While part of the class inevitably involves students learning how to use specific software applications, the more important goal is to expose them to multiple applications so that they are comfortable in moving to new software and adapting to changing software in the future.

Typically, the class moves from a beginning in Microsoft Word to PowerPoint and Excel and culminates in every student learning basic Web site creation and administration through HTML code and the use of a What You See Is What You Get (WYSIWYG) Web authoring software. Topics for each section are presented in Table 13.1.

TABLE 13.1 Sections and Topics for OUCHIE 415

Section	Content	Goal
Microsoft Word	Formatting, saving in multiple file types, inserting tables and images, desktop publishing, saving Word documents as HTML	Learners will be able to use Word to create documents for use in their classrooms including worksheets for students and class newsletters.
Microsoft PowerPoint	Creating presentations, applying themes and effects, inserting media objects, exporting PowerPoint as a Web page, creating classroom Jeopardy! games	Learners will be able to create instructional PowerPoint presentations that can be viewed locally and deployed online.
Microsoft Excel	Basic formulas, creating charts, using Excel for classroom management with grade books and other student records	Learners will be able to create and use classroom management tools with Excel.
HTML/Web Authoring	Creating basic Web pages with links using HTML coding in Notepad or an equivalent text editor, using a WYSIWYG to create more advanced sites with multiple pages, media content, and tables	Learners will be able to create, upload, and manage mutlipage Web sites with embedded media objects.

THE ENVIRONMENT

The OUCHIE computer lab has seats for 25 students and is equipped with relatively recent, although poorly administrated, iMac desktop computers. There is an instructor's machine at the front of the room connected to speakers and a digital projector, which projects onto a ceiling-mounted screen at the front of the room. Several windows are at the end of the room with the projector screen, which sometimes makes the screen difficult to see. The instructor's machine is a different type of Mac desktop from the students' machines, with a different configuration so the way things work on the instructor's machine is not how things work on the student machines.

The lab is managed by two individuals with the designation of system administrator. One is a full-time university staff member and the other is a graduate assistant who reports to the staff member. The full-time staff member is officially addressed as the Instruction for Education program Director of Information Protocols (the IE DIP). He has the reputation in the college of being very difficult to work with. The DIP's graduate assistant, the Special Protocols Instructional Technologist (the DIP SPIT) actually does like computers, but is unfortunately subordinate to the DIP and because of that reporting relationship he can neither learn how to be an effective system administrator nor initiate and undertake useful tasks in the lab environment.

From a system administration standpoint, the lab is not maintained to an acceptable standard for teaching and learning. Software updates are extremely slow to be deployed and often, updates changing the system configuration, location of files, default settings of programs, and sometimes even the versions of the programs themselves, are made without notice in the middle of the semester. This is confusing and more than a little frustrating to students and faculty alike, as they have to adjust their work in the lab without warning, often not knowing that a change has been made. Instructors often only discover the change to configurations when they begin class and students start asking questions about where files are or what happened to their menu bars. Compounding this update issue is the difference between the instructor's machine and the student machines, because the instructor's machine is not only not updated at the same time as student machines but even when it is updated, the configuration is still different, so the instructor cannot demonstrate on-screen where to find things.

As a final complication to the environmental factors of the computer lab, the DIP and the DIP SPIT adamantly refuse to allow anyone to have administrative privileges on the computers. This is frustrating for the Instructional Technology faculty who teach in the lab, many of who have industry experience in high-level system administration and some of who actively consult in the business world outside of their academic duties. This refusal to grant administrative rights forces faculty to go through a long and involved request process to have any changes made to systems, even to have open source software installed, and the actual work takes months to be done, if it is ever done.

THE CLASS FORMAT

OUCHIE 415 is a three-credit-hour undergraduate course that meets once a week for a period of 3 hours. The course begins at 5:30 p.m. and runs until 8:30 p.m. This keeps students and instructors on campus and in the classroom through the normal times for dinner, but because most of the senior education students are working on practicums and internships in local schools during the day, this is necessary to allow them to complete their studies. Thus, they spend their day in the classroom as teachers and then come to the university campus to step into the classroom as students.

THE STUDENTS

OUCHIE 415 has an unusual mix of students. About two thirds of the class are traditional undergraduate education majors in their senior year of study. The other third, however, are primarily working educators with many years of classroom experience who are coming back to either enhance their pay through continuing education or meet the highly qualified teacher requirements under the No Child Left Behind policy. This mix of students brings a unique combination of skills and experiences to the classroom, with the working educators generally having much greater work experience but far less background with technology, while the traditional undergraduate students tend to be more comfortable with technology but have little or no work experience at all, and outside of their internships and practicums no work experience in the education field.

From a resource view, all of the students have their own computers either at home or at their workplace where they can work outside of class on assignments. Approximately 80% of these personally owned computers run on the Windows operating system, whereas only about 20% are working on the Mac OS.

THE INSTRUCTOR

OUCHIE 415 is taught by a GA who is a doctoral student in instructional technology. The GA has a background in computer software and hardware support as well as system administration. Unfortunately, that system administration experience is in Windows, not Mac, operating systems, but he is a competent Mac user. The GA position is only partially funded and as such he does not have an office, is not able to hold office hours, and works for a campus information technology group. With serious demands on his time due to class work, research, writing, and traveling for conferences, it is important that the class planning and execution be done as quickly and efficiently as is possible. Also, direct support for students is difficult because of the lack of office hours, so he has an e-mail listserve in place and has access to Web space of his own to post things for the class.

THE CURRENT SITUATION

This case comes into the class with about 3 weeks left in the semester. The Word, PowerPoint, and Excel portions of the class have been completed and the class is now entering into work with Web authoring. The basic HTML has been covered and students are now learning how to use a WYSIWYG editor and manage files via a Web interface file manager and also a File Transfer Protocol (FTP) server. The class as a whole has done well up to this point, but with the move into Web site creation and site management, the vast differences in ability between students is starting to show more clearly.

INSTRUCTIONAL CHALLENGES

Because of the nature of the students' work and school-related activities, many of them are unable to come to campus to work in the computer lab during the week. The course is planned to provide students with some lab time during each session to work and have access to the instructor to ask questions, but since moving into the Web work, there has not been enough time for students to make good progress on the Web assignments in class and the number of questions is more than overwhelming for the single instructor. For reference, some student e-mails that arrived through the week between classes are provided below.

Case 1

To: thebigga@ouch.edu
From: notsosavvy@aol.com
Subject: FTP issues

Big GA,

I've been trying for the past two hours to see my web site through the FTP server we talked about in the last class but can't get it to work. How am I supposed to tell it where my site is and how do I log in? The online file manager takes forever to do anything with but I can't get this other thing to work.

Sincerely,

Frustrated Middle School Teacher

Case 2

To: thebigga@ouch.edu
From: tallscottishlass@ouch.edu
Subject: Links???

Big GA,

None of my links work! I just went and changed everything on my file the way we talked about in class to make the links relative to the page location or whatever and uploaded with the online file manager but they're still broken! What did I do wrong? My roommate says they work on her computer but they're still broken on mine. Why am I doing this again? Kindergarteners don't use the internet!

Red

Case 3

To: thebigga@ouch.edu
From: spitfire@ouch.edu
Subject: Embedded Video from YouTube

Big GA,

I'm having a little bit of trouble doing what I want to do with this web page. I want to actually use this for the class I'm interning with and we're doing a module right now on how caterpillars turn into butterflies. I searched YouTube and found a series of 3 videos that talk about the process and, one's really cool it actually does a time-lapse of the butterfly coming out of the cocoon and flying away, I wanted to put them in series on my web page so that the kids could play them in order. I know that the embed function in YouTube gives you a string of HTML code that you can paste into a web site but I'm not sure how to get it in the right place using the WYSIWYG and it's too hard to do in just code. My videos keep ending up in crazy places all over the screen! Can you show me how to get them centered up and aligned down the middle of the page, maybe with title headers above each one?

Thanks,

Dedicated

SPECIFIC PROBLEMS

The e-mails from students show not only the types of questions that are being asked but also the broad range of both ability and motivation that can be found among the students. In order to provide the learning experience that the students need, it is critical for the GA to provide the appropriate resources for students. The following issues detail some specific problems that the class is having.

- File management: OUCH has an online file management system that can be used inside a browser. It is an old system that dates back to the very first visual interface on the network and was designed to work with the university's UNIX system. Users have to navigate to the folder they want to work in and then manually browse to each individual file to upload items to the active folder. The inherent problems of this cumbersome system are compounded by some students' struggle to understand the file structure of Web sites. Ideally, an FTP client will be used, but making the move from an online file manager to an FTP client might be asking for too much from the more inexperienced students who are taking their first computer class.
- Browser cache: The e-mail message from Red is indicative of a problem that is seen in every lab session and one that is producing multiple e-mails every week. Students have trouble understanding the concept that browsers save, or cache, information on pages and that if they test a page, update it, then test it again without restarting their browser or manually clearing the cache, most often with just a page refresh, the changes they've made don't show up. This is very frustrating for the students and has appeared as a recurring problem, even after explanations from the instructor.
- Operating system compatibilities: Because so many students work with Windows on their home machines, they have trouble translating everything they see on the Macs in the classroom to their own computers at home.

- Software access: With the lab unavailable to so many of the students, there are issues of how they can complete their assignments on their own machines. Web authoring software and FTP clients are not standard programs included with most computers and requiring students to purchase many of the popular packages would be prohibitively expensive. Also, the multiple operating systems further complicate this issue because students need to see software that they can use on either a Windows or a Mac operating system for ease of instruction.
- Applicability: Several students have difficulty seeing how the class content relates to their intended profession. Many of the older students are uncomfortable with the idea of using technology in the classroom at all and as a result have trouble seeing its usefulness. Also, the younger students who plan to specialize with very young children, preschool to first grade, do not see how computers can be a useful educational tool for students at preschool level.

As with any course, there are myriad questions beyond those listed above, but the list covers all the major categories that have come to light in the class. For this specific course, the GA has two different sets of concerns. First, he wonders how to address the instructional issues. Second, he wonders how to address the instructional issues while simultaneously dealing with the infrastructure issues. While it is late in the semester, solving problems now would not only finish the class on a high note but also give the GA good material to use next semester.

DISCUSSION QUESTIONS

1. The field of business uses what is called a SWOT analysis (Strengths, Weaknesses, Opportunities, Threats). Strengths are defined as things an organization does well or advantageous resources available to the organization. Weaknesses are things an organization does not do well or deficiencies of organizational resources. Opportunities are things happening in the operating environment, in this case beyond the classroom to the school as a whole or off-campus, that provide the organization with a potential to expand or improve. Threats are things happening in the operating environment with the potential to harm the organization. Perform a SWOT analysis on OUCHIE 415.
2. What specific problems can you identify with the current state of OUCHIE 415?

3. What are some technical solutions that the GA could employ to solve problems in the class?
4. What are some instructional/course design solutions that the GA could employ to solve problems in the class?
5. What do you identify as the single most serious issue in the case?

SECTION 4

PROFESSIONAL DEVELOPMENT

CHAPTER 14

DESIGNING FOR THE FUTURE

At a Southern State University

David E. Stone
Southern Polytechnic State University, USA

VISION

Scott, a professor in the Electrical Engineering Technology program at Southern State University, had begun to use technology to enhance his classroom learning environment for his students. Scott observed that many of his fellow faculty members did not know how to use technology to enhance their teaching. While faculty are experts in the respective disciplines, many have not been exposed to newer technologies. While there were occasional workshops on technology for faculty, these workshops did not meet a need for greater depth and relevant application of technology for faculty. There were pockets of faculty members using technology in their instruction on the campus, but other faculty members did not know what technology was available or how to incorporate the technology into their instruction. Around the time of this observation, a funding source had become available, and campus administrators were requesting faculty proposals for projects that could improve teaching on campus. Scott decided to submit

Cases 'n' Places: Global Cases in Educational and Performance Technology, pages 181–158

a proposal for a program that would provide an opportunity for faculty to learn how to use technology to enhance their teaching. The funding source had no strings attached, which meant that the money did not have to be spent exclusively on specific categories, such as equipment or labor. This provided a great deal of flexibility in the proposal design. This flexibility allowed Scott to consider a wide range of support resources for the faculty development program. Scott understood that many faculty on campus perceived the addition of technology into their instruction as an additional burden to their already heavy teaching loads, and he knew that the proposal selection committee would value proposals that provided detailed plans and identified clear goals for the proposed program.

CONTEXT

During the late 1990s, the World Wide Web and other Internet technologies were gaining a tremendous amount of attention in both the popular media and on college campuses. These new technologies arrived rather quickly, and by the end of the 1990s there was plenty of media coverage describing the opportunities afforded by this new medium. The coining of the term "information superhighway" and the implications for business and society were widely discussed in both popular culture and academic literature. This phenomenon gained penetration rather quickly, as the Web began during the mid-90s, and quickly became established as a resource for both personal and professional pursuits. As universities began to grapple with the issues associated with the use of the new medium of the Internet, there was a pronounced need for faculty to become familiar with the new technology. On many campuses there were faculty development initiatives created to support the integration of technology into the curriculum, with the intent of improving teaching and learning. In the late 1990s, there were a number of new tools and systems that helped reduce the barrier to entry for faculty seeking to use technology in their courses. WYSIWYG HTML editors, PowerPoint, Portable Document Format, Visualization tools, digital cameras, scanners, and many online resources provided easier access to materials and technology for faculty.

SOUTHERN STATE UNIVERSITY

Southern State University (SSU) is located in a suburb of Atlanta in the southeastern state of Georgia. SSU was founded shortly after World War II at the request of business and industry, and the first students were primarily soldiers returning from World War II. The university was initially a unit of another engineering institution in the state, and operated as a 2-year unit of the engineering institution until 1980 when it became a senior college in the state university system. In the 1980s, the university began offering bachelor's degrees and master's degrees, primarily in science, engineering, technology, and mathematics. By the late 1990s, the enrollment of State University had reached nearly 4,000 students, with SSU's primary mission focused on teaching and the application of science and technology to solve "real world" problems. The university has traditionally catered to both traditional and nontraditional students, and has had dormitory housing on campus since its inception. In order to accommodate working students, there are many evening courses, which makes it difficult to find times where most faculty are present on campus. The students of SSU are interested in technology; they are attracted to science, technology, engineering, and math (STEM) programs that SSU offers; and expect that their instructors will use technology as part of their teaching. As access to the World Wide Web and Internet technology grew, the students' expectations grew. Faculty felt pressured by both their peers and students to use technology.

FACULTY PROFILE

The applied nature of the programs and close ties to industry make the students of SSU very desirable to potential employers who value the students' practical knowledge. As an extension of this philosophy, faculty had been selected for employment based on both formal education, as well as industry experience. State University has traditionally been viewed primarily as a teaching institution by the faculty of the university, and the primary measurement of faculty performance has been composed of their teaching and service record. The faculty of State University in the late 1990s taught about 90% of the credit hours taken by students at the university, with the remaining credit hours taught by part-time faculty. Faculty at SSU typically have a heavy course workload and complain about a lack of time to attend workshops or learn new technology. Of the approximately 150 full-time faculty, nearly 100 had achieved tenure. As a bachelor's and master's degree granting institution, the university did not require all faculty to have PhDs, and approximately 53% of faculty had earned doctorates. While faculty at SSU were well-versed in the technology that is used within their disciplines, they did not have much experience with instructional and presentation technology (Tippens, 2003). Many of the faculty members with a long history at the institution are comfortable with teaching via chalk and a chalkboard. Faculty are interested in the new technology that can be used to support teaching, but they have limited exposure to the technology. Faculty rarely have the opportunity to work with colleagues outside of their discipline, and while there are early technology adopters within departments, there are limited opportunities for faculty to discuss teaching methods (Tippens, 2003).

CENTER FOR INSTRUCTIONAL TECHNOLOGY

The university had recently created a Center for Instructional Technology (CIT) that was physically housed within the University Library and was a unit within the Division of Academic Affairs. A full-time manager, Susan, as well as two instructional service coordinators who were familiar with a wide range of digital media technologies staffed the center. The center included a faculty computer lab, equipped with 16 computer stations; a presentation classroom that was wired for recording; and staff offices. The center frequently offered short workshops on Web-page development, PowerPoint, scanning, portable document format, and digital media (such as Macromedia freehand, Adobe Photoshop, etc.). These self-contained workshops were offered to faculty and, if there was sufficient space, staff. CIT was equipped with a wide variety of state-of-the-art scanners, computers, video capture/editing stations, as well as digital and video cameras for checkout. The center housed the first digital whiteboard on campus, and served as a showcase for new technology on campus. CIT has advertised and delivered free workshops to faculty on Fridays and has provided one-on-one assistance for faculty as they work to integrate technology into their teaching. Susan, the CIT manager, is familiar with teaching theory and works closely with faculty in order to meet their individual needs. The faculty members who attend enjoy the workshops, but complain that they quickly forget what they have learned, and also do not like that they do not have access to the software in their offices. At this time, State University began to operate a course management system, which provided course tools for the Web. These tools included an internal discussion board for each faculty member's course, quiz and survey tools, as well as course content hosting (such as PDF files, etc.). Susan, as well as the two instructional service coordinators, was excited about the idea of a faculty development program, and was willing to conduct workshops and assist with any faculty development effort.

SUPPORT FROM THE UNIVERSITY SYSTEM

The University System of Georgia's (USG) Advanced Learning Technology (ALT) group funded multiple projects on campuses in order to jumpstart technology initiatives across the university system. One such program during the mid-90s provided laptops for faculty who participated in a faculty-development program. Another program was developed to support the development of the infrastructure required to create distance learning programs across the state. At this point in time, there was a willingness on the part of the administration to provide a wide range of support mechanisms to encourage faculty adoption of technology; and since there was external funding available for the project, the administration was flexible in the application of funds for this project. In 1996, the USG established a "Distinguished Professor" program that provided matching funds for campus-based activities that support teaching and learning. In 1998, Scott, an Engineering Technology professor, was named a "Distinguished Professor" and was able to secure the necessary matching funds from the SSU Foundation.

ENCOURAGING DIFFUSION OF INNOVATION

While major faculty-development initiatives at some institutions have been able to provide training for all faculty at an institution, funding limitations prevented such an ambitious initiative at SSU. Due to the short-term nature of the funding source, the faculty-development program may need to be funded via other means in the future. Regardless of the long-term funding source, the program should be designed to provide the maximum benefit for faculty at SSU.

BUILDING A PROGRAM

Scott believed that the workshops offered by CIT, while excellent, provided a limited view of the potential for the application of the technology. A major concern was the "scatter gun" approach to faculty training, which limited faculty's ability to see the big picture of technology integration within their teaching (Tippens, 2003). So, Scott began developing a plan for a faculty-development program, with Susan, in the Center for Instructional Technology.

CASE QUESTIONS

Develop a plan for a faculty development program that will help prepare faculty to begin to improve their teaching with technology.

In your plan, include the following items:

1. Describe the needs assessment process.
2. Identify potential political implications of developing a new faculty development program.

3. Identify the major program goals.
4. Identify the major program objectives. ("Goals" and "objectives" are synonymous, therefore making #s 3 and 4 identical/redundant. Best to delete one.)
5. Describe incentives or plans to motivate participation by faculty.
6. Describe the role technology will play in the development and operation of the program.
7. Consider the delivery format for the faculty-development program. How many sessions and how long will each session last? (Will this be a face-to-face workshop, series of workshops, online delivery, self study, and what percentage for each format?)
8. Consider the selection and composition of the program participants. (Are they from the same academic department; why or why not?)
9. Describe how the participants will interact with each other and their role in the program. (Will you include faculty in the program development process; can faculty suggest or plan new topics; how will faculty interact with each other?)
10. Identify structural changes required in the Center for Instructional Technology in order to support this program and the long-term success of faculty development.

REFERENCE

Tippens, S. (2004). *Born to teach with technology?* American Society of Engineering Education Southeast Section Annual Conference, April 4–6, Auburn, Alabama. Retrieved October 5 2009 from http://155.225.14.146/asee-se/proceedings/ASEE2004/ASEE2004SE.htm

CHAPTER 15

MANAGING AND SUSTAINING EXPECTATIONS OF INNOVATIVE ICT INTEGRATION IN DEVELOPMENT PROJECTS

Susan Crichton
University of Calgary, Canada

OVERVIEW OF THE CASE

Increasingly international development projects are recognizing the need to tackle the core issues of poverty and health reform through efforts aimed at improving basic education in underdeveloped areas through ICT.[1] This approach is seen as being a critical intervention, requiring systematic changes at both the macro- and microlevels—the overarching administration of education as well as at the individual rural school. These changes are neither quick nor inexpensive and require a systemwide commitment to long term, significant reform at all levels of practice. And, while laudable and necessary, these changes have the potential to result in unforeseen con-

Cases 'n' Places: Global Cases in Educational and Performance Technology, pages 187–172

sequences, impacting teaching and learning conditions, teacher evaluation and promotion, student assessment, and parental/community support.

The context for this case is the basic education system within the People's Republic of China (PRC). The PRC has the largest basic education system in the world with approximately 200 million students. Basic education consists of 6 years of primary school and 3 years of junior/ middle. From there, students can then enroll in 3 years of senior high school. Basic education (primary to junior middle) is compulsory, and the PRC reported in 2004 that primary education rates had reached 98.95%. While impressive, this rate is *not* consistent across the country (western rural rates are considerably lower), nor does it reflect the significant gap in the *quality* of education between large urban centers in the mo

re affluent eastern provinces and rural schools in more remote western regions, typically home to the majority of the PRC's ethnic populations.

In 2000, the PRC's Ministry of Education (MOE) introduced a New National Curriculum (NNC) to improve the quality of basic education. Central to the NNC is the transformation from teacher directed, knowledge-delivery-oriented instruction to student-centered learning designed to increase students' capacity to problem solve. Success of the NNC depends on the teachers' ability to teach in a child-centered way, which changes their role from lecturer/dispenser of information to facilitator of knowledge construction. This implies a major transition, as teachers typically teach in the manner in which they were taught and few, if any, have experienced student-centered instruction as learners. The problem is particularly challenging for teachers in rural areas, as they tend to have much lower teacher qualification standards than their colleagues in more developed, eastern areas.

Information communication technology (ICT) has been chosen as one of the strategies to assist the western areas to universalize and improve basic education. With the financial support from the Li Ka Shing Foundation, the MOE developed a project using basic ICT hardware to help teachers in rural schools to improve teaching quality through access to resources, teaching materials, and information. The project distributed ICT hardware to the remote rural schools and provided basic training on ICT use. Numerous international development projects (e.g., Canadian, British, Swedish educational initiatives as well as World Bank and Asian Development Bank pilot projects) were developed to support the implementation of the NNC and ICT policies in rural areas.

The Asian Development Bank (ADB) project, the focus of this case, was one of those projects. The goal of the project, in partnership with the PRC Ministry of Education (MOE), was to explore innovative and sustainable uses of ICT to advance universal access to basic education by improving equity, quality, and efficiency. As stated in the project end report

> Components of the project included (i) a broad assessment and identification of promising innovations and strategies for applying ICT support to existing education, with a particular focus on promoting universal access to quality compulsory education among disadvantaged populations including minorities, women, and remote communities in rural Hunan province; and (ii) a very modest and targeted pilot test of promising approaches and technologies. (Crichton, Wenbin, Hongwei, Qiong, & Spohr, 2006)

The ADB project placed particular emphasis on soft components (i.e., educational content and materials, training of teachers to use new ICT tools for innovative teaching, peer support networks, and monitoring and evaluation) rather than only in an investment of hardware and software, recognizing that without this professional development, ICT hardware/software often fails to deliver promised benefits in terms of advancing education objectives. The ADB project also sought to combine mature technologies (i.e., audio, television, and print) with newer forms of ICT (i.e., computers, digital cameras, and Internet) in order to address local education needs, ranging from training and information resources for teachers to broader provision of content to promote community development.

This case study will focus on the need to:

- Provide training programs for *all* education officials at various levels in the vision and practice of ICT for education helping them to empathize with the challenges of changed practice;
- Provide regular training for head teachers on the management of ICT for education at the school level, and encourage their active participation in teacher professional-development activities so they have a similar understanding of the link between ICT and curriculum reform; and
- Revise the evaluation of schools and teachers to focus on full and effective ICT utilization.

Specifically, this case study will share an approach used in the ADB project to encourage the use of reflection, dialogue, and digital documents for teacher evaluation and the importance of introducing these changes to those engaged in preservice teacher preparation and teacher evaluation.

THE CASE

Background

In summer 2003, I joined the ADB project, replacing the original ICT consultant and needing to make up the time lost by the Severe Acute Respiratory Syndrome (SARS) epidemic and other challenges encountered during the early stages of the project, which was situated in Fenghuang County, which is located in rural western Hunan province. A stunningly beautiful mountainous region, Fenghuang was difficult to access due to the transportation infrastructure and highly changeable weather conditions. Its agricultural-based economy has suffered in recent years due to increasing migration to urban centers—younger farmers felt there was greater opportunity in the cities and more money to be made. County officials welcomed our project, believing the future of the county rested in utilizing ICT to improve education in the hopes of increasing tourism (e.g., learning computer skills, multiple languages, and generally modernizing the region).

Rural schools had already received the basic Li Ka Shing Foundation package: a satellite receiver, computer, and basic IT skills (e.g., how to download content from the satellite and maintain the system). Some schools had created a multimedia room (e.g., converted the largest room in the school to a viewing space by adding a desktop computer, LCD projector, screen, speakers, and blackout curtains). During our needs-assessment tour of the county, we visited a variety of schools, observing basically the same thing: teachers downloading PowerPoint slides prepared in Beijing and showing them in the multimedia lab. While many of the teachers and principals proudly showed this innovative approach to ICT integration, others lamented that teachers were simply "walking a new road wearing old shoes," noting that the goals of the New National Curriculum (NNC) were not being met; PowerPoint was simply a temporarily more engaging form of teacher-directed education.

Significant Activity

Recognizing this gap between the goals of the NNC and the actual practices of the teachers (both in the school and at the teacher training institute), we designed a 5-day, hands-on workshop (see Appendix A: WORKSHOP Outline) where teachers could experience student-centered instruction (as students themselves) and develop their own teaching resources, learning various forms of ICT hardware and software along the way. We utilized the train-the-trainer approach, offering the workshop first to the instructors from the teacher training institute, then asking them to deliver the workshop to teachers selected from each of the county schools with peer support from the original trainers. Complete workshop materials were provided to each participant on CD-ROM, as encouragement/incentive that workshop participants would share their experiences with other teachers at their schools.

In the fall, following the summer workshops, we revisited the schools to see if there was evidence of transfer to practice, hoping to see lessons utilizing the teacher-developed resources and materials distributed during the workshop (e.g., digital cameras, portable radios with cassette players capable of recording, television sets on mobile carts with DVD players, and miscellaneous art supplies) supporting changes in teaching and learning.

Fortunately, to minimize transportation costs to the schools, county teacher evaluators traveled with us, observing the same schools and some of the same teachers. At each school, we were invited to observe a class, speak with the students, and watch a complete lesson. I was asked to formally critique each teacher's lesson during an open staff meeting. I can only imagine how intimidating this must have been for the teachers, but they were quite open and gracious, sharing their planning materials, lesson plans, resources, and assessment tools. I had not planned on this formal critique process—my comments were only verbal, delivered impromptu via an interpreter. When I was finished, I was asked to be more critical, less positive, as school administrators felt that evidence-based criticism was best for professional growth. After my second offering, the teachers thanked me while the administrators commented that Canadians, typically, were too positive. Following this, we were invited to watch students perform in another part of the school, but I noticed that the county teacher evaluators were keeping the teachers in the staff room, providing their impressions of the lessons they had observed. Asking one of my English-speaking colleagues to stay with me, we observed their criticism of the teachers' new lessons. In almost every instance, any innovation that the teachers had employed from the workshop was being criticized; almost everything student-centered in their approaches was viewed as inconsistent with the evaluation guidelines. In other words, our most innovative and eager teachers—those who had grappled with and made sense of the educational philosophy and instructional strategies of the NNC and who had been the bright stars of the summer workshop—were failing their evaluations.

Remedy for a Significant Problem

At that point, the ADB project modified its primary focus and target audience. By pure accident we learned that teacher evaluation criteria was based on competencies that were inconsistent with the NNC. The guidelines the evaluators used were entrenched in small booklets prepared by the county and mass produced. These booklets had not been revised and without the accidental discovery of their use, our project team (both foreign experts and Chinese experts from major urban institutions and organizations) would have remained oblivious to the gap between reform curriculum and teacher merit/promotion practices.

Building on the desire for evidence-based professional criticism, I began to prepare an evaluation instrument that would use digital documentation to illustrate changing teaching practices, believing this would model effective ICT use, help teachers and administrators see what NNC teaching and learning looked like, and create a model for sustaining the implementation of our workshop materials. Further, we believed that by talking about images and examples shown in the digital evidence, we could depersonalize the comments, abstracting them enough to reduce the emotion, speaking more about the activities and actions than the individual.

Once completed, we field-tested the evaluation instrument and observation process with instructors at the teacher training institute (see Appendix B, Evaluation Instrument and Observation Sheet). Modifications were made to the instrument, and we invited the instructors to join us in the schools, where we shared this approach with teacher evaluators and school administration. To aid in the evaluation process, we purchased additional digital cameras for county teacher evaluators and teacher-training institute instructors and offered a workshop on how to photograph classroom practice and discuss the content of the images.

Unfortunately, this final set of workshops and materials was the culminating activity for the ADB project. We know the materials got into the hands of approximately 50 county administrators and evaluators, but we really have no way of knowing if it has changed evaluation practices in any significant way.

CONCLUSION

The project concluded with positive evaluations from the majority of participants: teachers, administrators, county officials, and the Ministry of Education partners. County officials and some school officials had hoped we would have spent more money on hardware, and teacher-training officials wished we would have spent more time and money on their instructors, but that is typically the response when ICT projects are introduced—participants hope for more hardware components, believing students will naturally integrate it meaningfully into their practice, while research shows us that time and again it does not work that way.

Amid the sheer joy of getting to work with eager young teachers in rural settings, I learned two major lessons: innovations in the classroom consistently outpace administrative infrastructure, and often the most important learning happens unintentionally.

Regarding the first point, the teachers in rural Fenghuang embraced education reform for all the best reasons as they saw significant benefit in it for their students. When given ICT and professional development, they seized the opportunity and were fearless in their commitment to make their schools better and happier places. And they did that in the face of poor evaluations and significant risk to their careers.

Regarding the second point, we "outside" experts missed major pieces of the teaching and learning process. Without the accidental discovery of the evaluation guideline booklets, we and other projects helping to implement the NNC would have continued to ask teachers to do things that were not valued or recognized as good practice by those in positions of power. Sustainability and scalability of NCC implementation would have been stalled or stopped entirely. Once again, being an expert requires much more than subject-matter expertise.

AFTERWORD

The ADB project ended in 2006. Unfortunately, there was no follow-up evaluation planned, as the project was a pilot offered by the Asian Development Bank as part of a larger rural improvement initiative. My only hope that some of the materials are still being used rests in the fact that a major report, complete with annexes, including all the workshop materials and evaluation tools, was tabled to high-ranking officials in both the Ministries of Education and Finance. The report and annexes were also given to project partners from the major teacher-training universities and other international development-project leaders.

DISCUSSION QUESTIONS

- What are the system-level responsibilities for managers of development projects in terms of mitigating the negative unintended consequences of "good" project intentions?
- How can they come to understand these responsibilities?
- What are the responsibilities of the host country experts in terms of collaborating with the external expert?
- What critical elements support sustainability of ICT projects (e.g., need for ongoing professional development, recognition of the need to revise teacher evaluation practices when changes in pedagogical practices are encouraged, recognition of changes in student assessment when the focus of teaching and learning change)?

- What steps might you take to design an effective evaluation instrument for teachers?
  - What things would you need to know?
  - How might you field-test it?
  - How could you ensure that it was being used after the project was over?

NOTE

1. This is the title of a recent Asian Development Project (ADB)—TA 3958-PRC, which was completed in Xiangxi Tujia-Miaso Autonomous Prefecture, particularly Fenghuang County, in Hunan Province, People's Republic of China (PRC).

APPENDIX A: WORKSHOP OUTLINE

The format of this workshop blends theory with practice. Participants will leave the workshop with teacher-developed instructional designs and resources.

Session	Topic
Day 1	
Morning	• Welcome—Introduction to Workshop Format and Goals • Inquiry-Based Learning (IBL), Student-Centered Instruction (SCI), and the New Curriculum • Introduction to Teaching Using Inquiry Questions
Afternoon	• Crafting a Good Inquiry Question • Instructional Design template for the New Curriculum • Selecting Appropriate Resources to Support an Inquiry Question
Day 2	
Morning	• Evaluating Resources • Instruction Strategies for Inquiry-Based Instruction in the SCI classroom • The Art of Asking Good Questions
Afternoon	• Teacher-Developed Instructional Designs and Resources • The Value of Collaboration and Sharing
Day 3	
Morning	• Assessing Student-Inquiry Activities • Using the Instructional Design for Planning • Preparing Instructional Designs and Teacher-Developed Resources for Distribution
Afternoon	• Preparing Instructional Designs and Teacher-Developed Resources for Distribution (cont.) • Closing Ceremonies

APPENDIX B: EVALUATION INSTRUMENT AND OBSERVATION SHEET—PART 1

Date ______________________
Time ______________________

Name of school: ______________________
Grade: __________ Class: ________ Subject: ______________________
Name of teacher: ______________________
Number of students: ______________________
Other presenters: ______________________
If the lesson taking in the computer lab: ______________________
Number of computers & types: ______________________
Speed of the connection: ______________________

1. To talk with the teacher on your purpose of the observation and to know the background of the lesson (such as the activities arranged before, the plan of the lesson, and other relevant information):

2. Briefly describe the arrangement of classroom (includes the location of chairs and desks, decoration and group arrangement of students, and so on)

   A picture of Classroom arrangement (you may take a photo)

3. Records of observation (include classroom observation guide)

What to look for when observing a class	No		Yes	NA
1 The Classroom				
• Is the classroom pleasant and inviting?	1	2	3	NA
• Is student work displayed?	1	2	3	NA
• Are there resources available for the students to explore on their own?	1	2	3	NA
• Can the furniture be moved or arranged to support group work?	1	2	3	NA
• Is there access to technology?	1	2	3	NA
• Are there models or manipulatives for the students to use?	1	2	3	NA
• Is there evidence of project-based learning?	1	2	3	NA
2 Purpose or Focus of the Lesson				
• Is the purpose/focus of the lesson clear?	1	2	3	NA
• Is there a clear inquiry question guiding the lesson?	1	2	3	NA
• Does the teacher engage the students in the content?	1	2	3	NA
• Does the teacher ask the students to do something with the content in the lesson (e.g., make something, work with something, design something, work with peers)?	1	2	3	NA
• Does the student activity reflect the inquiry question?	1	2	3	NA

What to look for when observing a class	No		Yes	NA
• Is the student task worthwhile (i.e., does it foster significant learning)?	1	2	3	NA
• Is the teacher teaching from their lesson plan?	1	2	3	NA
3 **Pedagogical Relationships**				
• Do the students and teacher treat each other with respect?	1	2	3	NA
• Does the classroom appear to be a friendly learning environment?	1	2	3	NA
• Is it obvious that the teacher is doing something to establish an effective relationship with the students?	1	2	3	NA
• Does the teacher discipline the students in a respectful manner?	1	2	3	NA
• Are the students given responsibility for their own learning?	1	2	3	NA
4 **Teacher Explanations and Questions**				
• Does the teacher help the students with their individual learning needs?	1	2	3	NA
• Are the teacher's questions well-formed and open?	1	2	3	NA
• Does the teacher respond to student errors in a respectful manner?	1	2	3	NA
• Does the teacher respond to student errors by asking additional questions?	1	2	3	NA
• Does the teacher respond to student errors by simply giving the right answers?	1	2	3	NA
• Does the teacher use different instructional strategies to help students understand (e.g., oral explanations, diagrams, manipulatives)?	1	2	3	NA
• Does the assessment of the student activity match the focus/purpose of the lesson?	1	2	3	NA
• Is the assessment of the student activity consistent with inquiry-based learning (i.e., can students show their learning in projects, papers rather than just a written test)?	1	2	3	NA
• Does the teacher use resources s/he has handmade?	1	2	3	NA
• Does the teacher use resources s/he has made using ICT?	1	2	3	NA
• Does the teacher use resources s/he has downloaded from the IP satellite?	1	2	3	NA
• Does the teacher use resources s/he has downloaded from the Internet?	1	2	3	NA
• Does the teacher show video lessons prepared by others?	1	2	3	NA
• Does the teacher integrate the resources into their teaching (i.e., stopping and starting them when and where appropriate)?	1	2	3	NA
5 **Student Behavior or Actions**				
• Are the students active and engaged during the lesson?	1	2	3	NA
• Is there variety in what the students are asked to do?	1	2	3	NA
• Are the students given opportunities to demonstrate what they've learned?	1	2	3	NA
• Are the students given opportunities to work together?	1	2	3	NA
6 **Student Voice**				
• Do all students get the ability to talk and contribute in class?	1	2	3	NA
• Is there balance between the participation of boys and girls?	1	2	3	NA
• Is there balance between the participation of minority students?	1	2	3	NA

4. Executive Summary and Recommendations:
   Name of Observer ____________________________

APPENDIX B: EVALUATION INSTRUMENT AND OBSERVATION SHEET, PART 2

Example of Observation Sheet with Digital Evidence Included

Concepts	**Examples**
Physical space • How is the classroom furniture arranged?	
• Is student work displayed?	

Concepts | **Examples**

Purpose or focus

- What is the purpose of the lesson?
- Is the task worthwhile (i.e., does it foster significant learning)?
- How closely is the lesson connected to the curriculum?

Pedagogical relationships

- How do the students and teacher treat each other?
- What does the teacher do to maintain an effective relationship with the students?
- How does the teacher discipline the students?
- Are students expected to take responsibility for their learning?

Teacher explanations and questions

- How does the teacher scaffold the learning?
- Are the teacher's questions open or closed?
- Does the teacher use questions to lead to a point or to develop the purpose of the lesson?
- How does the teacher respond to student errors?
- How is the lesson consolidated or synthesized at the end?

Concepts	Examples
Student behavior or actions • How active or engaged are the students? • Is there variety in what the students are asked to do? • What is the quality of the student work? • What opportunities do students have to demonstrate what they've learned? • How well do the students work together? • Student voice: Who gets to talk and how much? Is there balance between boys and girls? What is the extent of the minority student participation?	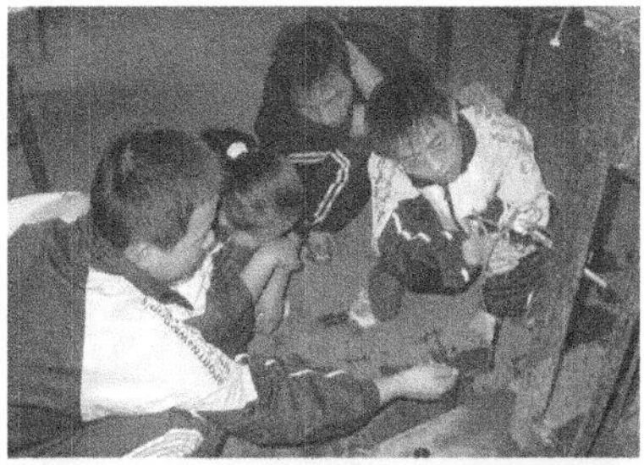 
Observations over time (throughout the school year) • Evidence of various forms of assessment being used by the teacher • Evidence of increasing student initiative or personal responsibility for the learning	Informal  Formal 

REFERENCE

Crichton, S., Wenbin, H., Hongwei, M., Qiong, W., & Spohr, S. (2006). *Focused synopsis of findings and recommendations from the final consultant research report on improving basic education in underdeveloped areas through ICT.* TA 3958-PRC, People's Republic of China—Ministries of Finance and Education, Asian Development Bank (ADB), 20.

CHAPTER 16

TEACHER PROFESSIONAL DEVELOPMENT IN AND THROUGH INFORMATION AND COMMUNICATIONS TECHNOLOGY

Kay Xuereb
University of the West Indies, Jamaica

BACKGROUND

As I entered the School gate, I was welcomed by students and staff. I went straight to the office at Blue Mahoe School and informed the secretary that I had arrived for my appointment to interview the Grade Coordinators. The School Principal was in a meeting when I arrived, but she still found time to welcome me and instructed the secretary to escort me to the library where the interview would take place.

I had visited Blue Mahoe School to investigate how the Information and Communication Technology (ICT) Policy from the Ministry of Education in Jamaica was being implemented at the school. The focus for this pilot study was the teachers, as they were the instruments of policy implementa-

Cases 'n' Places: Global Cases in Educational and Performance Technology, pages 201–181

tion in the school. Blue Mahoe School was a coeducational, government-funded institution, with 1,200 students enrolled, aged between 4 and 15 years old. The school had nursery, primary, and secondary sections with 40 teachers in total. The primary students were divided into age-specific year groupings or grades, each with its own Grade Coordinator, who was also one of the class teachers.

Established more than 100 years ago, Blue Mahoe School moved to its current location in a pleasant residential area of the capital city more than 50 years ago. The catchment area for the school was a diverse one in socioeconomic terms, which included the inner city and the rural outskirts. The school provided a supportive environment for staff and students and maintained close links with its local community. An annual arts festival was organized by the school and a number of cultural events were held throughout the school year. The school also participated in a number of local and national activities, which included spelling competitions, quizzes, and sports contests.

ICT AT BLUE MAHOE SCHOOL

The Computer Laboratory

ICT at Blue Mahoe School took place in the computer laboratory at the school. The computer laboratory was a classroom containing 11 computers and 1 printer. The computers were positioned on benches arranged along two sides of the room. The room had a window, but the glass only permitted those inside the room to look out; no one could look inside from outside. The solid wooden door was kept closed to the computer room when the room was occupied as there was an air conditioning unit inside. When the laboratory was not in use, the door was locked with a key. An iron grill was pulled into place in front of the wooden door and secured with a padlock at the end of every day. This fortification and the inability to see inside the room for most of the school day gave an illusion that what went on inside the computer laboratory was a mystery to all but those permitted to enter.

The laboratory had been set up for the primary and secondary sections of the school using donations of computers from the private sector, the local Member of Parliament, and the Ministry of Education. The computer laboratory contained 11 computers in total, 8 of which had been donated to the school. Two other computers had been won in a competition. One computer was reserved for teacher use only, and there was also a color printer.

ICT Lessons

A focus group interview with the six Grade Coordinators at Blue Mahoe School provided an opportunity for a discussion about the use of ICT across the school. The Grade Coordinators discussed the ICT resources they used with their classes. Each class had one timetabled lesson of 35 minutes in the school's computer laboratory every week. The computer laboratory at the school was the domain of the Information Technology (IT) teacher, Mr. Mitchell, and he taught ICT to the primary-level students as well as the secondary-level students in the computer laboratory.

Mr. Mitchell was interviewed separately from the Grade Coordinators. He explained that the once weekly session in the computer laboratory for each of the primary level classes constituted the students' ICT exposure for the week. This single session was prepared and delivered by Mr. Mitchell. The primary-level teachers could use the computer laboratory with their students, but Mr. Mitchell explained that they chose not to, leaving him to take their classes in the laboratory for ICT for one lesson per week. When questioned further, he elaborated that individual teachers from the primary grades only visited the computer laboratory to word process documents or to seek advice on personal computer issues from him in his role as the IT teacher. However, he wanted to assist the primary-level teachers and planned to meet with the Grade Coordinators.

The focus group interview with the Grade Coordinators was followed by individual interviews with a small number of coordinators. Criteria for the selection of coordinators to interview individually included their contribution to the focus group discussion held with all the Grade Coordinators. All grade levels were also represented, with at least one coordinator from grades 1, 2, and 3, and at least one coordinator from Grades 4, 5, and 6 because the primary level of the school was divided into two departments, Grades 1 to 3, and 4 to 6. The primary curriculum used in the school was also separated into an integrated curriculum for Grades 1, 2, and 3, and discrete disciplines for Grades 4, 5, and 6. Three out of the six Grade Coordinators were selected for an individual interview, the Grades 3, 5, and 6 Coordinators. During the individual interviews, the Grade Coordinators were asked further questions about the use of ICT at Blue Mahoe School. Ms. Andrews, the Grade 3 Coordinator, described the frequency of the lessons the students from the primary grades attended in the computer laboratory:

> The students go for computer classes; we have computer classes once per week. Presently it is suspended because of the lack of machines, but as soon as we get the lab back up and going, that would be back in place.

When asked if she had used the computer for teaching and learning, Ms. Cook, the Grade 6 Coordinator, explained that she had not used the computer "because they used to have computer classes, so they have a computer teacher, so he does the teaching not the class teacher."

Reliance on the IT teacher for the teaching of ICT was evident among all three of the Grade Coordinators. The teachers' dependency on the IT teacher appeared to be emphasized by the location of the computers in the computer laboratory. The computers had become the private domain of the laboratory teacher, and responsibility for computer use appeared to have been removed from the classroom teacher. The responses obtained from the Grade Coordinators indicated that they relied on Mr. Mitchell to use the computer technology with their students, and this absolved their responsibility for using ICT for teaching and learning.

Internet Use

Blue Mahoe School's Internet connection, provided free of charge by a private-sector telecommunications provider through the Ministry of Education Edunet project, was out of use at the time of the pilot study. Previously, Internet access had been available on the teacher's computer in the computer laboratory, and this was available to all the teaching staff. The principal intended to restore the Internet connection as quickly as possible.

FACTORS AFFECTING ICT USE AT BLUE MAHOE SCHOOL

Lack of ICT Facilities

The timetabled lessons in the computer laboratory were already suspended when the coordinators were interviewed because only three computers were working. This meant that ICT was not being used for teaching or learning at Blue Mahoe School. Ms. Brown, the Grade 5 coordinator, elaborated on the situation further: "We also don't have a functional computer lab right now, because the majority of the computers are not working."

She went on to explain that the IT teacher had been seconded to other teaching duties, as other teachers had left the school, so the school was without instructional technology. Ms. Cook explained why the primary grades were not using the computers: "We would like to keep up, but we don't have the facilities, we don't have the... for example the computer, which is the main one now, we don't have enough computers for the children to learn."

The number of working computers in the computer laboratory was an issue raised by each of the Grade Coordinators. All voiced their concern that minimal access to computers was affecting teaching and learning negatively. The limited number of computers that worked and the lack of access to the computer laboratory were cited by the Grade Coordinators as reasons why the school's computers were not used.

Teacher Ideas for ICT

Even though the computers in the laboratory were not being used, individual coordinators expressed their ideas as to how ICT could be developed within the school. Each of the coordinators appeared motivated to use computer technology and saw its potential for teaching and learning. Ms. Andrews' suggested how ICT could be used for literacy-skill development:

> There are a lot of CDs and computer programs available that I have at home as well, that I use with my daughter, that could be very effective in teaching literacy skills to the students, but because of the computer, or lack thereof, we cannot use them here you know, so if we have all that in place, we will be better able to use what we have to our advantage.

Ms. Brown thought that the students would benefit from hands-on, direct experience with technology: "I think if we had more instructional technology aids, like the computers more, just more hands-on things for them, it would play a more vital role than what we're doing now."

Ms. Andrews proposed that every class should have its own computer:

> I would like to see each classroom with a computer, the teacher being able to use it, the students being able to go there and being able to access information right there in the classroom using those technologies. Also like to see, as I say, more so that the students can have personal access to these things.

Ms. Cook also wanted a computer for every class and other ICT resources:

> Each classroom is equipped with computers... teaching different subject areas and finding information and so forth. The Internet, like you have a project and they have to go to the Internet to get information. If I am teaching a subject, I might need some information. I can get it from the Internet. They could set up a Web site. Getting to know the children in other schools, other countries as well, could help me to write my lesson plans too.

At Blue Mahoe School, two out of the three coordinators interviewed talked about having computers in their classroom rather than a computer laboratory and suggested that this would provide easier access to the technology for teacher and student. Research has demonstrated that a small number of computers placed in classrooms can be more effectively used for teaching and learning than more computers in a computer laboratory. However, it has also been acknowledged that locating computers in classrooms posed logistical, instructiona, and physical challenges (Gaible & Burns, 2005). At Blue Mahoe School, the computers were centrally located in a classroom, with all 11 school computers placed together in a computer laboratory for security and timetabling considerations. The designation of a classroom for computer use also meant that the room could be provided with an adequate electricity supply and air conditioning to maintain an ambient temperature for the computer technology in a tropical environment.

Continuing Professional Development in the Use of ICT

All of the primary-level teachers at Blue Mahoe School had received some training in skills and pedagogy in the use of technology during the first part of their Continuing Professional Development for the Revised Primary Curriculum (RPC). At the time of the interviews, the Grade Coordinators were waiting for the second part of their professional development for the RPC. In the RPC, ICT was described as a tool for aiding curriculum delivery. The RPC guidelines for teachers described the computer technology appropriate for each grade (MOEYC, 1999).

In addition to the Ministry of Education continuing professional development in the use of ICT, some of the teachers had also attended computer-skills courses organized by the Jamaica Teachers' Association and the private sector. Others had also undertaken computer courses as part of undergraduate degrees that they were pursuing part-time after their initial teacher training certificate. The Grade Coordinators explained that they and the teachers in their grades wanted to use computer technology, but even with their existing professional development in the use of ICT, they did not know how to use the computer for teaching and learning.

ICT Policy

Within primary education in the developing countries of the world, the role of Information and Communications Technology (ICT), particularly computer technology, has changed over time. Originally ICT was considered inappropriate in developing countries with limited resources (Lockheed et al., 1991), but in the last 15 years a number of projects using ICT at the basic education level have been piloted and developed in Africa, Asia, the Pacific, and the Caribbean region. Jamaica was one of the islands in the Caribbean region that embraced ICT and introduced computer technology.

The increase in computer technology in schools in Jamaica came about through private- and public-sector initiatives, with businesses, individuals, trust funds, foundations, and alumni associations providing sponsorship (Peart, 1998). The variations in computer provision among schools that developed prompted the Ministry of Education to create the policy in Information Technology in Education, which later became the Information and Communication Technology (ICT) Policy. The ICT policy clearly stated that facilities, equipment and personnel would be made available to permit access to ICT for all students, including those at the primary level (MOEYC, 2003).

Blue Mahoe School had a designated IT teacher and a computer laboratory. The School Development Plan had a literacy and numeracy emphasis as well as a technology component, and ICT had already been considered for skills development at the time of the interviews. The school principal, together with the School Board, was keen to develop the use of ICT within the school, especially at the primary level, as the school had been designated as a Demonstration School within the Primary Education Support Project (PESP). As part of the Demonstration Schools initiative, Blue Mahoe School had submitted its school activity plans, which focused on literacy, since literacy levels were low among the student population. Blue Mahoe School was expected to produce examples of best practice in literacy to showcase to other schools within their local cluster, regionally and nationally, as a Demonstration School.

The Principal's Vision and Support for ICT

At Blue Mahoe School, the Ministry of Education ICT policy and the RPC was being implemented under the leadership of the School Principal, Ms. Gibson. Her vision for the school placed great importance on ICT, and she encouraged the teachers and the students to use technology. She suggested that each teacher should have compulsory basic knowledge of the computer and be trained how to use a computer. The effect of technology on teaching and learning had become more apparent, as the principal stated:

> We are coming to realize that because our students are being exposed to technology because they are living in a technological age, we have to change some of the methods that are used to teach the students. More and more we are finding that when we teach, the students are more receptive, they learn more.

Ms. Gibson had already made plans for the computer laboratory at the school:

> We are now in the process of trying to secure funds to replace the computers. It has to be private sponsorship, the Ministry doesn't give us anything for that. While we can repair through our funds, we can't replace, we don't have enough, so when something goes wrong, we can fix it. In terms of replacement, that has got to be private funding.

As an interim measure, after the pilot study on policy implementation at Blue Mahoe School, the principal made arrangements for the computers in the laboratory to be repaired. A technician was employed to service and repair all 11 computers in the laboratory and return each to good working order. The repairs were carried out and the computer laboratory was returned to full strength. The principal then moved on to her vision for Continuing Professional Development for the teachers in the primary grades to enable them to use the newly repaired computers in the laboratory.

The school principal felt that Continuing Professional Development in the use of computer technology was an area that needed further development in the school:

> What needs to happen is if educational technology is to play its part, we have to look at how much we have available for student use. Yes, I know one computer can serve an entire class depending how it's used, but the teachers have to be trained on how to use it for the benefit of the students. I think that is one area that is lacking... introducing teachers to the technology and training them in the use of the technology.

The principal now wanted to provide her staff with the Continuing Professional Development that would prepare them to use the school's existing computer technology for teaching and learning. She had a large and diverse group of teachers with a broad range of teaching experience and computer literacy. Provision of appropriate professional development to enable each teacher to use ICT was a challenge that had to be met to give all the students at Blue Mahoe School access to computer technology.

DISCUSSION QUESTIONS

- What strategies for Continuing Professional Development could be used to encourage the teachers to use computer technology?
- What role would computer technology play in the Continuing Professional Development strategy selected?

- How could the Continuing Professional Development impact teaching and learning at Blue Mahoe School?
- Are there alternatives to professional development to encourage teachers to use computer technology?

CHAPTER 17

PROBLEMS AT MAPLE LEAF

Developing Constructivist e-Learning for Canada's Security Officers

Ellen Rose and Bev Bramble
University of New Brunswick, Canada

THE FIRST MEETING

The day of the project kick-off meeting had finally arrived. Dr. Fran Henderson hurried to the boardroom, determined not to show how nervous she was about this, her first big project since she was hired as Maple Leaf Security Training's Head of Education and Innovation. And after all, she told herself, stopping to pour her third coffee of the morning, there was no real cause for nervousness: she had 20 years of experience as a military training development officer, and the ink was barely dry on her PhD diploma in Adult Education. She had the experience and the credentials; what more did she need?

Fran breezed into the boardroom and, seating herself at the head of the table, took a moment to breathe deeply and survey the room. Seated to her right, with their backs to the view of the Ottawa skyline, were the two instructors from Maple Leaf's Saskatchewan office who would act as sub-

Cases 'n' Places: Global Cases in Educational and Performance Technology, pages 211–192

ject matter experts (SMEs) for this project. They had been chosen because they were by far the most knowledgeable and experienced of Maple Leaf's instructional staff. Cliff McDougall was a wiry man who was, she guessed, in his early 60s and therefore close to retirement. He sat slouched in his chair with his arms crossed, talking quietly to the other SME, Rob Lum, 50-something, who nodded periodically at his colleague's words but otherwise seemed to be preoccupied with the elaborate doodles he was creating on his pad of paper. Both men were former police officers and security guards and had been with Maple Leaf for over 20 years, although Fran understood that for both men, this was a first experience participating in an e-learning project.

On the opposite side of the table were the representatives from Prefex, the small e-learning company from Fredericton, New Brunswick, which had been awarded the contract for the instructional design and development work for this project, based on its innovative proposal for authentic video-based scenarios with just-in-time instructional scaffolding. Fran's doctoral research had entailed the development of a "constructivist andragogical" model for military and police training, so Prefex's ideas had won her over instantly. She called her approach constructivist andragogy because it combined Knowles' (1980) focus on adult learners' self-direction and experience as applied to solving authentic problems with the constructivist notion of "scaffolding," or supporting, learners as they encounter new material (a concept first introduced by Wood, Bruner, & Ross, 1976, and elaborated most notably by Vygotsky, 1978). Fran regarded this project as a proving ground for her constructivist andragogical approach to e-learning, which she believed would become a model for security officer training, perhaps even police training, not just across Canada but around the world.

Seated immediately to Fran's left was Prefex's President, Holden Sturgeon, a retired military training development officer. Fran had known Holden for years, and she knew that he was very capable but could also be brash and opinionated. Beside Holden sat Yoland Gagnon, a senior instructional designer, extremely competent but as soft-spoken and reticent as her boss tended to be loud and overbearing.

Fran smiled and cleared her throat. "Well, folks, we've got a lot of ground to cover today. We'd better get started."

The meeting began well. Fran welcomed the project team members, made the introductions, and handed out agendas. Everyone was cordial and smiling. Then came the first item of the agenda: an overview of the project. Firing up the PowerPoint presentation she had labored over for days, Fran launched into a description of Maple Leaf's Use of Force Model, which would be the subject of the e-learning. "As we all know," she said, "the Use of Force Model helps security officers determine the appropriate amount of force to use in potentially violent or dangerous situations. The primary outcome for this training is to ensure that, given an out-of-control situation or one that has the potential to go out of control, officers will use verbal communication, control holds, handcuffs, baton, pepper spray, and/or firearms to de-escalate the situation using the least level of force possible." Fran advanced to the next slide. "According to the Use of Force Model, an officer is expected to apply seven principles in determining whether and how to intervene in a potentially dangerous situation. The first is . . ."

Rob Lum's nondoodling hand shot up. "With all due respect, Dr. Henderson, is there anyone here who doesn't already know all this?"

Taken aback, Fran replied, "Well, Rob, I think it's important to make sure that we're all on the same page. If you'll indulge me, I'll just take a few more minutes of your time."

Fran's presentation continued without further interruption. Since Rob and Cliff were new to e-learning, she made sure to explain the rationale, in terms of both cost savings and pedagogical benefits, for delivering the Use of Force instruction online.

Following Fran's presentation, Holden Sturgeon displayed a diagram on the screen (Figure 17.1) that illustrated the constructivist approach Prefex proposed for the training. "In a nutshell," he said, pacing back and forth at the front of the room, "our idea is to create five interactive video-based scenarios that will place trainees in authentic, immersive situations with a minimum of instruction, get them acting on what they know, and figuring out what they don't know. Each scenario will have several decision points, and at each decision point trainees will have access to the particular set of tools that they might need to make that particular decision. We'll provide just-in-time, just-enough information, chunked into topic categories that make sense in the context of that particular decision and that particular scenario."

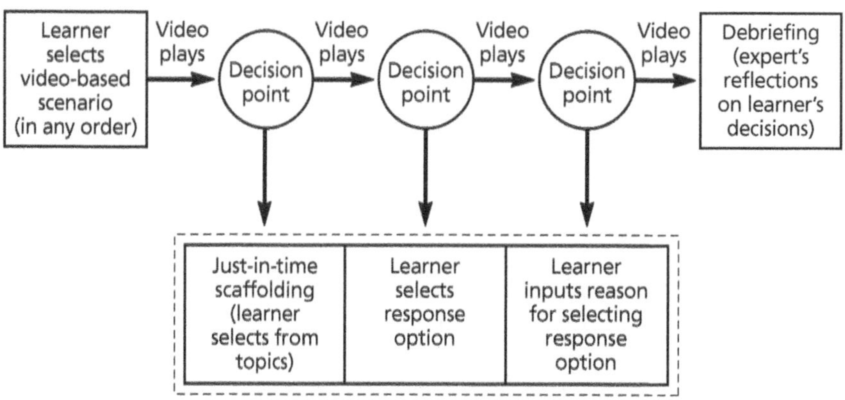

Figure 17.1 The constructivist instructional design flow proposed by Prefex.

Fran glanced at the SMEs. Was it her imagination, or had Cliff sunk even lower into his chair? “Excuse me, Holden,” she said. “Before you go any further, let’s just make sure that everyone here is familiar with constructivist learning theory.” She looked pointedly at Cliff and Rob.

Rob looked up from his doodles. “Eh? Oh, yeah, yeah, sure. We’re good to go, had a workshop on that a couple of years ago.”

Fran smiled inwardly. She knew that, when it came to training, Rob and Cliff were from the old school, favoring the traditional pedagogical approach to police and security officer training, based upon principles of behavioral psychology, which entailed delivering content via lectures to silent, obedient learners who were expected to absorb and then regurgitate the learned material. In this pedagogical model, scenarios or problems might be used, but only as a practical application of information that had already been learned (Figure 17.2).

In contrast to this behavioral model, the power of constructivism was that learning *began* with an authentic problem to solve, allowing learners to identify the skills and knowledge they needed in order to respond appropriately and effectively. Fran had no doubt that, once they realized the benefits of a constructivist approach, and particularly of her constructivist andragogical model, Rob and Cliff would come around to her way of thinking. “I’m glad to hear that,” she said, “because I see constructivism as the key to the future of Maple Leaf’s training.”

Rob and Cliff exchanged glances. “Could be,” mumbled Cliff.

The morning finished with lunch at a nearby Italian restaurant. The afternoon session went somewhat more smoothly, perhaps thanks to the mellowing effects of good pasta and wine. Fran outlined the logistics of the collaboration, which she had spent much time thinking through. She explained that Yoland would be the point of contact with the SMEs, who would be receiving release time in order to work on the project. Yoland would send storyboards in progress to the SMEs, indicating where information was needed, and then, when the storyboard for a scenario was completed, it would be signed off by Cliff and Rob. As the first storyboard was signed off, it would be handed over to the course developers, who would coordinate the video shoot and begin integrating interactive media into an

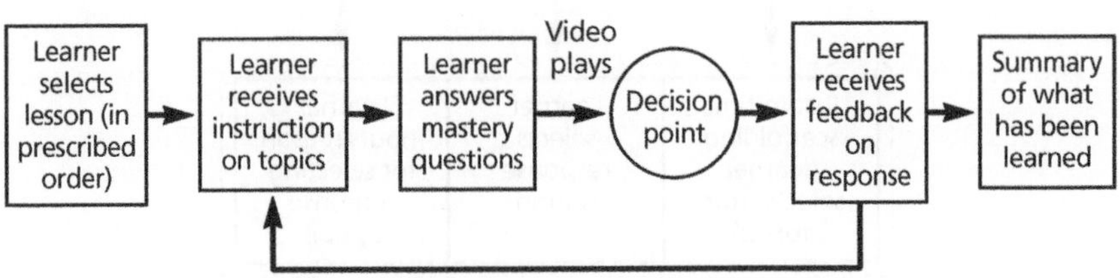

Figure 17.2 The instructional design flow desired by the SMEs.

e-learning prototype. The prototype would be reviewed and signed off on before work began on the scripting of the remaining four scenarios. In two months, Fran, Rob, Cliff, Holden, and Yoland would meet again in Ottawa for a final storyboard review meeting, at the end of which time Fran would sign off on the storyboards for all five scenarios.

The meeting wrapped up at 5:00, with plans for everyone to meet 2 hours later for dinner. Fran retreated to her office with a cup of coffee, her exhaustion buoyed by a glow of accomplishment. Sure, there had been a few rough patches throughout the day, but all in all, Fran felt that the first meeting had been a great success. Maple Leaf's Use of Force e-learning project was underway.

ONE MONTH LATER

Yoland hung up the phone and sat for a few minutes staring at the incomplete storyboard on her desk. It was full of errors and holes; Prefex's instructional designers had been unable to complete it because of a lack of input from the SMEs. But neither Cliff nor Rob had been available to take her call, and although she had left a message asking that one of them call her as soon as possible, she knew that they would not do so.

Yoland glanced at the Gantt chart posted on the wall above her desk. The deadline for the SMEs' sign-off of the storyboard for the first video-based scenario had come and gone, as had the date for beginning work on the prototype and the SMEs' sign-off of the storyboard for the second scenario. Now the deadline for the third scenario—tomorrow!—pressed like a heavy weight on the back of her head. She scrabbled in her desk drawer for some aspirin, then, sighing, she stood. There was no escaping the inevitable: she was going to have to talk to Holden again and make it clear that, unless they could somehow enlist the cooperation of Cliff and Rob, the entire project was in serious jeopardy.

Twenty minutes later, Yoland was seated in Holden's corner office, with its magnificent view of the Saint John River, maintaining her quiet composure despite the heavy aura of disapproval. Over the past 4 weeks, she had kept meticulous records in her day planner, and had therefore been able to give Holden a clear, day-by-day record of her efforts to obtain input from Cliff and Rob, which he was now reading:

> March 14—Project kickoff meeting in Ottawa with Fran Henderson, Holden, and SMEs Cliff McDougall and Rob Lum.
>
> March 15—Team meeting of Prefex instructional designers and developers. Process overview.
>
> March 16—Design work on scenario 1 begins.

March 24—E-mailed 20-page storyboard for scenario 1 to Cliff and Rob, with areas requiring their input indicated.

March 30—Still awaiting input from SMEs. Prototype review may impact instructional approach, but we are forced to begin design work on scenario 2 while we wait.

April 2—Called SMEs. Spoke to Cliff. He has looked at storyboard but needs more time to review and get back with input.

April 5—E-mailed 19-page storyboard for scenario 2 to SMEs for their input, with understanding that prototype review may result in changes. Explained importance of getting required information.

April 6—Holden advises that we proceed at risk with the design in order to maintain billable status of team members, so design work on scenario 3 begins today. I'm concerned that we are progressing too far with the scripting without having prototype review and may have to make significant changes later.

April 9—Heard from Rob, apologizing that they've been very busy and he didn't know when they would be able to get to the review of storyboard 1. Explained to Holden that we were not getting required information from our SMEs and prototype work is stalled. He made call to Saskatchewan; Cliff and Rob's supervisor assured him they are being given release time to review storyboards.

April 10—E-mailed Cliff and Rob explaining urgency of situation. No response. Called and left messages for both. Design team doing what they can with scenario 3 while we wait.

April 11—Finally, a strange e-mail from Cliff. He says he and Rob were expecting to get visual storyboards, not 20 pages of written information. Says he will get back to me when he has had more time to look at the storyboards. Apologized; very busy.

April 13—Called Cliff, left message. Called Rob, left message.

April 14—Still no word. Design team is beginning to script scenario 4, but instructional design work is proceeding at risk and is significantly impacted and slowed by lack of any SME input whatsoever.

Holden finished reading Yoland's record of her failed attempts to communicate with the SMEs and leaned back in his chair, steepling his fingers. "So, what's the problem? Why aren't they returning your calls and e-mails? Is it a personality conflict?"

Yoland shrugged helplessly. "How *could* it be a personality conflict? We never speak!"

"Okay," Holden said, "I think it's time to see what Fran can do for us."

Two days later, days of waiting anxiously but fruitlessly for word from the SMEs, Yoland was called into Holden's office for a scheduled conference call with Fran. Fran answered her phone on the first ring and got right to the point. "I had a conference call with Cliff and Rob yesterday," she said, "and, to be honest, I couldn't get a straight answer out of either of them. They kept going on about the storyboards being longer and more complicated than they'd expected and not having the time to read them. Rob kept saying, 'we're instructors, not computer programmers,' whatever that means."

Yoland's hopes sank.

"But," Fran continued, "I told them I didn't buy that excuse, since they're both getting release time to provide subject matter expertise for this project. So, here's all I can think of. You could try to shorten your storyboards, make them less complicated. Or—and I think this is probably the better option at this point—you could forego sending them the storyboards entirely, just talk to them over the phone, tell them what you need and get the information from them directly, so they don't have to take the time to read the storyboards and write down their responses."

"Without storyboards, we can't get sign-off from Cliff and Rob," Holden observed. "And, without SME sign-off, I'm not willing to proceed with work on the prototype of the first scenario."

There was a pause on the other end of the line. "That's true," replied Fran. "I guess we'll just have to proceed without the prototype. We'll get a final sign-off on the storyboards at the storyboard review meeting in May, and then begin development after that. Okay?"

"Okay," said Holden. "As long as it's understood that this is going to have a big impact on the dates for the final deliverables."

"I understand. Is this going to work for you, Yoland?"

"Yes," Yoland replied, already thinking about the additional work that this new method would entail for both her and her team. "It's worth a try. But," she added, recalling the frustrations of the past month, "it will only work if they'll return my calls and e-mails."

"Let me work on that," Fran said.

THE STORYBOARD REVIEW MEETING

Pausing to refill her coffee cup on the way to the boardroom, Fran recalled with a smile how anxious she had been 2 months ago at the project kick-off meeting. She felt much more confident and relaxed now, knowing how unnecessary that anxiety had been. For despite a rough beginning, the project had progressed very well, thanks to her suggestion that Prefex forego sending the storyboards to Cliff and Rob. Yoland had been able to gather all the necessary information through lengthy phone calls with the SMEs, and in the end she reported that they had been reasonably helpful. With that problem solved, Fran's attention had been diverted by other training projects, so she looked forward to this opportunity—a mere formality, she felt—to review and sign off on the five scenarios that Prefex had storyboarded for the Use of Force e-learning.

Entering the boardroom, Fran took her place at the head of the table, and welcomed everyone back. "Well, we've got a lot of ground to cover, so let's get started."

This was Yoland's cue to rise and distribute spiral-bound copies of the storyboards for the five scenarios. After 2 intense months of familiarizing herself with the content and getting to know the SMEs, Yoland was also feeling more confident. She knew the scenarios inside out, and she felt that she and her design team had done exceptional work.

"Okay," she began. "Scenario one is called 'Airport Security.' The situation is that you're an airport security officer who spots a suspicious-looking man lingering outside the preboarding screening area. As you approach him, the woman with him sees you coming and yells, 'Jack, the cops are here!' Jack turns and swiftly reaches into a bag he is carrying. Now, this is the first decision point. Depending on what you say and do, the scenario can go one of three possible ways..."

"That's not right," said Cliff.

Startled, Yoland looked up from her notes. "W-what do you mean?"

"That's just not right," Cliff repeated. "How will they know the correct thing to do? You're throwing trainees into this situation and you haven't even taught them the Use of Force Model. How can you expect them to know what the correct procedure is?"

"But..." Yoland looked to Fran and Holden for help.

Fran spoke up, struggling to keep her voice calm and even. "Cliff, you know we're using a constructivist andragogical approach to this training. We established that at our first meeting. The whole point is to put the trainees in authentic situations and scaffold their decision-making."

"But it's hardly fair to ask them to make a decision when they have no basis upon which to make it!"

"And besides," added Rob, looking up from the doodles with which he was decorating the margins of the storyboards, "what if they do the wrong thing? You learn what you do."

Fran and Yoland exchanged dismayed glances.

"Whoa, whoa, hold on a minute," blustered Holden. "Let's not get off track here. This is *constructivist* training we're talking about. The principles are a little different from what you fellows are used to, but the theory is sound. Trainees have got a complete set of just-in-time tools to support them in making the right decision. And even if they don't, well, people can learn from their mistakes. That's what trial and error is all about!"

Cliff was shaking his head stubbornly back and forth, and Fran noted with some alarm that his face had grown quite red. "No," he objected. "That's just wrong. You don't want their first experience with the courseware to be a failure. That's just not right."

"Okay, okay," said Holden. "Can I make a suggestion here? Let Yoland keep talking us through the storyboard; once you see where we're going with the scenario, you'll get it, okay?"

"Well, okay," Cliff said, while Rob nodded his assent.

Yoland continued. "The correct action, at this decision point, is for you to stop Jack before he reaches into the bag so that you can see his hands and what they're doing at all times. If you don't do that, then Jack will either pull a bat or a shotgun out of the bag and start . . . "

"But," said Rob, "I understand what Cliff's getting at, because if trainees make the wrong move at this point, that's going to disincentive them from the beginning."

"Rob," Holden said, sounding exasperated. "What makes you think they're going to make the wrong decision? There's a whole set of tools to scaffold their decision-making. And anyway, a lot of the trainees are ex-police officers. They're going to be familiar with the Use of Force Model."

"They're supposed to be" said Cliff, "but that's not always the reality. No," he shook his head stubbonly, "they need some basic instruction before they get thrown into these situations."

Fran was overwhelmed by a panicked feeling that the whole project was unraveling before her eyes. If the SMEs wouldn't sign off on these storyboards, then the project was derailed. She could make concessions and have Prefex design lessons on the Use of Force Model—but then the training would just be more of what Maple Leaf's training had been for years: instruction, practice, and feedback. It certainly wouldn't be the exemplar for constructivist andragogical security officer training, combining authentic scenarios with appropriate scaffolding that Fran had envisioned. She turned to the SMEs. "Cliff, Rob, you knew this was a constructivist e-learning project. We established that at the beginning, and you've been working with Yoland for the past two months! Why are you posing these objections *now*?"

DISCUSSION QUESTIONS

1. Identify the people supporting and resisting implementation of a constructivist training solution for the Use of Force e-learning. Why do people resist the implementation of new approaches to training? What mistakes can be made if instructional designers are unaware of the political tensions to which new training approaches can give rise?

2. Discuss Fran Henderson's performance as Maple Leaf's new Head of Education and Innovation. How did she facilitate or impede acceptance of the constructivist andragogical approach to the e-learning? What might she have said or done at the first meeting to encourage the SMEs to support and even take ownership of the new approach to training?
3. Given the constraints in the case, should Fran Henderson and Prefex's instructional designers insist upon a constructivist approach, or should they respect the wishes of the SMEs, even though it might result in what they feel is an instructionally inferior product? Is there a compromise position they might negotiate?
4. How can instructional designers gather information from SMEs who are unable or unwilling to provide the necessary information?

REFERENCES

Knowles, M. S. (1980). *The modern practice of adult education: From pedagogy to andragogy.* Englewood Cliffs, NJ: Prentice Hall/Cambridge.

Vygotsky, L. S. (1978). *Mind in society: The development of higher mental processes.* Cambridge, MA: Harvard University Press.

Wood, D., Bruner, J., & Ross, G. (1976). The role of tutoring in problem solving. *Journal of Child Psychology and Psychiatry, 17,* 89–100.

SECTION 5

TECHNOLOGY IMPLEMENTATION AND ADOPTION

CHAPTER 18

HATCHING THE COCOON

Assiut University Students' First Step to the World of ICT

Hanan Salah EL-Deen EL-Halawany
Assiut University, Egypt

Learn to build all your roads today because tomorrow's ground is too uncertain for plans.

After a while you learn that even sunshine burns if you get too much. So plant your own garden and decorate your own soul, instead of waiting for someone to bring you flowers.

—Canfield, Hansen, & Kirberger, 1997, p. 7

INTRODUCTION

This is the story of a group of Egyptian young students who dream of a better future and wait for a sunny tomorrow to shine and scare away all their nightmares of unemployment. Still, despite their struggle against their agonies and hardship, a cloud of pessimism conceals the horizon of their future. They are a bunch of soldiers without weapons who fight against

Cases 'n' Places: Global Cases in Educational and Performance Technology, pages 223–208

a vicious army called world capitalism, which has subjected all economic activities in Egypt to its dominion, leaving most of the disadvantaged, marginalized, and subordinated groups an easy target for unemployment and despair.

In this piece of inquiry, I will try to take you in an adventure toward the East, to a land that once upon a time was called the Sun of Civilization. A land whose soil can tell you stories of great people who walked upon it. A soil where any child with a sand shovel can find a thousand-year-old artifact, play with, then throw away because he is tired of history and wants a computer or video gaming system. A land whose people are occupying the same spots their great grandparents inhabited for thousands of years around the Great River Nile, honoring the Nile and working under the burning sun to receive its gifts.

Now life has dramatically changed as Egypt stands on the intersection between underdevelopment and modernity. The scene has changed in a way that if you stand on the banks of the Nile in Cairo, the capital of Egypt, you will see the glimmering towers of the World Trade Center, including some of the fanciest stores, restaurants, and offices of modern Egypt. Looking down though, you will also see poor large families who live in tiny boats by the banks of the Nile. Thin and poorly dressed, these families apparently spend their days and nights on tiny canoes no longer than fishing poles. Yet, if you look down you will find shiny objects in the center of some boats, upon looking more closely, you will realize they are battery-operated televisions. Even those impoverished families living in tin canoes are grasping at modernization through media. This contrast within contrasts is the best elaborative introduction to Egypt today (Warschauer, 2003).

Sprouting from this dominant theatrical controversy, Students In Free Enterprise (SIFE) emerges. It mirrors the confusion and perplexity overwhelming Egyptians nowadays. Therefore, the expedition with SIFE Assiut seeks to find some answers to a very critical question that will determine the future of Egypt as a knowledge society: How do average university students perceive their future through Information and Communication Technologies (ICTs)? Searching for answers requires following different paths through which I will document and analyze how members of SIFE Assiut perceive ICTs in relation to their activities in SIFE and their future.

The final portrait will not only scrutinize the performance of an international nonprofit student organization, but it will also shed light on how globalization, with its heavy fist, intertwines with national cultural and economic transformations to shape the young Egyptian generation's negotiation of their future in relation to ICTs.

THEORY AND STRATEGY

Equipped with my ethnographic toolkit and situating my argument within Bourdieu and Bernstein's (Bernstein, 1973, 1996; Bourdieu, 1993) social and cultural reproduction discourse, I will try to analyze two teams of SIFE Assiut's negotiation of identity and power through certain sociolinguistic styles concerning ICTs. This negotiation mirrors the ongoing discourse between globalization and national transformation into free market economy (Collins, 2000).

In Bourdieu and Passeron's *Reproduction in Education, Society and Culture* (1977), the relation between institutional expectations and language was theorized and analyzed in terms of *cultural capital*: institution-sanctified symbolic resource, forms of knowledge, and ways of speaking. These forms of cultural capital were found to be unequally distributed among members of SIFE and interacted with the implicit pedagogic messages of the SIFE organization in a way that might benefit the privileged and handicap the unprivileged (Bourdieu, 1991; Niehoff & Ganzeboom, 1996; Street, 1999). A scenario not only is implemented on the individual but also on national and global levels.

Within this context, I will examine my informants' words and reactions in different situations as they negotiate their identities and power relations through elaboration and self-examination of their utilization of ICTs in two projects carried out by two teams of SIFE Assiut. Meanings will be drawn for individuals, SIFE as a student organization, and Egyptian higher institutions as national and international agents.

SIFE Assiut: The Cultural Setting and Study Context

Changing the world, we create global partnerships between business and higher education that prepare university students to make a meaningful contribution toward a better world of business entrepreneurs and business leaders by challenging to address real world business and economic issues in their communities (Teach-Learn-Connect-Inspire-Empower).

This statement is written on a big banner hanging over the heads of four young, good looking keynote speakers in one of SIFE Assiut's seminars held under the title "Stocks . . . Banks . . . Insurance: New Opportunities

Emerge and Money Waits for Reaping." The first speaker is a bank representative, the second is a broker's company representative, the third is an insurance company representative, and the fourth is the faculty advisor of SIFE Assiut. Attendees are a group of no more than 30 students; among them are SIFE Assiut members. The guest speakers are addressing the audience as investors. Each of them has put in a moderate effort to convince students to invest in their sector—banks, stock market, or insurance. The irony in this event not only exists in the fact that most of the audience are low-income students, but also in the fact that the organizers, the financial literacy members, have specified 10 seats in the front row for businessmen and 40 minutes during the costly coffee break for the guest speakers to meet businessmen in Assiut and discuss business, as promised on the Arabic leaflet. However, the shocking fact was that those 10 seats remained empty throughout the whole event, and the extravagant French snacks were consumed by the audience and SIFE Assiut members.

SIFE is a global nonprofit organization active in more than 40 countries. Working in partnership with business and higher education, SIFE establishes student teams on university campuses. These teams are led by faculty advisors, and they are challenged to develop community outreach projects that reach SIFE's five educational topics: market economics; success skills; entrepreneurship; financial literacy; and business ethics (SIFE, 2008).

The SIFE Assiut team started in 2007. Through their involvement in planning and implementing different projects in their community, members of SIFE develop their awareness of their community's needs and problems and work with local enterprises and personnel to empower the local community and individuals to take charge and recognize their role in solving their problems and improving their community. At the same time, they are trained in different skills to become entrepreneurs driving a free market in an IT society (SIFE Assiut, 2008). In this study I will focus on two projects: the Slum project, Candle Village, and the Financial Literacy Project.

The Slum project, Candle Village, "aims to solving the economical problems of a certain sector in Assiut society whose most of its members are unemployed. The full picture of the society after finishing the project and achieving it's goals each person who could have been an extra load on his society will be self employed and capable generating enough income through making scented candles" (Slum Project team, 2008, p. 1). The Slum project team consists of two girls from the school of Art with English majors, three English Commerce students, and the leader, Ibrahim, a fourth-year Arabic Commerce student.

The Financial Literacy project is an educative project that seeks to spread a new financial awareness among the Assiut community. It aims "to teach people what money is, how they can get it, and how to use it in a way that enhances their local community," explained Hassan a third-year English

Commerce student and a member in the Financial Literacy project. In observing the conduct of the two teams, I noticed that the Slum project team is heterogeneous and functioned with equal roles. The Financial Literacy project team is homogeneous but lacks uniformity. It consists of six English Commerce students and their leader is Mahmoud. Mahmoud is a second-year English Commerce student and an old member in SIFE Assiut, 13 months. Although he is the youngest member in his team, he controls the rest. He is a very dominant and manipulative character, who tries to subject the project to meet his personal interest: "it is my chance to let the world know of my existence, especially as I'm the one who designed *my project,* and I also *apply it.* My affiliation with SIFE allows me to enter banks and contact big companies and billionaires, and this is what I like about SIFE."

In the course of action, the two teams use ICTs, mainly for communication, in a way that expresses the symbolic power some possess, whether illusionary or in reality. In the meantime it reflects their bewilderment between equilibrium and hegemony. These are the two dichotomies upon which I will develop my analysis and draw conclusions.

THE FIRST DICHOTOMY: ICT BETWEEN REALITY AND ILLUSION

The dissemination of ICTs and the Internet in developing countries has been associated with promises of development, prosperity, and equilibrium (Wheeler, 2004). It is expected that they are to empower individuals in the exercise of their right to receive, produce, and circulate information and ideas beyond national borders (de Castell, Bryson, & Jenson, 2002; Noble, 1998; Watson, 1998).

The most optimistic viewpoints see ICTs as providing developing countries with an opportunity to "leapfrog" stages of development and be at par with the level of development in the West (Sunden & Wicander, 2006). One evidence is a recent study that found a relationship between access to mobile phones and economic growth, with its impact more significant in developing than developed countries (Waverman, 2005).

On the other hand, an opposing view about ICTs warns that they "will only increase existing inequalities and power relations" (Aiyepeku, Iwayemi, & Ajiferuke, 1994). Evidence of this is seen from cases showing that areas that have long benefited from excellent physical access, and have been dominant politically and economically are the ones benefiting from greater access to information technologies (Niles & Hanson, 2003). The idea that development results from linking poor nations to ICTs, the Internet in particular, is considered a myth (Disraeli, 2001).There are questions regarding the real effects of ICTs on national development, considering the limited evidence regarding its correlation (Heeks, 2003).

The view from the middle-ground considers that ICTs can play a role in a country's development if applied appropriately (Soeftestad & Sein, 2003).

In the context of the current study, all my informants hold a strong conviction that those who master ICTs and can manage information will survive and find a good job opportunity, while those who do not will perish economically (Technology Development Center, 1997, p. 79). Ibrahim, the leader of the Slum Project team, explained, "Without computer skills, you won't have a chance in the labor market. In my second year in my postsecondary education, I got the chance to earn a summer internship in Bank Naser. They told me that if I succeeded in learning a specific computer program responsible for money transactions among banks, I will certainly earn a job opportunity in any banks I wish to work for"

This is the main motivator that encourages most students to join SIFE. As Hassan, a third year English Commerce student and a member in the Financial Literacy project, expresses, "Joining SIFE is useful for me because I'm good in communication that will help me to establish relationships with a businessman who can teach me about life skills, teach me how to use the computer in pulling out information, data."

Hassan's words reflect how vulnerable Egyptian youth are to the role ICTs play in securing employment chances for them in Egypt. However, most have failed in translating this recognition into real-world strategies. In their daydreams, they imagine that these preliminary IT skills they developed through SIFE will enable them to obtain a prestigious job: "It came to our minds that we might establish a Human Development Center. I discovered I'm a good leader so I can be the manager. Maha and Rana can work as trainers. Ali, a second-year student in the school of medicine, is the IT person. I never thought like that. That is why I say that SIFE has helped us to enhance our self-confidence to do such daring things," shared Abdel Monem, a graduate student in English Commerce and a former SIFE member.

In reality, these daring actions have shrunk to the extent that filling an application on the Internet has become a triumph. Mohamed, a member in the Financial Literacy project recalled the following with joy: "I searched for a summer training opportunity in different banks and filled the application for an internship in a Saudi British bank. They responded by thanking me and apologizing for not having any vacant positions."

The above quotes reveal the controversies and perplexity SIFE Assiut students' experience in their understanding of the nature of SIFE and its mission, which asserts that students, through their involvement in SIFE activities, have to develop a profound personal growth that will prepare them to lead sustainable enterprises and build stronger futures (SIFE, 2008, p. 4).

In the midst of this disappointment that swept over me, a beam of light and hope shines again when some of my informants talk about real on-ground strategies to refine their IT skills. Hamam, a third-year student in English Commerce and a member in the Slum Project team, comments, "I did use the Net before for searching specific Web sites that culturally attract me. Before SIFE, I didn't have an e-mail account, now I created one to keep in touch with SIFE members. Now I'm working to get my ICDL—The International Computer Driving License—certificate, so I can become more efficient in using computer."

Apparently Hamam plans to echo and extend the prevalent image of SIFE as an egalitarian and empowering students' organization that helps its member to perceive ICTs as engines of growth and tools for empowerment, as they offer unlimited access to information and invite a profound rethinking of the purpose of education and its relevance to national labor market transformation (Guttman, 2003. p. 9). At the same time, it opens the Egyptian universities' eyes to the importance of focusing on interdisciplinarity or transdisciplinarity, not only in research study, but also in university life including on-campus students' activities.

In a similar vein, many of my informants, through participating in SIFE, recognize their need to work on their language skills, especially English, not only to boost their choices in the labor market but also to be able to fully engage in all SIFE activities that require fluency in English. Mohyee, a third-year law student and a member in the Financial Literacy team, explains how languages can expand and vary his working opportunities. "Upon joining the faculty of law, I had to choose either to take an English or French course. I preferred taking French so I would have two languages. See, this will help as I'm from Luxor." Mastering different languages is very essential for working in tourism, which is a very profitable economic sector in Luxor.

THE SECOND DICHOTOMY: ICT BETWEEN HEGEMONY AND EQUILIBRIUM

The observation of SIFE Assiut performance unveils cycles of hegemony, starting from the individual cycle until reaching the global cycle, as I will explain next.

Hegemony vis-à-vis Equilibrium on the Individual Cycle

The recruitment criterion that is adopted by SIFE Assiut members reflects hegemony rather than equilibrium. In reference to Bourdieu's (1991) symbolic power, the elite members of SIFE Assiut have invested their power to exclude the unwanted individuals from being members in a way that contradicts with the rules of SIFE.

The SIFE handbook states that there are several strategies for recruiting new members. First, current members in SIFE should participate in their colleges' events to spread the word about SIFE. Second, they should encourage faculty members to make announcements about SIFE in their classes. Third, members should create personal invitations to join SIFE and distribute them to their friends or other student leaders on campus. Fourth, members can create a SIFE bulletin board to include a sign-up sheet, current projects, media coverage, announcements, and the team's meeting time and place (SIFE, 2008).

Unsurprisingly, the only strategy adopted by the majority of SIFE Assiut members is recruiting friends. This is very explicit in the homogeneity dominating the two teams, who are either friends or colleagues. This has also been reflected in the way they use ICT to create a "castaway system" (Sernau, 2001, p.190), which turns SIFE into a closed organization, especially when we consider that all members of the Financial Literacy project are selected by Mahmoud, the leader, and they are all his colleagues. In the meantime, the Slum Project team members are all friends, and their families are socially acquainted, as they are all children of staff members in the university. Therefore, to circulate information and announcements, members usually use their personal e-mails or cell phones. As for chatting, they use Facebook, the most popular Web site among Internet users in Egypt (Egyptians use Facebook to deter censorship, 2008), instead of posting information on the SIFE Assiut homepage, which is neglected and has become out-of-date.

However, this closed society has secured an intimate and empowering environment, which can be easily witnessed in observing the Slum Project team. They perform relying on friendships, loyalty, and responsibility toward each other. They have distributed chores among themselves based on their experiences. Maha and Rana, because of their English skills, are responsible for translating reports into English. Ali is the IT manager, who explains,

> For our project, we will create our Web site that will have an easy domain. So in any search one can find it easily. It will be in three languages, Italy, French, and English. It won't cost much, only 150 Egyptian pounds, including the domain and dot net. Also, we can sign an agreement with Google where they can post an ad through our Web site, but this will cost more. We can also post an ad through Facebook or Yahoo; it is not expensive at all. Or we can do this through e-Bay.

Ibrahim and Kamel, the Commerce students, are responsible for preparing the SWOT—strengths, weakness, opportunities, and threats—report, and the marketing plan.

Accordingly, the Slum project team uses the virtual space of the Internet to hold conferences, exchange information about their project, as well as socializing. Maha explained, "We used the computer to chat with each other, and once we held a conference and we talked together."

Counter to this, different members in the Financial Literacy project confine their use of the Internet to socializing with girls. Mahmoud, the leader of the project, stresses, "In our society, I cannot encourage commingling between boys and girls; therefore the Net presents a secure space for both boys and girls to get together." This view is common among his team members as well.

Mahmoud's statement lends support to a very critical issue raised in different studies, arguing that the uses of the Internet and other communication technologies in most developing countries are often restricted to entertainment (Rohozinski, 2004; Teitelbaum, 2002). This has led me to challenge the illusion propagated by different studies claiming that the adoption of Western media, particularly the Internet, encompasses the potential to accelerate national development efforts and to bring about favorable sociocultural changes (Fandy, 2000; Gher & Amin, 1999; Hudson, 2000; Huff, 2001; Wei & Kolko, 2005).

The paradox in the rush by developing countries to embrace network technologies is that ICT importers hardly understand the culturally mediating characteristics of the technology (Bowers, 1998). Bowers asserts that computer technologies select Western cultural patterns for amplification, while other cultural experiences are reduced or eliminated altogether. He further contends that socializing non-Western people into the patterns of thinking amplified through the use of ICT "is a form of cultural domination" (p. 115). In the context of the current study, English language, as the language of Western technology, is scrutinized for being the medium of the Western global hegemony as I will explain next.

Hegemony vis-à-vis Equilibrium on the Global Cycle

The ability to benefit from the computer is restricted to those who master English, due to English-language computer science terms, English operating systems, English resources on the Internet, and such (Warschauer, 2005). Mastering English requires adjusting Arabic normal ways of doing things and ways of thinking to Western norms; for instance, writing from left to right instead of writing from right to left.

Complying with SIFE regulations, all documents have to be written and presented in English, which in return has restricted membership to those who master English. Abdel Rahman, a third-year English Commerce student and a member in SIFE, discloses, "Last year, new members were recruited immediately before the national competition on the expenses of other active and hard working members because of their good looks and their English."

Although English is the second language in Egypt, and the government has introduced it in all levels of education, this has born little fruit due to a lack of trained teachers, overcrowded classes, and most importantly, the focus on English for writing rather than for communication (Warschaur, 2003, p. 13).

Most significantly, English has started to invade the Arabic language. Albriini (2006) records the intrusion of English technological jargon into Arabic vocabulary. He notes that such statements as "cancel almawdoo" (cancel the topic), "arsillak message" (shall I send you a message?), "systemu mu'attal" (his system is broken), are commonly used, even though Arabic equivalents are available. Such terms are becoming the colloquial speech of Egyptian youth, including my informants. They even write Arabic using English letters while they are chatting on the Internet.

The issue here does not concern English as a language but as a sign of global homogenization of the Western culture. Harvey (1983), in this respect, warns that "computerization cannot be allowed to become a new form of cultural imposition—neocolonialism is not acceptable, even in an automated package" (p. 269).

A NEW HORIZON

Approaching the end of my journey, evidence from this study sustains the claim that human development is about much more than the rise or fall of incomes. It is about creating an environment in which individuals can develop their full potential and lead productive, creative lives in accordance with their needs and interests (UNDP, 2001, p. 9).

This can only be achieved through establishing a partnership between public-skill training organizations, represented in universities, and other organizations such as SIFE, which hold considerable promise for more relevant and better quality skills-development for youth, and hence better employment outcomes. Realizing this promise calls for finding ways to improve the effectiveness of these public/private partnerships (National Center for Educational Research and Development, 2001).

Upon that investment in human capital then, education has thus moved to center stage in strategies to promote economic prosperity, fuller employment, and social cohesion. As a result, education is increasingly considered an investment in the collective future of societies and nations, rather than simply in the future success of individuals (OECD, 2003). This awareness has prompted Egyptian universities to recognize that they are playing a paramount role in shaping the more sophisticated forms of human capital (Fergany, 2000).

As for SIFE, we have a very common Egyptian proverb that says who "lacks power cannot provide it." Through their involvement in SIFE, students are expected to assist the disadvantaged groups in their local communities and contribute to the overall welfare of their society. How can we expect them to do so while they are powerless? Therefore, SIFE can play a very important role as a nonformal education organization through directing its activities to income generating and poverty eradication projects carried out by the students and for the students. Anyway, this is not a new trend in education, as attacking poverty has become an international concern in the paradigm of "education and learning for sustainable development," taking into consideration the reality that almost half of the world's population lives in poverty (World Bank, 2000).

This is the case where ICTs can be viewed as crucial in the development agenda (International Telecommunications Union [ITU], 2003). Specifically, as it has been strongly argued that ICTs can contribute significantly to poverty alleviation (David & Foray, 2002), and hence expand opportunities for economic development (Prosser, 2000; World Bank, 1999). At that moment only, access to information will provide people with the opportunity "to undertake production, engage in labor markets, and participate in reciprocal exchanges with other people" (Ellis, 2000, p. 31).

Lastly, users of ICTs should recognize the cultural and language biases accompanying them in different multicultural contexts. Therefore, efforts should be directed to preserve the local culture through creating ICT applications that are pertinent to the local context; that is, how well the proposed innovations fit within the importing culture in a way that preserves genuineness and authenticity.

REFERENCES

Aiyepeku, W. Q., Iwayemi, A., & Ajiferuke, I. S. Y. (1994). *Information technology & capacity building for the global environment: Africa case study.* Retrieved April 16, 2008, from http://www.africa.upenn.edu/Padis/AiyebExe.html

Albirini, A. (2006). Cultural perceptions: The missing element in the implementation of ICT in developing countries. *International Journal of Education and Development Using Information and Communication Technology (IJEDICT), 2*(1), 49–65.

Bernstein, B. (1973). *Class, codes, and control* (Vol. 2). London: Routledge & Kegan Paul.

Bernstein, B. (1996). *Pedagogy, symbolic control, and identity: Theory, research, critique.* London: Taylor & Francis.

Bourdieu, P. (1991). *Language and symbolic power.* Palo Alto, CA: Stanford Univ. Press.

Bourdieu, P. (1993). *The field of cultural production.* New York: Columbia Univ. Press.

Bourdieu, P., & Passeron, J. (1977). *Reproduction in education, society, and culture.* Beverly Hills, CA: Sage.

Bowers, C. A. (1998). The paradox of technology: What's gained and lost? *Thought & Action, 14*(1), 49–57.

Canfield, J., Hansen, M. V., & Kirberger, K. (1997). *Chicken soup for the teenage soul.* Deerfield Beach, FL: Health Communications, Inc.

Collins, J. (2000). Bernstein, Bourdieu and the new literacy studies. *Linguistics and Education, 11*(1), 56–78.

David, P. A., & Foray, D. (2002). Introduction and general perspectives: An introduction to the economy of the knowledge society. *International Social Science Journal, 54*(171), 9–23.

de Castell, S., Bryson, M., & Jenson, J. (2002). *Object lessons: Toward an educational theory of technology.* Retrieved April 15, 2008 from http://firstmonday.org/issues/issue7_1/castell/index.html.

Disraeli, B. (2001). *Information technology for the development of youth in Africa.* [Online]. Retrieved October 5, 2005 from: http://www.ayf.de/documents/Dixit.doc

Egyptians use Facebook to deter censorship. (2008, April 30). *Middle East Times.*

Ellis, F. (2000). *Rural livelihoods and diversity in developing countries.* Oxford, UK: Oxford University Press.

Fandy, M. (2000). Information technology, trust, and social change in the Arab World. *The Middle East Journal, 54*(3), 378–394.

Fergany, N. (2000). *Arab higher education and development: An overview.* Retrieved April 23, 2004 from www.almishkat.org

Gher, L., & Amin, H. (1999). New and old media access and ownership in the Arab World. *Gazette, 61*(1), 59–88.

Guttman, C. (2003). *Education in and for the information society.* Geneva: UNESCO Publications for the World Summit on the Information Society.

Harvey, W. B. (1983). Educational technology and third world development. *Journal of Educational Technology Systems, 11*(3), 265–270.

Heeks, R. (2003). Information systems perspective on ethical trade and self-regulation. *Information Technology for Development, 10*(2), 123–138.

Hudson, M. (2000). A pan-Arab virtual think tank: Enriching the Arab information environment. *Middle. East Journal, 54*(3), 362–377.

Huff, T. E. (2001). Globalization and the Internet: Comparing the Middle Eastern and Malaysian experiences. *The Middle East Journal, 55*(3), 439–458.

International Telecommunications Union (ITU). (2003). *World telecommunication development report. Access indicators for the information society: Executive summary.* World Summit on the Information Society (WSIS) & International Telecommunication Union (ITU). Retrieved June 15, 2008 from http://www.itu.int/ITU-D/ict/publications/wtdr_03/material/WTDR2003Sum_e.pdf

National Center for Educational Research and Development (NCERD). (2001). *Education development: National report of Arab Republic of Egypt from 1990 to 2000.* Cairo: NCERD.

Niehoff, T., & Ganzeboom, H. (1996). *Cultural socialization and social reproduction: A cross-national test of a cultural theory of socialization.* Paper presented at the 91st Annual Meeting of the American Sociological Association, New York.

Niles, S., & Hanson, S. (2003). *A new era of accessibility*. APA I, 15. Retrieved May 20, 2008 from www.urisa.org/files/Nilesvol15apa1-4.pdf

Noble, D. (1998). Selling academe to the technology industry. *Thought & Action Journal, 14*(1), 29–40.

OECD. (2003). *Financing Education–investments and returns: Analysis of the world education indicators 2002 edition.* Chronicle of Higher Education. Retrieved June 4, 2008 from http://chronicle.com/daily/2003/02/2003021902n.htm

Prosser, T. (2000). *The Law and Regulators.* Oxford, UK: Clarendon Press.

Rohozinski, R. (2004, March 24–28) *"Secret Agents" and "Undercover Brothers": The hidden information revolution in the Arab world.* Paper presented at the Fifth Mediterranean Social and Political Research Meeting, Florence & Montecatini Terme.

Sernau, S. (2001). Moving up: Education and social mobility. In S. Sernau (Ed.), *World apart: Social inequalities in a new century* (pp. 89–213). Thousand Oaks, CA: Pine Forge Press.

SIFE. (2008). *Global handbook and training manual 2007–2008.* Retrieved June 5, 2008 from www.sife.org

SIFE Assiut. (2008). Retrieved June 5, 2008 from www.sifeAssiut.org

Slum Project team. (2008). Slum project: Candle Village. SIFE Assiut.

Soeftestad, L., & Sein, M. K. (2003). ICT and development: East is east and west is west and the twain may yet meet. In T. Krishna & S. Madon (Eds.), *The digital challenge: Information technology in the development context (voices in development management)* (pp. 63–82). Aldershot, UK: Ashgate.

Street, B. (1999). New illiteracies in theory and practice. *Linguistics in Education, 10*(1), 1–24.

Sunden, S., & Wicander, G. (2006). *Information and communication technology applied for developing countries in a rural context: Toward a framework for analysis factors influencing sustainable use.* Retrieved April 13, 2008 from www.diva-portal.org/diva/getDocument?urn_nbn_se_kau_diva-748-1__fulltext.pdf

Technology Development Center. (1997). *Technology: A tool for developing education in the 21st century.* Cairo: Ministry of Education.

Teitelbaum, J. (2002). Dueling for Da`wa: State vs. society on the Saudi Internet. *The Middle East Journal, 56*(2), 222–231.

United Nations Development Program (UNDP). (2001). *Human development report 2001: Making new technologies work for human development*: Oxford University Press.

Warschauer, M. (2003). *The allures and illusions of modernity: Technology and education reform in Egypt, 38*(11). Retrieved May 20, 2008 from http://epaa.asu.edu/epaa/v11n38/

Warschauer, M. (2005). Dissecting the "digital divide": A case study in Egypt. *Journal of Educational Resources in Computing, 5*(4), 1–12.

Watson, D. (1998). Blame the technocentric artifact! What research tells us about problems inhibiting teacher use of IT. In G. Marshall & M. Ruohonen (Eds.), *Capacity building for IT in education in developing countries* (pp. 185–192). London: Chapman & Hall.

Waverman, M. (2005, March 12) Economics focus: Calling across the divide. *The Economist,* 9.

Wei, C., & Kolko, B. (2005). Resistance to globalization: Language and Internet diffusion patterns in Uzbekistan. *New Review of Hypermedia and Multimedia, 11*(2), 205–225.

Wheeler, D. L. (2004). *The Internet in the Arab world: Digital divides and cultural connections.* Retrieved June 13, 2008 from http://www.riifs.org/guest/lecture_text/Internet_n_arabworld_all_txt.htm

World Bank. (1999). *World development report 1998/99: Knowledge for development.* Washington, DC: International Bank for Reconstruction and Development.

World Bank. (2000). *Bangladesh education sector review* (Vols. I, II, III). Washington, DC: Oxford Press Limited.

World Summit on the Information Society (WSIS). (2003). *WSIS plan of action Geneva 2003— Tunis 2005.* Retrieved June 14, 2008 from www.itu.int/wsis/docs/geneva/official/poa.html

CHAPTER 19

PRINCIPAL WILLIAM'S VISION

Critical Issues for Institutionalizing Educational Technology

John A. Gedeon
University of the West Indies, West Indies

BACKGROUND

In 2000, Professor Williams was promoted from his post as Dean of Social Sciences to the Principal of a large university in the English-speaking Caribbean: *Windward Islands University* (WIU). Professor Williams first came to the university in 1970 with a PhD in Economics awarded from a British university. He made his way up the ranks and became Head of Department for Economics in 1990 and later Dean of Social Sciences in 1995.

As Williams took office, total enrollment was at 8,000 students at this prestigious institution, which has granted graduate, postgraduate, and doctoral degrees in popular disciplines over its 40-year history. WIU, while only having one physical campus, serves five satellite islands in the Windward region though its Distance Programme Unit (DPU). Historically, these islands were served by a mixed-mode delivery system consisting of printed

Cases 'n' Places: Global Cases in Educational and Performance Technology, pages 237–221

learning materials and tutorials conducted by use of audio-conferencing using telephone connections from learning centers on each island.

The Windward islands are the most southerly islands in the Caribbean, stretching from Dominica in the north to Trinidad & Tobago in the south, where the main campus is located, because of the island's industrial, and hence, influential prominence. The other English-speaking islands are St. Lucia, St. Vincent, Barbados, and Grenada. The government of Trinidad & Tobago, buoyed by recent increases in wealth in its petroleum sector, declared in 2000 that it plans to subsidize the local tertiary sector in terms of tuition. For WIU, this is forecast to double enrollment in the home physical campus from 5,000 to 10,000 over the next 4 years.

Technology is playing an ever-increasing role in education and can be conceptualized as being used in either a face-to-face situation that could be termed as educational technology (ET) or technology used at a distance (distance education or DE). Technology, of course, is not just networks, equipment, and software, but the *process* that defines their roles. Institutions of higher learning have many reasons to employ technology—some weak, some strong, some implicit, some explicit. Those not familiar with organizational theory may not appreciate the powerful change role that technology adoption can engender. Some have compared it with a Trojan horse that looks harmless on the surface, but can have far-reaching consequences on an organization's direction, market, processes, structure, and culture.

THE VISION

As the new leader, Principal Williams, had to formulate his vision for the direction of the university. Coming up through the ranks, he had seen and been frustrated by all types of problems and politics that are typical of institutes of higher learning. He was most upset by a bureaucratic structure that was tacitly designed to preserve the status quo.

Being progressive, he had always wanted to solve problems and move forward. The system, the administrators, and many of his colleagues appeared not to share his innovative mindset. They valued stability, predictability, and tradition. Yes, they would grumble about things that irritated them, but by and large, saw them as permanent fixtures in the system that had to be endured from time to time.

Since the global introduction of the personal computer into schools in the early 80s and the Internet in the early 90s, institutions of higher education in the Caribbean region have been adopting technology in some form. Technology, of course, was first used for administrative functions like payroll and HR, then later spread to the classroom. WIU did not want to be left behind in the adoption of technology, but was not quite sure about what role it could or should play in academics and wider institutional goals.

While tradition had largely carried WIU through its history, WIU was now on the doorstep of the 21st century. Personal computers were now part of the mainstream infrastructure in progressive schools. The Internet was 7 years old, and universities in developed nations were venturing into Web-based learning systems in a serious way. "We can't be left out of the revolution and sidelined," he deliberated.

He remembered teaching his students about the Industrial Age, which started with the invention of the steam engine in the 1700s, and how it eventually gave rise to the Information Age in the 1960s with the advent of the computer (an electronic, not mechanical machine). Each age had its enabling or driving technology. The 1990s saw a further transformation to the Knowledge Age. The interactive networking of many "cells of information" via Internet protocols, as well as the increased sophistication of the computer, now enables the current age.

That is all nice theory, but where does that leave us, he wondered? As dean, he had heard a lot of speeches from the former principal that spoke to the current age, but when he thought about the current systems, culture, and infrastructure, it clearly represented the *previous* age with some Industrial Age holdovers, too.

Principal Williams knew enough about leadership that maintaining the status quo in the face of increasing competition from universities outside the region was not a long-term strategy. He knew from his limited background in systems theory that a successful organization was one that aligned itself to the realities of the *current* environment, while pursuing its strategic objectives.

The previous Strategic Plan 1995–1999 had barely mentioned technology, and when it did, it was mostly for administrative purposes. What did he want to accomplish in the next 5 years with technology to position WIU for the 21st century? What was technically possible, financially possible, and culturally possible? There were so many other pressing needs on campus that demanded resources, too. How could a new vision be rationalized?

What type of educational technology should be introduced or expanded on campus, and what approach should be used? How could the satellite countries be served better via distance technologies?

HISTORY OF TECHNOLOGY USAGE

Not being in the technology field, Principal Williams called in his *Educational Technologist* to get an idea of just exactly what ground educational technology (ET) had covered to date. The technologist provided the following definition for the principal:

> The theory and practice of design, development, utilization, management, and evaluation of any *process* or *resource* for teaching or learning in any learning *environment.* (adapted from AECT, 1994)

ET adoption therefore includes using technology in traditional f2f (face-to-face) classrooms, computer labs, teaching & learning online (DE), and e-learning on any other platforms (mobile devices, CD players, etc.). It includes both digital and analog systems (nondigital, traditional equipment such as overhead projectors, chalkboards, etc.). Sometimes, the ET said, the learning happens in more than one environment in the same course and this has been termed as *blended* learning (f2f and online components), or *distributed* learning, which has two or more environments, but one of them is not necessarily online.

The principal asked the ET for a report on what the university had done with ET and DE over its history up until the present (2000). Some of the main points from this report are summarized as follows.

For traditional classrooms, "Chalk-n-Talk" was the dominant technology used since the university was formed in 1960, as it required little resources or skills and there was not much other technology at that time. Overhead projectors were introduced in 1970 as soon as they became both fashionable and affordable.

Beyond the traditional classroom, the first distance courses to the satellite islands started in 1975 using a comprehensive printed study manual and audio-conferencing tutorials situated in learning centers. This was a best-fit (not best-practice) solution for the technologies available at the time.

Moving into the digital age, the first computer lab was set up in 1985. It was first used more for assisting students typing papers than for teaching purposes, as faculty had received no training in conducting sessions in a lab. Later in 1994, the Internet was used as an educational resource and for e-mail, but not as a platform for an online classroom, as this software had not been developed yet. Other distance technologies such as closed-circuit TV, radio, satellite, and microwave technologies had never been employed.

Institutionally, there had been no central committee or unit that oversees the planning, operations, and evaluation of ET activities. There were a few ET resources on campus, but not enough to assist the number of faculty on a one-to-one basis or support them in any sophisticated use of technology (making a video, animation, fancy graphics, etc.).

To make matters worse, many academics did not possess a teaching certificate for traditional f2f teaching, let alone teaching with technology or online teaching. There was nothing in the system that rewarded teachers for using technology or compensated the added time it takes to design or use technology in their teaching process. The last Strategic Plan (1995–1999) stated that academics need to "use more technology in the teaching and learning process" but did not make direct reference to using online classrooms.

WHERE ARE WE NOW?

The principal called an exploratory meeting for the promotion of ET/DE with his executive team:

Administrative

- Registrar
- Bursar
- Auditor General
- IT Head
- HR Director
- Marketing Director
- Head of Planning & Development

Academic

- Heads of Academic Departments (HOD's)
- Deans
- Provost of Academic Affairs
- Chief Librarian
- Director, Distance Programme Unit (DPU)
- Head of Instructional Support Unit (ISU)

To clarify their roles and relationships, WIU's organizational chart can be found in Figure 19.1 and departmental functions in Table 19.1.

Principal Williams began by providing the following agenda:

1. ET/DE—What have we achieved so far?
2. How does it fit into our educational process?
3. ET/DE—Where are we going with it next?
4. What issues do we need to address to make it successful?

The meeting started with a review of the ET's report as outlined earlier. IT remarked that they have a lot of software and server space, but that there

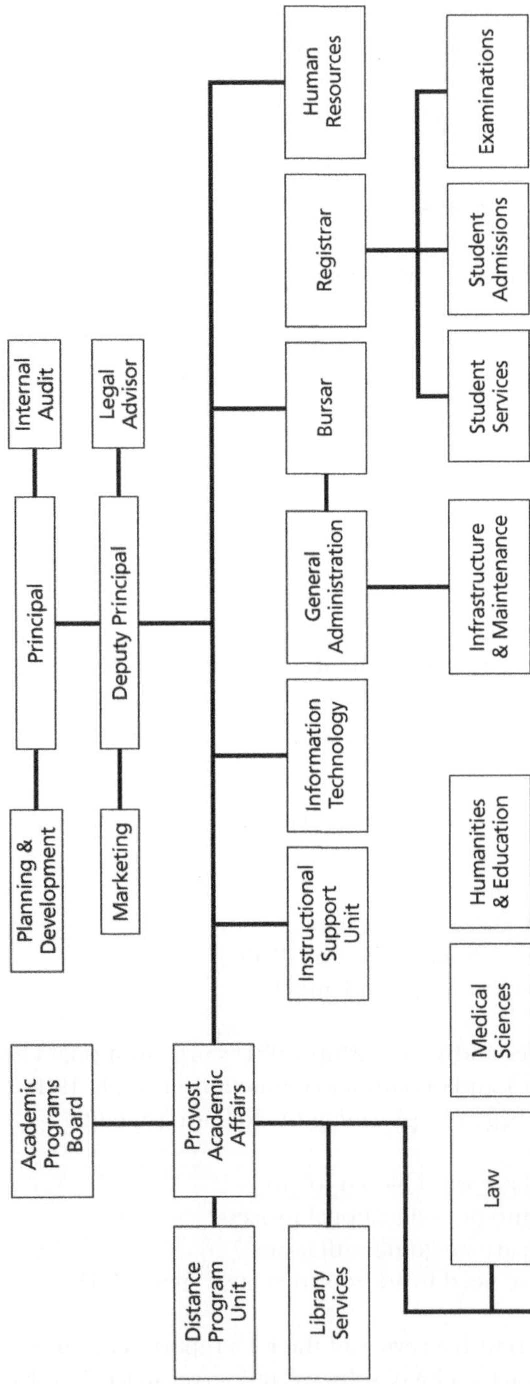

Figure 19.1 Windward Islands University organizational structure.

TABLE 19.1 Functions of WIU Departments

Department/Unit/Group	Functions
Faculty/Schools/Academic Departments	There are six faculties depicted in Figure 19.1 that develop and deliver all the academic programs to students, conduct and publish research, and participate in outreach programs and projects with the in region. They are each headed by a dean and are subdivided into departments, each headed by a Head of Department (HOD).
Distance Program Unit (DPU)	Responsible for the design and delivery of 100% distance-delivered courses and programs, whether print or Internet based. Students in the same course may be in several different islands, there are no face-to-face classroom requirements, but they may be required to attend tutorials or proctored examinations at a local resource center.
ICT Unit	The Information and Communications Unit is responsible for all digital systems, including networks (intranet & Internet access); the purchase, installation, training for, and maintenance of computer and software systems and related peripheral devices. It also maintains the WIU's operational databases.
Instructional Support Unit	Provide training, consultation, and latest research to inform practice for faculty to improve any aspect of the teaching and learning process, including the educational use of technology. Anchors the *Scholarship of Teaching & Learning* program by which faculty research and share findings on how to improve classroom practices locally.
Academic Programs Board	Is responsible for the certification of new courses and academic programs, ongoing quality assurance, and periodic program reviews (every 3 years).
Library Services	Provide physical and virtual informational resources and research services for students and faculty.
Student Services	Provides a range of services such as career, personal, and financial counseling, health services, recreational activities and programs, etc.
Office of the Bursar	Management of the financial resources, budgets, and investments of the university. Oversees general administration not covered by other departments and the purchase of assets and supplies and the construction and maintenance of physical infrastructure.
Office of the Registrar: Admissions	Provide initial admission, ongoing registration, and payment services to students.
Office of the Registrar: Examinations	Provide examination protocols, oversee the examination process, and certify students eligible for graduation.
Human Resources Unit	Manage the hiring, training, promotion, of employees and contract staff and all routine personnel processes.

(continued)

TABLE 19.1 Functions of WIU Departments (continued)

Department/Unit/Group	Functions
Planning & Development	Responsible for facilitating the drafting and the execution of the strategic plan to ensure that all departments are aligned to produce a synergistic performance.
Marketing	Provide promotional services for the university in order to attract staff, enroll students, promote public events, and manage the public-relations function.
Internal Audit	Conduct financial, physical, and performance audits to safeguard university assets and see that units are complying with policies and procedures in the achievement of their outputs.

were only sporadic requests from the academic staff for it. It was generally felt that online courses were really the business of the Distance Programme Unit (DPU), but some early adopters had used their own server space (owned or rented) to put parts of their course online.

One HOD remarked that since classrooms were not equipped with multimedia projectors, screens, or laptops, that setting up, breaking down, and dragging around that equipment for up to three classes per day was just more than the average lecturer could bear.

Another HOD argued that teaching is *not* a core function of the university and proceeded to give the following evidence. Research and publishing are the routes to tenure, promotion, and professorship and the university does not require that faculty possess a teaching certificate or its equivalent when they are hired. There is little or no oversight or review of the faculty's course content and how it relates to the overall program. There are no serious provisions in place to monitor traditional teaching, let alone using technology. Teachers can get any type of ratings from student evaluations without serious consequence. While the university does provide an Instructional Support Unit (ISU) to assist faculty, it is totally voluntary. Besides, he said, technology takes time to learn, time to develop materials, time to deliver and type responses, and time to learn new versions. The return-on-investment is really not worth it. It is a distraction to our main job of research and publishing.

A more sympathetic dean said that he knew several lecturers who would like to use technology, but there appears to be a lack of ET/DE policies, procedures, and protocols documentation at the institutional level; the same is certainly evident at the departmental level. While there was an ET role for the ISU to play, they were seriously under resourced.

The principal soon started to realize that it was the department heads' own personal experience and feeling about technology that had a large impact on how their departments adopted or did not adopt technology. For many of them, no clear vision and commitment to educational technology was evidenced by lack of encouragement and support. He remembered some lecturers had commented that their heads were very traditional and either provided no support for the ET initiatives of the faculty, or in some cases, saw ET/DE as a threat to the faculty's "substantive" duties.

Faced with increased enrollment and a fixed number of classrooms, the registrar argued that more virtual classrooms needed to be created to accommodate students. The Auditor General added that the more we put online, the less furniture, equipment, supplies, and classrooms we would have to purchase, monitor, secure, maintain, and account for. The bursar noted that a heavy initial investment in hardware, software, networks, and training would be required and that the campus had other pressing needs like leaking roofs and infrastructure that needed serious upgrading or repair.

The chief librarian chipped in that distance students would need equivalent resources as those on a physical campus enjoyed. She lamented that the budget was not keeping up with expanding WIU physical-information needs in terms of books and periodicals, let alone online database subscriptions that would be required in a virtual learning environment.

The Director of HR believed that if WIU provided "proper" ET/DE tools, that faculty would find a way to teach themselves how to use them in the teaching-learning process and that maybe a few Educational Technologists may have to be hired to support them.

Given the reduction in regional government subventions to WIU, the Marketing Director saw the need to expand WIU's reach both within and beyond the states being currently served to leverage the limited faculty and courses offered. The director, Distance Programme Unit (DPU), agreed with marketing on this point, but noted that while they had staff to develop fully online courses, they were limited in delivering them due to the limited number of e-tutors available.

The Head of Instructional Support Unit (ISU) mentioned that so far everyone was discussing distance education with almost no mention of the use of technology in the classroom, computer labs, and other non-Web-based e-learning. She noted that some faculty were using technology to solve their problems and not necessarily improve student learning, especially by using an online classroom. Many, she said, were just placing course documents and materials online, but lecturers were not present in a pedagogical sense. While that was OK if that is all they were using it for, it was still a low-order use of technology. Many faculty did not have a teaching certificate for normal f2f teaching in a low-tech environment, let alone advanced teaching and technology skills required of 21st-century institutions, she went on to note.

Finally, the Head of Planning & Development said the previous Strategic Plan gave very little guidance on the way forward. It stated that "we must increase the usage of technology in the teaching-learning process." He stated that we need clear strategic goals in this area and then find the funding for the resources needed to support the thrust.

The principal summarized the meeting by stating that we have come a long way from the pretechnology era and that the different stakeholders see both the advantages and issues facing the management team in making more formal and deliberate arrangements for technology use. He announced the formation of a committee to pull together all the ET/DE perspectives, goals, and issues and come up with a 5-year plan that would be integrated into the campus's formal strategic plan covering the period 2000–2005.

Privately reflecting in his personal journal after the meeting, Principal Williams was not so optimistic about the way forward. While many views shared were fairly accurate, he thought that many comments were stated in a way that the participants were "telling the boss what he wanted to hear." Academic freedom, habit, bureaucracy, no "fire at the door," and no formal requirements for basic teaching proficiency would make technology adoption for academics, who saw it as more unrewarded work with little benefits, a challenging endeavor.

THE COMMITTEE'S FINDINGS

After working on the ET/DE plan for over 6 months, the committee submitted a progress report on issues discovered as they collected data. These are summarized below by institution, department, and faculty.

INSTITUTIONAL ISSUES

1. There has been no consensus on why WIU is seeking to expand ET/DE activities and initiatives; what is the rationale?
2. No one has "institutional ownership" of the ET/DE function; it is scattered about in bits and pieces with no central organizational plan, control, budgeting, or evaluation processes.
3. There are no campuswide or departmental policies on the use of ET/DE.
4. There are no procedure manuals for ET/DE tasks that show faculty how to perform common technology tasks.
5. There are no written quality standards for integrating technology into the curriculum or standards for online courses (DPU has a rough checklist, but is by no means comprehensive).

6. The WIU monthly management reports have no performance indicators to either define or measure success of the ET/DE function.
7. WIU has no communications plans to keep everyone informed on progress, problems, and accomplishments in ET/DE.
8. No one has been recognized or celebrated by the university newsletter, award functions, or other for accomplishments or innovations in the use of ET/DE.
9. It appears that if university management just announces it (change by proclamation), that bureaucratic machinery and faculty will automatically align itself with the new ET/DE thrusts (maybe an untrue assumption).
10. ET/DE training has been sporadic, not comprehensive, and mostly on demand.
11. Besides necessary components missing, there is no process to institutionalize the ET/DE function so that it becomes sustainable regardless of institutional leadership changes.

DEPARTMENTAL ISSUES

1. The budgeting process has no sections devoted to ET/DE expenditures; they are currently captured under the "ad hoc" expenses classification heading; department heads must "cannibalize" funds from another area to support ET/DE activities.
2. Some departmental heads refuse to make any ET/DE policies at their level until equipment, software, training, and support systems are put into place and a budget allotment is dedicated specifically for these activities.
3. The system, as exists, discourages faculty from experimenting with or using technology as research, and publication is rewarded; designing, developing, and conducting courses with technology is very time-consuming and appears only to benefit the students (not a powerful motivator for many faculty).
4. Administration and support units have not given serious thought to how they, and indeed the whole university, must change and will be changed by the technology-adoption process.

FACULTY ISSUES

1. Nowhere in the annual appraisal form for academics are there any items or points for the use of ET/DE.

2. While many faculty understand that technology can do a lot, they do not have the motivation, knowledge, or skills to pursue it.
3. Many faculty do not have basic teaching skills or a teaching certificate.
4. It appears that faculty will continue to teach the way they were taught, which is often outdated, teacher-centered, and counterproductive in many instances. Online teaching demands the "next level" skills in all of the above areas, plus skills in many more areas and handling of issues not present in f2f instruction.

In summary, the current approach appears to be, "you can fool around with technology in teaching, but you will get little support, no time off, no incentives, no budget, and still be held accountable for your traditional duties."

Now the committee had to decide on how to proceed and create a technology plan given the local culture, constraints, and traditional systems.

DISCUSSION QUESTIONS

1. What may one deduce are some rationales (implicit or explicit) that the WIU is interested in expanding the use of both ET and DE?
2. What has been the administration's implicit ET and DE implementation strategy up to 2000? Is there evidence that this strategy is aligned to WIU's rationales (in Question 1)?
3. What are some valid rationales for introducing/expanding ET/DE in a university and what are those rationales' relationship to the implementation strategy? In other words, what variables may change in employing different strategies?
4. Up until 2000, outside of the DPU, only the "early adopters" have been utilizing technology, now this must become a mainstream process. What are the differences between motivating the former and latter, and what characteristics should a successful strategy have to promote mainstream adoption?
5. Identify all the university departments/units and stakeholders that would be affected by the introduction/expansion of ET & DE. Select four of them (or these may be assigned by the instructor so they are all covered) and outline the fundamental ways they would have to change; make your answers department specific.
6. Given what you have determined needs to be put into place to fully support ET/DE adoption, what *change management* processes and

structures need to be put into place for a successful *implementation* of ET & DE initiatives?

7. How can the whole ET/DE endeavor become *institutionalized* so that the change is permanent or sustainable regardless of changes in institutional leadership?

CHAPTER 20

DRAMA, THEATER, AND E-LEARNING

Robyn Philip
University of Sydney, Australia

Jennifer Nicholls
Macquarie University, Australia

BACKGROUND

Jenny and Robyn have been working together for over 12 years as colleagues at the same metropolitan university in Australia. Jenny is a senior academic in education and teaches drama to students from a wide range of programs: creative arts, education (0–8 and K–12), and the arts. She has a background as a director in drama and theater and retains close links with the current theater community in the city and internationally. Robyn is an educational developer with a background in education and the humanities. She has long-time experience with the design and implementation of distance, blended, and e-learning courses across many disciplines. She has worked in various centralized departments of the university, an e-learning research center, and lately as a freelance external consultant.

The two began their collaboration when Jenny was required by her Head of Department to change the delivery mode of her First Year

Cases 'n' Places: Global Cases in Educational and Performance Technology, pages 251–231

drama course to meet the needs of a new cohort of students entering the established course. The new program, the Bachelor of Creative Arts, was designed to help students gain skills and knowledge across a broad range of subjects, such as philosophy, accounting, marketing, and sociology, as well as their chosen specialization (e.g., drama, dance, music, art), and to become conversant with emerging digital technologies and their application. Consequently, Jenny was required to incorporate the use of new information and communications technologies and prepare the course for distance students, as well as provide for her regular on-campus students, who attended practical workshops each week. Jenny had no experience working with the new e-learning technologies; in fact, few at the university had this experience. So she sought advice from the centralized distance education unit, which offered educational design support. This was where she met Robyn, who was assigned to her project as educational developer, or instructional designer, as it was then called.

EARLY INITIATIVES

Jenny's experience of distance education to date had been of traditional print-based packages. These well-designed and presented packages were sent out to students who studied on their own. There was little interaction between teaching staff and students over the semester, other than a compulsory session on campus midway through the semester. Until this time, the technologies were not available to support ongoing interactions. Print was a very good basis for the courses, but multimedia and teleconferencing, which might have offered opportunities for interaction among the students and with staff, were expensive options. Audio cassettes were the only other media traditionally available to enhance the mainstay—print.

Jenny was adamant that active student participation remain a key element of her course. In her mind, drama was, after all, a practical subject, requiring personal, real-time interactions. She could not see how this could be achieved via the new online Learning Management System, WebCT, as she did not understand its affordances at first, and knew of no one using the platform for e-learning in her discipline. Few staff used e-mail and even fewer accessed the Internet with any regularity. After a lengthy period of discussion and negotiation with Robyn, Jenny began to see that there might be possibilities for the new technologies in the drama course, but was still reserved in her enthusiasm for the project and its demands on her time. But both Robyn and Jenny were keen that the adoption of these technologies not be implemented in an *ad hoc* way or as "add ons." Consequently, they worked through a thorough process of curriculum redesign, revisiting the aims and outcomes of the course, considering resource types and strategies for approaching activities and assessments. There was much discussion over assessment because this is where the issues of access and equity, central tenets of distance education praxis, came under review. Assessment tasks were the place where student activity could be assured.

Jenny became interested in using the capabilities of the Web to give students the opportunity to "talk" to each other outside of the regular face-to-face class hours students were expected to attend. She and Robyn began to devise an assessment task that would see students working collaboratively online. This presented a number of dilemmas. How could they ensure that all students had access to computers so as to complete the task? What about the distance students who often had more problems than the on-campus students accessing reliable and suitable technology? At the time, few students, either distance or on-campus, had easy access to computers from home or work, particularly for any length of time. There was a bank of computers in the library for students to use free of charge, but usage was restricted to short periods so as to ration the resource across the university community. Local libraries offered Internet connection on a fee-for-service-basis, but also for restricted periods. Those who had access to computers at work acknowledged that they were often not permitted to use them for private study purposes. And what if a student claimed not to be able to access a computer at all during the semester? Would an alternative assessment task have to be set for these students, and how would their absence from the online task affect other students' participation?

After much discussion about ensuring equity and access, one of the four assignments set for the course was the review of a professional theater production. If students could not attend a *professional* (rather than amateur) production, then they could not complete the course. This was seen as an essential element of their learning that could not be compromised. Critique of the theatrical performance was traditionally completed as an individual essay. However Robyn and Jenny thought that converting this essay to an online collaborative task would add depth to the discussion. Would the drama students learn more about the production by reading and reflecting on the recorded observations of their peers? Or was this a task better completed on one's own? Was it more academic to write an essay rather than post short, considered reflections to an online discussion? Did spelling and syntax matter? The structured online assessment task developed was adapted from a relevant model recently trialed in the law school at the university. At the time, most courses trialing (piloting) online methodologies used a model for discussions, which was very loose in structure. This meant that discussions often took their own course, which could be quite positive; however some never got started and most grew out of control, posts often becoming irrelevant or too long and rambling, which made them time-consuming and difficult to mark. Jenny was not keen on increasing her workload and that of her tutors to unmanageable proportions, so she took these lessons-learned into consideration when designing the first assessable task for her students.

Students signed up for one of four plays that were currently being presented in the local city. These groups of 10 students were then assigned an online tutorial group. Over a period of three weeks, students were expected to contribute four responses of 150 words to a threaded online discussion. Students were expected to read, reflect, respond and build on the postings of others. They were required to begin two new threads (ideas) and respond to the postings of others. This meant that individual comments needed to be woven into the whole conversation online, making for a well-structured, group learning task. As Jenny and other tutors monitored the discussions, they noted an immediate improvement in students' critical thinking and analytical skills compared with students' essays in past years. Students were effectively scaffolding each other in their writing skills and in their understanding of play production in an online environment. Student feedback verified Jenny's observations.

> What others said sparked new ideas and viewpoints other than my own.
>
> It pushed me to look further into the play, and in fact I enjoyed the play more, and it broadened my knowledge of drama.
>
> A good exercise in developing analytical and critical skills.
>
> You spent short amounts of time reflecting and learning from others' views, better than an essay, you get immediate feedback and more insight (student comments from the surveys).

MOVING FORWARD

Building on the success of the First Year course, Jenny and Robyn developed an online history-of-theater course called Genres of Theater, for Second Year students. They wanted to provide opportunities for students to engage with multiple resources based on individual preferences, multiple types of interactions, and multiple forms of communication among learners, teachers, and others beyond the classroom. They believed this strategy would provide many pathways through the course for students. To realize this conceptual approach, the following resources were added to the WebCT Web site: scanned scholarly readings accessible from the library's e-reserve collection, a comprehensive image bank of theatrical stages, costumes and characters, and links to the best available theater and education Web sites that supported the learning modules. In addition, 27 digital video clips were specially created to demonstrate acting styles and scenic conventions of various theater genres along with interviews with the actors and theatrical designer. These were distributed to students on a DVD as well as streamed from the Web site. Students were required to participate in synchronous and asynchronous peer-to-peer discussions throughout the semester. Virtual visits from invited experts and practitioners from the local theater scene also provided a fresh perspective for students. There was a noticeable lively dynamic in the chat rooms for these special conversations.

While students were expected to take responsibility for their own learning in this distance education course, Jenny and Robyn did not want them to be left to flounder in a completely unstructured environment. Both were familiar with the demands of distance education and knew the risks of either too much or too little structure. Therefore, regular commitment to a structured online discussion task was believed to be important. Students were expected to be present in the course for themselves and others via the group tasks. However, students could choose how and when they accessed the online course, its resources, and interactions with other students. They also had a range of innovative assessable project tasks with flexibility in submission dates to choose among.

Students had 2 weeks to study each of the five theater-history modules and then 2 weeks to respond to a question posed by the instructor. In this way learners were regularly engaging with course content and other students enrolled in the course. Responses were marked twice over the semester, ensuring timely feedback.

The second assessment task was a conventional essay chosen from a range of topics. The final assessment was a project. Project choices ranged from completing a director's portfolio on one of the set play texts to viewing a current production in the city and participating in a follow-up synchronous chat session with the play's director in preparation for an essay; or a particularly innovative project that involved students sharing production ideas with students from another country studying a similar online theater-history unit.

Students' feedback on the course gathered through systematic evaluation was once again positive.

> Watching the acted scenes clarifies what is in the readings, and we can visually see what we have read.
>
> The interviews with the artists helped me to understand the practicalities of performance from an actor's point of view.
>
> The degree of flexibility was excellent. I had to travel overseas for two weeks, and this unit worked in perfectly with this. I was actually able to post my 17th-century French theater postings from Paris—how ironic!
>
> As such, this innovative unit allowed me total flexibility and communication through modern technology to gain a thorough, comprehensive, and easy ap-

> proach to this subject (as a wife, mother, and full-time university student, this was invaluable, particularly in my second-to-last semester before graduating) (student comments from the surveys).

It was apparent that the constructive alignment (Biggs, 2003) of activities and assessment with the expected learning outcomes and goals of the course optimized the learning environment for the students and helped contribute to a lively dynamic within the virtual classroom.

ANOTHER CHALLENGE

Having successfully implemented online technologies into two drama courses and completed regular evaluations as part of their action research cycle, Jenny and Robyn were often invited to present the outcomes of the course development to staff interested in new approaches to learning and teaching. This was at various showcasing opportunities within the university, at conferences, and at sessions for outside organizations. Jenny often talked with colleagues in her faculty about the innovations she was undertaking and students' responses. Robyn, working through her centralized department, was able to pass on the lessons learned to other disciplines across the university. In doing so, the colleagues acknowledged the need for a team approach to their projects, as they had worked closely with Web developers, video producers, library personnel, and e-learning training and support staff.

After many years of working together, meeting routinely to discuss and reflect on outcomes and plan strategies for curriculum development, Jenny and Robyn then moved onto the Third Year drama course that Jenny offered at the university. This course is offered to students as a practical drama course on campus. Students must attend for 3 hours a week. The class comprises usually about 20 students, and many have either completed some drama through the Department of Humanities or Cultural Studies, or one of Jenny's First or Second Year courses. The course, Performance: Theory and Practice, is about devising theater (playbuilding). In groups, students select a play theme, they then devise, script, produce, direct, perform, stage-manage, and promote the play, which is staged somewhere on the university campus. The venue might be in the drama studio, for example, or unconventional performance spaces such as the student cafeteria, in the grounds of the university, in a lecture theater, or in a staff and student parking lot. The plays often attract eclectic audiences, invited audience members, plus astonished casual passers-by.

To achieve the outcomes of the course, students require skills in working as a team, commitment to the group, the ability to contribute strongly as individuals and negotiate, problem solving skills, a knowledge of the principles for devising theater, imagination, and critical thinking skills. In the first week of the semester, students discuss and share with the whole group the skills they could bring to the building of a play: this is called a skills inventory. Skills may include playing a musical instrument, dancing, gymnastics or circus skills, or other skills related to production elements such as proficiency in desktop publishing, access to wardrobe departments, transport, and such. Before the next workshop, students are required to think about an interesting idea for a play. At the ensuing workshop, students share their ideas and then agree on two or three concepts for plays. Individuals then commit to one of the ideas, and for the rest of the semester work with their team to develop and present an original play for public production. Each week students work on their plays during class, sharing ideas and discussing progress with the teacher, who acts as a facilitator and mentor. Sometimes drama or theater professionals are brought into the class to share their knowledge with students. This often takes considerable planning and management on the teacher's behalf to organize, but it is well worth the effort for the inspiration it provides for students to be in contact with those who are actually working in the industry. In the past, Jenny has arranged for a scriptwriter for children's theater to visit, a director of street theater, and a producer from an experimental theater company to come in and speak with the students.

In previous offerings of the course, students have worked on their plays during class time with a few extra rehearsal sessions in the evenings or on the weekends. Outside class time, students gather performance ideas, develop characters, and begin scene writing on their own in preparation for each week's rehearsal time.

In addition to the face-to-face drama class, which comprises workshops and rehearsals, students keep an individual record of work done in class. Traditionally, students of drama who devise original plays for performance as part of their course requirements often accompany their practical work with a reflective journal or diary that documents and analyzes the process of devising a play from inception through to performance. This has usually been done as an individual task. The reflective journal is both a reflection and analysis of that process from the individual's perspective. Although the journal is predominantly text based, students have included other resources such as photos, images, Web links, costume designs, and reference to scholarly texts, such as books and journal articles that deal with performance styles, genres, play production, and acting.

After many years of systematically evaluating and reflecting on the impact and effectiveness of online collaborative writing tasks on students' skills in critical thinking, Jenny and Robyn began to reconsider the educational value of an individual journal for the Third Year drama students.

They knew that many of their students used social networking tools on a daily basis and as educators were interested in utilizing the affordances of these collaborative tools to support educational processes, reflection, and knowledge sharing. Improvements to the technologies, their ease of use, their potential to support multimedia texts, and the ready access students now have, meant that Robyn and Jenny were keen to go beyond the tools of the Learning Management System (LMS) and try the new and emerging Web 2.0 technologies to support the playbuilding (devising theater) processes of the classroom.

They began researching blogs and wikis. They realized that blogs could be used as individual tools for reflection. But could they be used as a tool for group blogging? While the literature on individual blogging was starting to emerge, little was available on group blogging. Was a wiki a better option for group processes? How would assessment of a blog compare with an editable wiki? Were these technologies really better than standard LMS discussion tools? Was an individual paper-based reflective journal a fairer alternative after all? What criteria do you use to mark wiki or blog contributions? Robyn and Jenny began documenting the limitations and affordances of the old and new technologies. They began thinking about the possibilities that students could use the technologies outside of class time to continue the collaborative process of devising theater. They could seek out and share ideas and resources and discuss theories as they built their plays together beyond the face-to-face tutorial times. Not only could these technologies be used as a space to share reflections and analyses of the creative process, but they could become an integral tool for playbuilding.

DISCUSSION QUESTIONS

1. What technology do you think would be the best choice for the new Third Year course to facilitate creative and group processes and aid assessment? Why? (You should think about the curriculum and technical innovations of the earlier drama courses in answering this.)
2. What challenges are Robyn and Jenny likely to face if they make changes to the assessment and the technologies to facilitate playbuilding?
3. What are the strengths and weaknesses of the collaboration of Jenny and Robyn, given their different backgrounds?
4. What educational theory underlies the design of the three drama/theater courses? What evidence is there to support your answer?
5. How important was evaluation to the progressive curriculum innovations implemented in this case? In your opinion, do you think it

would have been possible to implement the technological innovations without systematic evaluation? Why or why not?

6. What were some of the key reasons for Jenny's change in attitude to the use of new technologies in drama? In your experience, are all educators likely to adopt technology so readily? Why is this?

CHAPTER 21

INSTRUCTIONAL PROBLEMS WITH A CHIROPRACTIC TECHNIQUE COURSE

Preliminary Use of Video and Associated Issues

Aaron Powell
Palmer Chiropractic College, Florida Campus, USA

INSTRUCTIONAL CONTEXT

The setting is a small chiropractic college in the southeast United States. Chiropractic is a direct-access primary health care profession that focuses on diagnosis, treatment, and prevention of specific biomechanical and neurological disorders of the spine, or "chiropractic subluxations." Chiropractic emphasizes manual therapies, most notably spinal adjustment and other joint and soft-tissue manipulation to reduce or eliminate these subluxations to improve the function of the spine and the neurological pathways associated with the spine.

Cases 'n' Places: Global Cases in Educational and Performance Technology, pages 261–241

The student body of the college is fairly diverse. All students have a bachelor's degree and basic premed course prerequisites upon entering the program. The program is quite rigorous, with an integrated curriculum scheduled for the entire 13 terms, 4 terms a year with no term off. A cohort signs up for the same classes every term and sticks together throughout all 13 terms. The curriculum is so intense and tightly packed that if a student falls behind or fails in a course, it is difficult to recover and stay with the cohort due to scheduling issues and the workload. The college is fairly new and has had some typical issues associated with launching a new campus and curriculum.

The campus is pretty well equipped with technology, with a student laptop program, wireless network, and a course management system (CMS). Professors have laptops with which they interface with the classroom technology, video projection, and audio support. There is a small computer lab in the library. There are many smaller conference style rooms that have TVs with built-in VHS/DVD players. These rooms are used for class sections, large-group work for processing case studies, and other active learning activities. The CMS is WebCT CE 6, which is a Web portal that provides students access to learning content electronically from anywhere, 24/7, assuming the students have access to a computer with Internet connection. This content can be in the form of text documents, PowerPoint presentations, and various multimedia formats. However, a majority of faculty members use the system only for distributing a syllabus and schedule, and for managing grades, the minimum of what is expected of them by the administration.

There is an Information Services department with a busy staff of three, who mostly provide hardware support for classroom technology and student laptops. They have limited equipment they can check out to faculty, namely portable A/V carts and 10 basic digital video cameras. The campus is supposed to have an instructional technologist, but the position has experienced some turnover in the last few years and has been vacant for about a year.

The students in this case are only in the second quarter of their chiropractic education. The course covers neck and lower-back chiropractic adjustments. Specifically, the curriculum includes the following: 29 cervicothoracic (neck and midback) technique set-up variations; patient positioning; doctor stance; which part of hand to use on patient and hand positioning; stabilization of areas not being adjusted; positioning of area of patient to be adjusted to maximize correction of the segment (vertebrae or other bone); verbalization of the type, direction, and affect of thrust (the doctor's adjustment of patient). Based on the descriptions of this instructional content, one can imagine the complex psychomotor skills involved, let alone the foundational cognitive knowledge and skills required.

The learning outcomes for the course are on the syllabus, which is posted on WebCT with a separate schedule as to when the outcomes are covered. The class is divided into lab hours and lectures that cover topics such as taking patient histories and red flags, or signs of serious health issues that need immediate attention. For this content, the instructor has distributed PowerPoint presentations on CD, available at the library's reserve desk. IMPORTANT NOTE: These files were not posted to the CMS, because it was the instructor's *mis*understanding from the previous IDT person and Director of IS that it was too much material for the system to handle.

The class has 60 class hours spread over the 10 week term:

- 10 hours for radiology
- 20 hours for lecture
- 20 hours for technique
- 10 hours for testing/practical exams

Technique is the central focus of the course, yet at 20 hours, it only gets one third of the time available. For technique sessions, a large amount of time is taken up by physical demonstrations of various chiropractic procedures, as detailed in the instructor's custom-created course packet and technique manual. Each session has students demonstrating procedures on student volunteers and then doing set-ups and practice in front of the instructor for feedback, which also takes a lot of time. Therefore, the predominant instructional problem is a lack of time to sufficiently cover all the material and give students the practice they need to polish their skills under the instructor's supervision. Twenty hours to cover the techniques simply hasn't been enough, and some of these hours are devoted to nontechnique issues such as instrumentation (heat sensing device), and special tasks (the use of special tables). The problem with a lack of time is compounded by large class sizes. The course is divided into four sections of up to 20 students. This is a large class for technique; all these students have trouble getting the best view of the demonstrations and, most importantly, getting time with the instructor after the demonstrations to confirm they have the technique correct. The instructor is able to check only two or three technique set-ups per student per session, depending on how well the students have prepared. When the classes are smaller, the students feel less stressed in their ability to learn from the lessons.

The course centers on two practical exams with students demonstrating their skills. There are two or three 1-hour review sessions per practical exam. Students are allowed 3 minutes and 45 seconds to complete three chiropractic adjusting technique set-ups. This takes 2 hours for each section. The average score for the exam is 85%. The students who achieve a score in the 80%–89% range (grade of B) have estimated that it takes 10 to 15 hours of preparation, which can include review of the technique manuals and utilization of upper-quarter students and tutors for support. There is no way for students to really "study" for the technique procedures for the exams, as written descriptions can not fully represent the complicated psychomotor skills required. Rather, the skills take practice, for which students have had to rely on memory of the demonstrations, some pictures in the technique manual, and assistance from peers and teaching assistants. The help they get from peers is always suspect, as the peers may have errors of their own. The availability of teaching assistants is very limited.

Some of the students have stated that they feel lost. The students ask for out-of-class tutoring, which demands a lot of the instructor's time, of which he has very little to spare. This is how one student described the learning problems:

> It is difficult, because many times I only see the individual techniques only once. It is hard to know if I am doing it correctly. Also the class size is large, approximately 20 students, so the professor is only able to check our positioning only once, maybe twice, to confirm if we are using proper technique. Also, I cannot see the details of where the instructor has his hands oriented while setting up since it is not practical to get in the way of the other students to see close up. This is frustrating.

The instructor and his students observe that the material is not *that* complicated, but that there is just so much of it. There has been some feedback from students and faculty that the instructor is very thorough, which may take up more time than might be thought required for the content. At the same time, it has been recognized that for this foundational knowledge in the field of chiropractic, it is good that the instructor is so detail-oriented and drills his students so rigorously on the material.

The instructor has observed in his students a lack of depth in understanding of prerequisite concepts, even including an inability of students to find many basic anatomical landmarks. He has observed students having trouble creating a mental image of a particular listing—a diagnosis, a description of how a bone is out of position or not moving correctly. They learn listings in the previous term, but it seems quite a leap for students to go from "knowing" the listings to actually applying them. He feels it is possible that students have not been challenged enough in their past educational experiences. The curriculum is so packed with material that there is little time to reinforce knowledge that students should already have. The curriculum demands a fast pace. The instructor empathizes with the students' feeling that they are always moving on to new material, but this is necessary to get it all covered within the term.

ADDRESSING THE INSTRUCTIONAL PROBLEMS

The obvious solutions of decreasing class size and increasing class time are not institutionally feasible. Though there is potential for reducing the curriculum load of the course, it was also not an option during the course of this case. Work-study funds are available for only two teaching assistants. Even if enough teaching assistants were funded for equal distribution over four course sections, academic and personal scheduling conflicts for the tutors preclude such a solution. Further, as they are still students, the teaching assistants also need monitoring to be sure they are teaching their peers correctly. The instructor has often heard from a student, "Well, the TA told me to do it this way," which turned out to be an incorrect way. This monitoring of tutors takes additional time. Bottom-line: the instructor must be self-reliant and come up with instructional solutions within the confines of space and time that he is allotted by the institution.

The instructor questioned students on how these instructional problems could be addressed, how he could support them in studying more independently. Some suggested videotaping his demonstrations of techniques. The instructor had referred students to technique videos already available at the library. However, students have complained that these videos do not have the same sequencing required for this course's exams. They find the videos difficult to use because they are not aligned with the instructor's organization of the material, and they lack the detailed information and close-ups of certain techniques to fully capture their nuances. The students expressed a need for step-by-step videos that correspond with the instructor's step-by-step technique manual. The instructor understood that video was really the only solution that would give the students the ability to review, study, and accurately practice the complex psychomotor skills involved with the techniques.

The instructor had considered producing his own videos, but his only experience was with home videos of his children with his personal DVD video camera. Creating videos that needed to be planned and sequenced seemed more complicated, particularly without the necessary support from the institution (no instructional technologist). Also, producing the videos seemed time-consuming, adding to the time burden. A few students volunteered their help with video production, and he did have his personal camera that he knew how to operate. He also thought it could be a good learning exercise for the students who participated, giving them an opportunity for stronger metacognitive processing of the techniques.

INSTRUCTOR'S PRELIMINARY SOLUTIONS

For the instructor, the steps to produce the video seemed to be as follows: determine and obtain resources (equipment, personnel), create outline of video content, shoot video, and distribute. These steps had to be expedited since the video was intended to be a learning tool to help the students with upcoming practical exams of the course. The instructor was not aware of cameras the college had available, or he did not see any reason not to use his own. He was not aware of any limits of this camera, particularly from an editing/distribution standpoint. As indicated, he didn't have a lot of time to plan or work on the project, so he was operating in a mode that he thought was the easiest means to the end result. He was responding to the immediate needs of the students, who had a comprehensive exam in 2 weeks and were uncomfortable with their ability to prepare in time with the limited resources available to them.

The instructor addressed student complaints of the library videos by using outlines of his step-by-step manual to provide an organizational scheme for the videos. Template outlines with the technique names and versions were created with Microsoft Word. Multiple copies were created, each with a particular technique highlighted in yellow. He had short video recordings of these outlines before each technique, to function as titles in the video.

The idea of editing the videos was not even considered. All shots were one take, even without any in-camera editing. Basically, all shots were final. Of course, he made errors or left out some things. It would have been extremely time-consuming to do the entire sequence of shots over again, so instead, he prepared worksheets to accompany the videos to describe anything that was missing or needed revision.

Some of the students contributed to the concept and design of the videos by providing opinions on how some of the techniques could be shot differently and better visualized. This contribution included drawing with a wax pencil on the patient to identify specific landmarks. Other contributions included the following: determining angle of video shot, necessity for close up shots, and suggesting multiple angles of video for complex technique set-ups. In addition, these students conceptualized and shared different ways to explain the listings associated with the techniques and suggested providing additional lecture and demonstration sections on different types of listings. In addition, the students suggested interludes of humor, such as the instructor wearing a ridiculous wig in one video. As expected, the student engagement with the video production was a significant learning opportunity. Videos on 14 cervico-thoracic adjusting techniques (with 29 total variations) were the result of the work. The work took 6 hours in design and preparation and 18 hours for production.

There were quality issues with both the audio and video. Audio was captured with the built-in microphone of the camera. Such a microphone is suitable for capturing sound all around, omni-directional. However, for targeting specific voices, it does not work well, as it picks up a lot of ambient noise. In the final videos, the audio fades in and out a bit. Video quality issues were mostly related to lighting. Some of the video is a little muted, as the camera had a small lens that did not do a great job in capturing light, and no lighting was used during production. There was some video shake as well, as a tripod was not used. Of course, because the videos were not edited, content was an issue.

Distribution of the videos posed a significant problem. Since the videos were not edited or compressed, they were quite large at 2–3 gigabytes. At first, a USB flash drive was passed around the class for students to load them on their laptops, but this was time-consuming and met with compatibility problems when some students had playback issues. Later, a student volunteered to burn a DVD of the videos, which was made available at the library; then there were read issues with the DVD, or files disappeared because a rewriteable DVD was used and files were somehow deleted. Certainly some of the issues were user related, but there were definitely some player compatibility problems with the file formats from the instructor's DVD camera. It seems they were not finalized in the camera, so they were of unusual file types—.ifo or .bup—not compatible with some players. The instructor solved this by having students download a free player, WinDVD, which is no longer freely available. All these distribution problems were time-consuming and frustrating for the students and instructor.

FORMATIVE ASSESSMENT OF VIDEO SOLUTION

Despite the challenges listed above, video provided significant advantages for student learning. Student response to these videos was obtained informally, both verbally and in written feedback via e-mail or anonymous, institutional evaluations. The overall response was quite positive, though there were some definite problems. Students appreciated

- the ability to see the techniques demonstrated in a step-by-step fashion that corresponded with the technique manual
- the ability to repeat the video demonstrations as needed
- the extra time the videos provided to study and review the techniques
- the ability to pause and zoom in on the video frames to obtain a view not practical in class
- being able to use the videos later in the program to review for clinic entrance exams

They did not appreciate

- the professor's errors that required a textual addendum that had to be utilized with videos
- the poor sound quality at times, making it difficult to understand easily
- camera movement at times, particularly of the titles, difficulty to read
- the apparent reliance on video over actually teaching
- lack of videos for some techniques
- when practicing the techniques based on the video, having no assurance that they were doing the set-ups correctly (unable to self-monitor)

The instructor appreciated the student feedback and realized there was significant room for improvement in the video production and methods of using the videos for the course. He was particularly mindful of the usability issue of students having to remember to refer to the worksheets for corrections as they watched the videos. With finer attention to video production, the instructor felt this and other technical problems could be addressed.

He was concerned about the feedback that said that he relied too heavily on the video over instruction. The purpose of the video lessons was to give students extra guidance outside of class. The instructor took advantage of this facility, as the extra class time allowed him to focus review sessions more on mastery of the techniques. It was expected that students would develop basic skills by watching the video. However, the instructor has observed among some students a lack of self-assessment skills for confirming their techniques to be in alignment with what the videos present. Students appear to need practice with the videos and even some initial supervision in utilizing the videos to their best advantage. Of course, this assumes the students utilize the videos at all, which was a problem as well—students not wanting to do "homework," apparently a common problem associated with the millennial generation.

ENTER THE INSTRUCTIONAL TECHNOLOGIST

As the instructor was further considering how he would proceed with handling the problems associated with this course, the college hired a new instructional technologist.

An instructional technologist working with an academic institution may rarely get to address a course from scratch. Many instructional decisions have often already been made by the time an instructional technologist gets involved, which was the situation in this case. Also, a professor will often have an attachment to the way he or she does things, a strong sense of ownership in the current design of a course, and a possible reluctance to make significant changes, again the situation in this case. At the same time, the Instructional Technologist was fresh out of his PhD program and had some strong opinions.

The Instructional Technologist was first concerned about the *mis*understanding between the instructor and campus staff regarding the CMS and the supposed restriction of distributing course content via the CMS, whatever the electronic file format or size. It appears the issue was more with the wireless network and 40–80 students targeting a larger file all at the same time. Many faculty felt that it was necessary for students to load the lecture's PowerPoint to their laptops at the start of class, to follow along with the projected version. It was apparently the notion that this method justified the laptop program. The Instructional Technologist challenged this strategy for a number of reasons. Technically, these particular PowerPoints were relatively small in file size. What were his other concerns? Consider less passive and more active strategies for PowerPoint lectures. Note: if and when it is required that students all have access to a larger file from the CMS, they could download it for homework rather than all at the same time at the start or end of class.

With the addition of an Instructional Technologist to the faculty, the instructor immediately started to seek assistance. He initially presented only the technical issues. The instructional problems that led to them surfaced only gradually for the instructional technologist. Here are some questions he considered with the instructor:

1. What other changes could be made to the course and delivery, outside of class, to address the instructional problems or to enhance learning potential?
2. What other changes could be made within course meetings to enhance learning potential?
3. Are there different ways for handling various components, such as assessments, that you would recommend?
4. Other than video, are there other instructional tools to address the instructional problems presented in this case?
5. How do you solve the various production, technical, and distribution problems for the video? What are some other strategies for incorporating them into the curriculum?
6. What are other ways of using video for the course?

CHAPTER 22

INDIAN COMPANY CONTRACTS WITH PUBLIC SECTOR U.S. CONSORTIUM FOR 3-D VISUALIZATION APPLICATION DEVELOPMENT TRAINING

L. Roxanne Russell
India, China & America Institute, USA

CASE BACKGROUND

A private company based in India, NextGen Ed, has contracted with the Institute for Advanced Learning (IAL), a consortium of three U.S. state universities, a community college, and one of NASA's Space Centers, to train up to 50 employees to build applications that produce 3-D graphical representations for fully immersive virtual environments. NextGen Ed plans to produce software and build virtual environments for thousands of higher education, primary, and secondary institutions in India, the United States, and Europe.

Cases 'n' Places: Global Cases in Educational and Performance Technology, pages 271–251

The IAL actively marketed the 3-D visualization training to NextGen Ed and sought a training contract in order to maintain funding for its VizTraining Center. The plan for NextGen Ed to enter the 3-D visualization market was prompted by their decision to take advantage of this training program. According to the contract, the IAL will offer this 3-D visualization training exclusively to NextGen Ed and participate in the application development process. The entire budget of the IAL 3-D visualization program will be funded by NextGen Ed for the duration of the initial 1-year contract.

PROJECT DESCRIPTION

3-D Educational Technology Product

Open Graphics Library (OpenGL), a cross-language, cross-platform Application Programming Interface (API) will be used for constructing applications that produce 3-D graphical representations for a virtual environment. Users are fully immersed into a virtual world within a Cave Automatic Virtual Environment (CAVE), a physical environment constructed by joining multiple screens onto which 3-D images or video are projected. Users navigate the virtual environment with the aid of stereoscopic glasses and a control wand similar to a typical joystick or sensory hand gloves. The virtualization allows users to move around within a virtual environment exploring high-resolution animated concepts or objects, such as chemical structures, geological features, LCD crystals, or even tidal waves from all angles. Users are given a sense of floating around these simulations and may experience the simulation from a complete sphere of perspective. The CAVE environment was the first Virtual Reality (VR) technology to provide a simultaneous 3-D immersive experience for multiple users. The number of users that may be immersed within a CAVE environment is limited only by the size and necessary hardware required to run the software within that CAVE.

OVERVIEW OF NEXTGEN ED'S 3-D VISUALIZATION PRODUCT PROJECT

Project Team

- India Management
- Chief Operations Officer (COO), Ashish Jain
- U.S. Management
- President of U.S. Operations, Harish Krishnan
- Senior Project Manager, Vinay Gubbi

- Visualization Scientists in Training
- 16 honor-level college graduates
- 4 female, 12 male
- Single
- <30 years old
- 2 team leads
- Sree Reddy, oldest student and point of contact for COO
- Anand Priya

First Year Project Plan

- Invest >$600,000 into training a team of 3-D visualization developers
- Cultivate a staff of 10–12 fully trained developers
- Start the training of additional 20+ developers
- Produce a completed, commercially viable product for the education market
- The fist wave of trainees will produce an off-the-shelf application as part of the training program

OVERVIEW OF IAL'S VIZTRAINING PROGRAM

Faculty and Staff

- Director, Dave Porter
- Chief Scientist, George Lindsey
- Primary Instructor, Dr. Mai Srisai
- Instructor, Dr. Gunjan Sinha

Participant Expectations

- Good knowledge in C or C++, data structures, and college level mathematics
- Experience in OpenGL and image processing a plus

Goals

Train students to

- Adapt graphics to scientific data
- Modify existing and produce new visualization programs
- Transport a visualization program among commodity computers to commercial grade large graphic displays

Curriculum

- 12 month timeline
- Introduction
- OpenGL framework
- CAVE programming
- General techniques
- Porting to desktop
- Real-time, real-world projects

CASE NARRATIVE

After 6 months of planning and preparation, the IAL's VizTraining team eagerly gathered in their state-of-the-art classroom, ready to greet the first group of students from NextGen Ed. Three days earlier, Vinay Gubbi, NextGen Ed's Senior Project Manager, had welcomed the students at the airport after their 15-hour flight from India and immediately taken them to NextGen Ed's U.S. headquarters for orientation, including a presentation by a cross-cultural competency specialist. Vinay spent the next day driving the students two states away from headquarters to their company-provided homes near the NASA Space Center. On the third day, four of the students, who had international driver's licenses, were given certified driving lessons so they could drive the two vans provided by NextGen Ed. These students were to be responsible for transporting their teammates to and from the IAL each day and for the purposes of daily living. Vinay then took all of the students to the closest city for a visit to a discount department store and an Indian grocery store and helped the students settle in.

On the fourth day after their arrival in the United States, the students walked into the IAL VizTraining classroom. Dr. Mai Srisai, Primary Instructor, quickly noticed that only 12 of an expected 16 students had arrived. Vinay explained that 4 students were having minor visa problems and would arrive in another week.

Harish Krishnan, President of NextGen Ed's U.S. Operations, began the first session with a speech encouraging the students to stay focused, be serious about the training as work, and to ignore the temptations of U.S. entertainment and lifestyle that would be nearby. He announced that it was NextGen Ed's goal to have a product ready for the market in 1 year, and this goal rested largely on the students being ready to develop applications within 8 months.

Dave Porter, Director of IAL, then welcomed the students and assured them that the focus of his team was to provide a quality education and create a collaborative, productive learning environment. He invited the students to introduce themselves and show on a map of India where they were all from. In their introductions, the students revealed that they were from all over India and that none of them knew each other prior to this program.

Dr. Srisai introduced herself and let the students know that she herself was a former student of the IAL VizTraining program and that this was her first teaching experience. George Lindsey, IAL's Chief Scientist, joked that he was the antique of the group because he had been with the IAL since its inception and had over 21 years of experience in the field. He explained that he had worked with several smaller groups on projects just like this one. Finally, Dr. Gunjan Sinha, IAL Instructor and non-resident Indian, introduced himself as an Associate Professor in the consortium and offered himself as a resource to the students for handling the culture shock of adjusting from India to the United States.

After the first week of classes, Dr. Sinha met with Dave to discuss some concerns and complaints that the students had shared with him. Sree Reddy, NextGen Ed student team lead, had shown great anxiety in explaining that she and the students were all surprised by Harish's announcement that he expected product development to begin in 8 months. She was also concerned that Vinay had already placed them in work teams and asked them to immediately begin meeting about product development goals each week. She explained that they had been assured by Ashish Jain, Chief Operations Officer of NextGen Ed, that this first year was to be strictly training, not development, and that this stipulation was clearly stated in their contract. Dr. Sinha had also heard from some of the students that even after a full week of training, most of them were hoping to start over from the beginning when the visa-delayed students arrived, because they felt overwhelmed by the introductory material.

In response to this information, Dave scheduled a meeting with Dr. Srisai and George to discuss the problems. He asked if they thought an expedited training schedule to suit Harish's expectations was possible. Dr. Srisai did not think an expedited schedule was likely to work, and, on the contrary, believed they may have trouble keeping up with the current schedule. Though she had forwarded *The Red Book*, the OpenGL Programming Guide, to the team in India responsible for preparing the students and explained that the students were expected to have read it upon arrival, it seemed none of the students had read it. The students were already asking her to slow down. George insisted that the students absolutely needed to master the basics before getting into the "mess" of actual development and that rushing the training was a recipe for disaster. Dave assured Dr. Srisai and George that the timeline would not be expedited, and they decided to have an informal meeting with the students the next week to get any other concerns out in the open.

After his meeting with Dr. Srisai and George, Dave wondered who to call at NextGen Ed to discuss this problem. He needed to act fast to reassure the students and maintain a productive learning environment. However, he had been having some trouble determining who was in charge of the students. Vinay, his point of contact for student-related issues, did not have any decision-making power. Harish, though a decision maker, showed little interest in the actual training logistics or the students and was focused solely on product development; he was currently on a trip to procure hardware for building the CAVEs. Dave decided to call Ashish in India, as he had been the primary person responsible for recruiting and entering into a training agreement with the students. Much to Dave's relief, Ashish assured Dave that the students, not the product, were currently the top priority and that they were not expecting the timeline to be expedited. Ashish expressed his full support for allowing the students the time and space to focus on learning and promised to internally address the issue of Vinay's directive for the students to form work teams and begin product development meetings.

At the end of the second week of classes, all of the students and the IAL VizTraining team gathered and Dave announced that he had reassurance from top level management at NextGen Ed that they should not feel pressured to hurry their training or begin development. He then asked the students to share their impressions of the first couple of weeks of class and air any concerns or complaints. Only the two student leads spoke up. Sree expressed concern that the classes were going too fast and asked if they might have more time to complete the initial assignments. Anand Priya, the other student lead, said that instead of slowing down in the presentation of the material, that they would actually prefer to see less material being presented in PowerPoint and demonstrations and be let loose to experiment more. He said that Indian professors did not give them such detailed information, but let them have more freedom to explore and experiment. Sree interrupted Anand to say that this may have been Anand's experience, but his was the opinion of only a few of the students. She said she knew that most of the students preferred more detailed instruction. Anand shook his head in disagreement but did not say anything further.

Dr. Srisai asked to hear from other students. None of the students spoke up. Dr. Sinha broke the silence by saying that he had heard both opinions about class style from some of the students, but that in either case, he had gotten the impression from all of the students that they were not ready to move on to the next bit of material but would prefer to continue to work on the beginning material. He asked if this were true. Several of the students nodded in agreement. Sree answered that it was not that they were not fast learners but that the challenges of settling in to their new homes and beginning with this material had slowed them down a bit and that, yes, they would like to start over, possibly when the visa-delayed students arrived. Dr.

Srisai agreed that they could review at the beginning of the next week to help the new students catch up, but that they would need to move through the material quickly and get back on schedule.

During the third week of class, the visa-delayed students finally arrived. Their visas had been delayed when the U.S. Consulate called into question the approval of all of the H3 visas that had been granted. H3 visas are not to be used for trainees attending degree-granting programs. Because the IAL, in its broader context outside of the VizTraining program, conducts classes that are part of degree-granting programs with its university partners, the visas for this group of students had been flagged. Dave was able to provide specific charter information about the consortium to confirm that they were not a degree-granting program and that the training program was not a class included in the degree-granting program agreements with their university partners. The visas were released. Ashish then began working with the U.S. Consulate in India to admit NextGen Ed into a special program between the United States and India that allows a large number of Indian employees to enter the United States for business purposes through an expedited visa process.

At the beginning of the fourth week of class, Vinay called to ask Dave why his team lead Sree had claimed that she was not forming work teams or holding product development meetings, because Dave had assured her that was no longer a requirement. Dave answered that he had not mentioned the work teams or meetings to the students; acting on Ashish's directive, however, he had reassured the students that they were to be focused on learning for now and not on product development. Vinay asked Dave to allow the NextGen Ed team to discuss project goals with the students.

Vinay also told Dave that he was surprised to hear concerns from the students that Dr. Srisai was losing sleep over having to revamp the curriculum because the students were not catching on and not doing their work. Dave said he did not know where that rumor might have come from but that it was not true as far as he knew. Vinay then thanked Dave for the team's help in smoothly transitioning the visa-delayed students into the program and asked when Dr. Srisai would have evaluations of the student's progress available. Dave suggested they schedule a meeting between the VizTraining and NextGen Ed teams to discuss progress reports after the first 6 weeks of class. Vinay agreed and said that since there was such a heavy investment for each student they needed to know who was not passing muster as soon as possible.

In the fifth week of class, Harish called Dave to ask if one of the VizTraining team members could come to India to meet with some university professors about their needs in 3-D visualization training. He expressed NextGen Ed's urgent need for determining the best content for the first application in order to get demonstrations ready to market the product.

Harish suggested Dr. Srisai come since she was familiar with the technology and in charge of the student's instruction, so she could help the professors determine what might be done with a 3D product and then immediately begin to tailor the student's instruction toward a product targeted at those needs. Dave shared his concerns about Dr. Srisai being absent from class, but agreed to consider the idea and discuss it with Dr. Srisai.

Dave called a meeting of the VizTraining team to discuss Harish's request. Dr. Srisai said she was willing to do whatever the client needed. However, she added that even though she was spending weekends revamping materials to suit the students, the class was already behind and that she thought the class would get too far behind if she left to travel to India. Dave asked George if he thought this trip might benefit the student's training in the long run. George said he did not think so because the students needed to learn the basics regardless of what content would be put in place in the future. Even though he himself preferred the apprenticeship-style training that he had led in the past, where the training was basically part of highly experimental research and development toward a project, he had not tried this method with a group larger than three team members. He concluded that he did not think it would be appropriate with these large groups of students that would be coming in waves to try to tailor toward a specific outcome early in the curriculum. Dave then asked Dr. Sinha if he felt he could keep the class on course in Dr. Srisai's absence; he said he could. Dave decided to fulfill his client's request and asked Dr. Srisai to prepare materials and assignments for her absence.

Dave called Harish to tell him Dr. Srisai could prepare to visit India in a week or so. Harish was pleased and agreed that Dr. Srisai's trip would be as short as possible. He then asked if they were prepared yet to share progress reports. Dave said that those had been planned for the 6-week mark but would now need to be postponed until after Dr. Srisai's return from India. Harish asked for informal assessments, but Dave answered he did not feel knowledgeable enough about student progress to comment. After the call, Harish asked Vinay to call Dr. Srisai directly and ask for progress reports.

Vinay called Dr. Srisai to ask for the progress reports, and she echoed Dave's reminder that the progress report meeting had been planned and that they would go over them upon her return. Vinay asked for her informal observations. Dr. Srisai said that she thought that although some students did not seem to be catching on, she knew they would eventually be able to and that overall the students were dedicated and working hard. Vinay asked which students, and Dr. Srisai said she did not feel comfortable revealing that information until providing the progress reports. Vinay asked what measures were being used to evaluate their progress. Dr. Srisai answered that she had not put any formal evaluations in place but that she was keenly aware of each student's strengths, weaknesses, and progress from her own observations. Vinay asked how many assignments had been turned in and evaluated. Dr. Srisai hesitated to admit that actually no assignments had yet been completed, but that they were all working diligently. Vinay encouraged Dr. Srisai to have something more formal in place for the progress report meeting because NextGen Ed needed to make decisions about which students would continue in the program.

Eight weeks after beginning the training program, the IAL's VizTraining team anxiously gathered in their state-of-the-art classroom, ready to meet with the NextGen Ed team about the students' progress and plans for the remainder of the program. Dr. Srisai had returned from a 10-day trip to India 2 days earlier, preparing progress reports during her return flight. Members of the IAL's VizTraining and NextGen Ed teams had also prepared several questions to cover with each other in the meeting.

DISCUSSION QUESTIONS

1. Whose needs should be the primary concern of the Institute for Advanced Learning's (IAL) VizTraining team: the IAL consortium? NextGen Ed? the students? the ultimate users of the technology? How do such priorities impact design and delivery decisions?
2. If you were a member of the IAL VizTraining team, what questions would you ask NextGen Ed at the progress report meeting? What questions would you ask the IAL if you were a member of the NextGen Ed team?
3. What issues and challenges of this case seem attributable to the cross-sector nature of this training program? How would you improve the efforts of both the IAL VizTraining and the NextGen Ed teams to address those challenges?
4. What issues and challenges for the training team seem attributable to cultural differences? How would you improve the efforts of both the IAL VizTraining and the NextGen Ed teams to address those challenges?
5. Would the services of an instructional designer before the beginning of the program have mediated any of the current issues or problems? Would the hiring of an instructional designer at this point benefit the progress of the program and better prepare the teams for the next group of students?
6. What features of the relationship between the United States and India make this cross-sector, cross-border training scenario possible?

CHAPTER 23

BENJAMIN AND HARRIETT WENT UP A HILL

A Modern Day Nursery Rhyme

Paul A. Walcott
University of the West Indies, Barbados

Jamillah M. A. Grant
Southern University New Orleans, USA

AN INTRODUCTION

Benjamin and Harriett went up a hill
To create an e-portfolio
Benjamin had fun
Harriett had none
But both reflected afterwards

This is a true story of two dreamers, Harriett and Benjamin (pseudonyms) who talked in metaphors, and since one had a young child and the other

Cases 'n' Places: Global Cases in Educational and Performance Technology, pages 281–268

had as many children as the old lady in the shoe, they go from one metaphor to another to present their visionary ideas.

We Have a Dream[1]

Once upon a time, in a distant land, during the summer of the year 2005, two dreamers met on a corridor to discuss the possibility of helping faculty members create and publish their electronic teaching portfolios (e-portfolios). They pondered how they could improve the academy by getting faculty to reflect on their teaching.

Harriett had been trying for the last academic year to get faculty members to reflect on their teaching practices through paper-based teaching portfolios, without the success that she had hoped and wondered whether faculty would be more interested if technology was infused into the process.

Harriett and Benjamin at that time had no idea how true this would prove to be.

The Dream Team[2]

These two dreamers could not be more different!

Harriett was an instructional development specialist who had only joined the university at the beginning of the previous academic year and had spent most of her time mentoring faculty members and conducting workshops on teaching and learning. Being the sole member of the instructional development unit (IDU), she had the full responsibility of planning and running these workshops. From time to time, in order to offer more diverse workshops, increase attendance at workshops, and help to manage her workload, Harriett offered workshops in collaboration with other faculty members.

On the other hand, Benjamin was a lecturer in computer science who, strangely enough, had also joined the university in the fall of 2004. He taught courses in e-commerce, Web technologies, and software engineering and had a very keen interest in teaching and learning. Although Benjamin was a new faculty member, he was carrying a full teaching load, supervising several undergraduate students, creating a new postgraduate program in e-commerce and attempting to establish a credible research program; in other words, Benjamin also had a very heavy workload.

The skills of these two individuals and their ability to network with other faculty members would prove to be an invaluable resource for this ongoing project; nevertheless, they were both operating from a "marginal position."

R.E.M. Sleep[3]

During this impromptu meeting, Harriett and Benjamin began to brainstorm, which resulted in a flurry of questions in quick succession. Needless to say, R.E.M. sleep was accompanied by a barrage of questions that bounced through Benjamin's subconscious.

"What should the contents of an e-portfolio be?"

"What technology should we use to create these e-portfolios?"

"Which faculty members might be interested in creating e-portfolios?"

"What could be a possible start date?"

Harriett, with a voice quivering with excitement, asked, "Is this possible?"

Benjamin hesitated; not because he was not excited at the prospect of such a project, but he was concerned about the technical details. Many thoughts began to race through his mind.

"Should we use tools, because tools are sometimes more trouble than they are worth?"

"Should we start from scratch or reuse something already created?"

"Which technology would be the easiest to teach?"

Although Benjamin at the time had more questions than answers, he was adamant that it could be done and in a relatively quick timeframe.

Harriett and Benjamin parted.

Benjamin had a lot to think about. The ball was now in his court. He needed to go away now and find... A SOLUTION.

EXPLORING WONDERLAND[4]

The university where Harriett and Benjamin worked was located in a developing country and had an enrollment of over 20,000 students split over three campuses. Their campus (see Figure 23.1), the smallest of the three, had approximately 5,000 students and over 100 faculty members. The disciplines offered at this campus were law, social sciences, pure and applied sciences, education, the arts, and medicine. Most of the faculty members were located at the central campus, however faculty members from the School of Medicine were located at a nearby hospital, a few miles away.

On campus, five general-purpose computer laboratories were provided for the student population. These computers were running a Microsoft Windows operating system such as Windows 2000 Professional or Windows XP Professional, with software such as Microsoft Office, Macromedia Dreamweaver, and Microsoft FrontPage. A wireless network was also available at several hotspots on campus, which were utilized by a comparably smaller number of students with notebook computers.

Figure 23.1 Going up the hill. A photograph of a part of the university. Notice that a traveller may choose the "yellow brick road" or the more adventurous and treacherous path, the grassy slope.

Despite the university having a Web site for some time, not having a Webmaster resulted in improper maintenance and a disorganised layout, which impeded navigation. The lack of central control and limited support also made it difficult to determine who should be contacted if a problem arose.

Most faculty members had a desktop computer in their office. Most of these machines were also running a Microsoft operating system such as Windows 2000 Professional or Windows XP Professional, with software such as Microsoft Office, Macromedia Dreamweaver, and Microsoft FrontPage.

AND HE IS BOWLED . . . WHAT A GREAT DELIVERY[5]

So we had figured out what we wanted to do and had some great ideas about how we could help individuals create their e-portfolios, whether they were faculty members, administrative or technical staff, or students; or so we thought. Afterall, creating an e-portfolio could not be hard, or could it?

"Hook, Line, and Sinker!"

Let us recap what we were trying to do. Our main goal was to get individuals to reflect on what they were doing and why they were doing it.

To accomplish this however, we realized that we needed to utilize a "carrot and stick" approach. The "stick" was the reflection (which people generally hated to do, especially if they thought that they had not accomplished much); and the carrot—"oh yes, the sweet taste of a juicy orange carrot"—was learning to use the technology. Incidentally, while they were learning to use the technology, they were also constructing their e-portfolios, reflecting on practice, and having fun.

We would later discover that we had chosen the correct lure; we interviewed two participants who said that the primary reason for creating an e-portfolio over a traditional portfolio was the opportunity to learn the technology (Walcott & Grant, 2006a).

A Leonardo da Vinci Moment: The Master Plan

Harriett and Benjamin met later to discuss their approach to what they would call an "E-portfolio Initiative"—I know, the name was really not that enticing.

They agreed that they would first focus on faculty and staff members and deliver the instruction using a workshop format. Some faculty members were already accustomed to this mode of instruction, since workshops were occasionally being offered. The e-portfolio workshops were to be held in a multimedia room equipped with computers, a white board, and a computer projector. Each participant would be assigned to a computer. The room layout, we would later learn, also helped to encourage collaboration and cooperation.

Faculty members and staff were to either receive a personal invitation to the e-portfolio workshops or would receive an invitation poster (sent to all staff and faculty members) by e-mail. Before coming to the workshop, participants would be required to assemble artifacts for their e-portfolios, including courses taught, a list of publications; and content specific e-learning Web sites.

"Format A:"[6]

Harriett and Benjamin decided on the following format for the workshops:

The Contents of an E-Portfolio

They would first talk about the content of an e-portfolio. Some of the primary parts of the e-portfolio were the individual's profile and their philosophy—a teaching philosophy for faculty members or a personal philosophy for nonfaculty members. Faculty members' e-portfolios would also contain research interests, research publications, and course descriptions, at the very least. The content of e-portfolios varied with the interests of the portfolio author. Some were complex with hyperlinks to content specific sites, while others were simple text descriptions.

Web Publishing

Part of the e-portfolio workshop included a brief overview of the way the Web was used to publish documents. The learning outcomes of the Web publishing section included discerning: the difference between the Internet and the World Wide Web (WWW); the difference between a client and server computer; and the storage, distribution, and viewing of Web pages.

Why Use Web Pages?

A basic description of the Internet would be necessary because Benjamin had decided, after pondering "for many a moon," that the best way to implement the e-portfolios was to design a template that would be used by participants to create their e-portfolios. This template was built using HTML and cascading style sheets for a number of important reasons:

- The e-portfolio needed to be easy to deploy
- The e-portfolio needed to be available for viewing by a large audience
- The approach needed to be simple to understand
- The technology needed to be open-source (nonproprietary) and freely available

Creating a Web Page

Benjamin recognized that a completed e-portfolio could be deployed by simply copying the HTML files to a designated folder on the Web server.

Since Benjamin was also teaching an HTML course, he believed that he would be able to show most faculty members how to create a Web page. After the participants understood how Web pages were stored and viewed, it was necessary to show them how they were created. To simplify matters, Benjamin decided only to utilize the subset of HTML tags presented in Table 23.1.

TABLE 23.1 The Subset of HTML Tags Used by Participants to Create Their E-Portfolios

Opening Tag	Closing Tag	Description
<html>	</html>	Specifies the opening and closing of an HTML document
<h1>	</h1>	Specifies a level 1 header, e.g., <h1>Chapter 1</h1> Headers <h2>, <h3>, <h4>, <h5>, and <h6> also exist.
<head>	</head>	Specifies the head of an HTML document
<body>	</body>	Specifies the body of the HTML document
<title>	</title>	Specifies the title of the Web page and is found in the head part of an HTML document, e.g., <title>My Web page</title>
<p>	</p>	Specifies a paragraph, e.g., <p>This is a paragraph</p>
<div>	</div>	Specifies a division, e.g., <div>This is a division</div>
<ul>	</ul>	Creates an unordered list (bullet points) of items e.g., <ul> <li>Item 1</li> <li>Item 2</li> </ul>
<ol>	</ol>	Creates an ordered list of items. e.g., <ol> <li>Item 1</li> <li>Item 2</li> </ol>
<strong>	</strong>	Displays text in bold, e.g., <strong>Bold</strong>
<em>	</em>	Emphasizes text; displays it in italics, e.g., <em>italics</em>
<a>	</a>	Creates hyperlinks e.g., <a href="http://www.google.com">Go to google.com</a> e.g., <a id="beginning">In the Beginning</a> . . . <a href="#beginning">Jump to In the Beginning</a>
<img>	</img>	Display Image, e.g., <img src="banner.jpg" alt="My images"/> *The "/" in the opening tag, in this special case, closes the tag*
<table>	</table>	Creates a table e.g., <table> <tr> <td>A</td> <td>B</td> </tr> <tr> <td>C</td> <td>D</td> </tr> </table>

Toolset Used

Since nearly all members of faculty, staff, and students had access to the Microsoft Windows Operating System, it was decided that the simple text editor Notepad and the Internet Explorer browser would be used. During the actual workshops, participants found Notepad very easy to use to edit HTML documents, since it had the look and feel of familiar Microsoft software.

In addition, in order to keep the Web page creation process easy to learn and fun, an online tool called Tryit Editor would be used (see Figure 23.2). Through the use of this editor, participants would be able to create simple Web pages and view the HTML code and the rendered page side-by-side. At the press of a button, any changes to the HTML code would immediately be seen on the rendered page. This type of visual feedback greatly improves learning (Walcott, 2007).

Constructing the E-Portfolio

After providing an opportunity for the participants to get familiar with these tools, they would be required to customize the e-portfolio template and construct their e-portfolio (the latest version of this template is available at http://www.cavehill.uwi.edu/staff/eportfolios).

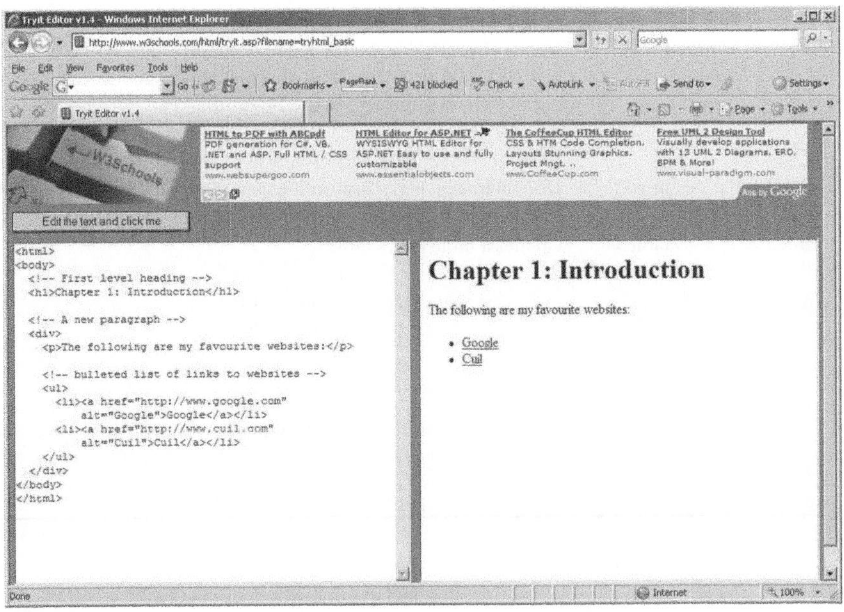

Figure 23.2 The Tryit HTML Editor from W3Schools.com.

After participants completed their e-portfolios, each would be required to peer-review the other participants' e-portfolios, highlighting broken links, spelling, and grammatical errors; indicating clarity or content issues; and providing improvement suggestions.

"I Love it When a Plan Comes Together"[7]

During our discussions, we identified three different methods of administering e-portfolio creation sessions. The first approach was to offer a 2-day workshop where individuals reflected on practice while constructing their e-portfolios. The second method was to run a 2½-hour e-portfolio creation session where the focus was more on the creation of the e-portfolio. The third method was to demonstrate the creation of a part of the e-portfolio within a 2-hour session, and allow the individuals to complete the e-portfolio outside of the session.

We tried the first approach for the first time back in 2006. Five participants attended a 2-day workshop where they were required to assemble and summarize their teaching portfolio, construct a simple Web page, and design and construct their e-portfolio. This group was a diverse one comprising three males and two females from three different faculties; four were faculty members and one was a staff member. During this session, the group shared their teaching philosophies and strategies, as well as methodologies for increasing student engagement. A postsession interview of three of the five participants revealed that two of them had in fact attended the session because e-portfolios required the use of technology.

Comments from participants indicated that the workshop was successful; for example, one participant said that it was good for academics to have Web pages in order to provide easy access to scholarly activities.

We used the second approach during a workshop at the Fourth Pan-Commonwealth Forum on Open Learning (PCF4) held in Jamaica in October 2006. Eighteen conference attendees participated in this session. The group comprised 12 females and 6 males from various universities worldwide. Participants were required to construct a simple Web page, use the e-portfolio template (HTML template) to construct their e-portfolios, and evaluate their e-portfolios. Due to the time limit, participants were not required to write their teaching philosophy in the session, but to reflect on it and utilize the online resources provided to complete it.

We utilized a questionnaire to examine how comfortable participants were writing HTML and using Microsoft Notepad before and after the workshop session. We found that the comfort levels increased in the use of both of these technologies.

The final approach was used by Benjamin. A 2-hour laboratory session of a final year undergraduate Information Systems course was used to demonstrate the construction of an e-portfolio. Students were expected to include their personal philosophy, their educational background, and achievements, as well as their work experience in their e-portfolios. This session was attended by 21 computer science students: 19 males and 2 females. These students were allowed to complete their e-portfolio outside of the laboratory session and have them peer-reviewed by their colleagues.

This session was viewed by students as an exercise that enhanced their skills for the job market. Some of them were learning these skills for the first time and many reflected on their futures.

Some of What We Learned

After running this initiative for some time, we were able to identify three clear groups of individuals, namely students, members of staff (nonfaculty), and faculty members. Each of these groups had separate needs. For example, faculty members were interested in exposing their teaching philosophy and research, staff members were interested in revealing their personal philosophy and work experience, while students were more interested in highlighting their skills and achievements. Our sessions were designed in such a way that participants were able to add or remove content as they required.

At least one common thread was seen throughout all of these e-portfolios, and that was the individual's philosophy. This was something that we were clear on from the outset. Getting individuals to reflect on their philosophy required them to reflect on two fundamental questions. First, "Why do you do what you do?" and second, "How do you do what you do?" These questions were relevant whether the individual was a student, staff member, or faculty member.

Despite these groups having separate needs, we found that we were able to run sessions that included both staff and faculty members. We never tried to mix staff, faculty members, and students.

GOING UP THE HILL

It was tough going; so many problems crying out for solutions! We had scheduling difficulties, issues of encroaching on faculty members' time, problems convincing faculty of the value of the exercise, attrition, and problems finding a suitable venue.

We had problems!

Schedule: Tuesday @ 4 p.m., No . . . Wednesday at @ 9 a.m., No . . . What About Next Week?

The first problem was "When was the best time to offer these e-portfolio creation sessions?" "Should we offer them once a year or several times a year?"

"Should we offer them at the beginning or during semesters?"

"Should we offer these sessions during summer?"

What was the best time to offer these sessions?

Truthfully, we did not have a clue. Actually, we did not anticipate the full range of scheduling difficulties at all. We did not really imagine that it would be so difficult to get faculty members to sit down together.

Time: "Like sands through the hourglass, so are the days of our lives."[8]

The issue of time was a major problem. Faculty members were already feeling overworked and burdened. Many were teaching either a large number of classes or very large classes, which were consuming their time. That, along with administrative responsibilities, made it even more difficult. Remember also the importance of research in the advancement of the faculty members' careers. "When exactly do I find the time?" we often heard echoing in our ears. Time was a problem for everyone.

To make this already bad situation even more complicated, the university timetable did not have scheduled any noncurricula time; that is, time when all or most of the faculty members would be available. In fact, there was no guarantee that you could find a time when all the faculty members in the same department did not have a scheduled class.

Value: Identify what a person spends their time and money on, and you will know what they value.

"What's so important about an e-portfolio?" We have heard this question far too often. Some faculty and staff members seem to place little value in spending time developing them. Creating an e-portfolio appeared by many to simply be extra work and time-consuming. It was therefore difficult to motivate them and to obtain buy-in.

The reflection required during the creation of an e-portfolio can be painful, yes painful, when you ask yourself the question, "What have I done for the last year?"; especially when the answer is "routine teaching and administrative work."

It was the reflection that was of great value to some individuals. During one e-portfolio creation session when we began working on our publication section, one faculty member exclaimed, "I have no publications!" "Let us just put it this way," but by the end of that session, we had identified a reasonable list of publications for this faculty member, including two self-published books. Self-worth is another hidden value of e-portfolios!

Attrition: The Swinging Door

We had a problem getting some individuals to complete their e-portfolios. In fact, in one e-portfolio session, only one participant completed an e-portfolio. Unfortunately, this was our fault because we decided to run a pilot session for the PCF4 conference in Jamaica. The session length was therefore only 2½ hours. We learned from this session and were able to streamline the process. Unfortunately, the penalty was a discontented audience and incomplete e-portfolios.

Not completing e-portfolios was not always our fault. In some cases faculty members were only able to attend a part of the session and therefore were unable to complete their e-portfolios. Many times we had to work around the fact that there was a constant flow of individuals coming in and going out of sessions. Some started their attendance during midsession rather than at the beginning.

Venue: Oh Where, Oh Where Shall I Go?

If figuring out when to schedule e-portfolio sessions was difficult, figuring out where to hold them was even more problematic. A problem mostly left in Harriett's capable hands. This problem was present for most workshops not only the e-portfolio. Unfortunately the situation regarding the lack of venue still remains a problem today. There was only one room available to the IDU, albeit not exclusively. Other entities in the university also utilized the room. This clearly limited our flexibility.

STILL GOING . . . AND GOING . . . AND GOING[9]

We felt like the Energizer bunny in those commercials where he just keeps on beating his drum. Although the problems that Harriett and Benjamin faced seemed insurmountable, they struggled on, holding fast to their dream.

"We were just a couple of ants trying to eat away at a rubber tree plant. We had high hopes."[10]

Benjamin was totally frustrated; Harriett echoed, "I am sooo tired." Yet, they laughed and joked, not to be discouraged as they labored on.

"We had high hopes."

"Make it fun," Benjamin kept repeating to himself as he flopped down in a chair exhausted after completing another 2-day e-portfolio creation workshop. Even he was "sooo tired" but did not give voice to his fatigue.

"We just had high hopes."

MIRROR, MIRROR ON THE WALL, WHO HAS REFLECTED MOST OF ALL

So what did we learn? The responses were varied, but all very positive.

We learned that the technical skills of faculty and staff varied significantly, but that by carefully streamlining our sessions, we could teach them the Web publishing skills needed to create their e-portfolios. We also learned that these technical skills are "a little intimidating at first" but that this fear can be overcome in a relatively short time (within a session).

Many faculty members reflected on their scholarly work and publications and recognized that "self-development [was required] to be on the cutting edge."

Many important lessons were learned from our student participants.

One student said, "In my opinion, creating this e-portfolio is a good way to market yourself." This student saw the value of making an e-portfolio to portray a particular image through the artifacts placed on his e-portfolio.

Another student had a similar view and said that the e-portfolio could "be a great asset in the world of work" and could complement her résumé.

There were other slants as well. For example, one student commented that he had "absolutely no solid background in the area of Web site designing" and felt that this had been crippling him. The student concluded however that "this e-portfolio designing activity is seeking to fix that."

Yet another student indicated that the e-portfolio creation process "encouraged my thinking and self-reflection."

Clearly, from the students' point of view, the e-portfolio creation process had numerous benefits, including the learning of technology and self-development.

THE HILL TOP . . . HALLELUJAH!

Now that we have streamlined our e-portfolio creation process, our next step is to increase the number of completed e-portfolios. This means minimizing attrition; providing the carrot.

Thankfully, more faculty, staff, and students are beginning to recognize the usefulness of reflecting on practice while creating an e-portfolio. We still have a long way to go though.

THE JOURNEY CONTINUES

"Take care. We have to go." We have about seven staff members from the library awaiting us to help them create their e-portfolios. By the way, it was them who asked us to do it!

DISCUSSION QUESTIONS

1. Is an e-portfolio more than just an electronic CV? Is an e-portfolio really useful?
2. Identify the different technologies that could be used to create an e-portfolio. Rank-order the cost of ownership (in terms of money, development and maintenance time, human resources, and so on) of these technologies to the e-portfolio creator and your institution. Is it too costly?
3. What types of technical skills are required to create an e-portfolio? Does your institution provide opportunities to learn these skills? Identify the courses or the source of this training if your institution has and recommend possible changes to the curricula in order to provide this type of training.
4. Does the creation of e-portfolios as part of a group help to foster constructive collaboration and cooperation? Does it improve the quality of the e-portfolio?
5. Publishing personal information online has serious privacy implications, such as cyber-stalking and spam. Do the benefits of publishing an e-portfolio outweigh these potential risks, especially for individuals in developing countries? What kind of information should an individual avoid publishing?
6. Given the obstacles Harriett and Benjamin faced, propose an approach that could have been more successful.
7. What do you think would be an effective way for an individual or institution to market its e-portfolios?

REFERENCES

Barrett, H. (2000). Create your own electronic portfolio using off-the-shelf software to showcase your own or student Work. *Learning & Leading with Technology, 27*(7), 14–21.

Danielson, C., & Abrutyn, L. (1997). *An introduction to using portfolios in the classroom.* Alexandria, VA: Association for Supervision and Curriculum Development. Retrieved August 28, 2008 from http://pdonline.ascd.org/pd_online/portfolio/1997danielson/ch1.html

Gathercoal, P., Love, D., Bryde, B., & McKean, G. (2002). On implementing Web-based electronic portfolios, *EDUCASE, 2,* 29–37.

Gibson, D., & Barrett, H. (2003). Directions in electronic portfolio development, *CITE Journal, 2*(4), 559–576.

Johnson, G., & DiBiase, D. (2004). Keeping the horse before the cart: Penn State's approach to e-portfolio. *EDUCAUSE Quarterly, 27*(4), 18–26.

Lambert, J. (2007). *Digital storytelling cookbook.* Berkeley, CA: Digital Diner Press.

Lorenzo, G., & Ittelson, J. (2005). An overview of e-portfolios, *EDUCAUSE Learning Initiative (formerly NLII)* Retrieved July 31, 2006, from http://www.educause.edu/ir/library/pdf/ELI3001.pdf

Strudler, N., & Wetzel, K. (2005). The diffusion of electronic portfolios in teacher education: Issues of initiation and implementation, *Journal of Research on Technology in Education, 37*(4), 411–433.

Walcott, P. A., & Grant, J. M. A. (2006a). *Helping new faculty to document their scholarship through the creation of e-portfolios.* Proceedings of the International Conference on Education and Technology (pp.135–140). Calgary, Canada,.

Walcott, P. A., & Grant, J. M. A. (2006b). *Creating e-portfolios through collaborative and technology-mediated learning.* The Fourth Pan-Commonwealth Forum on Open Learning (PCF4). Ocho Rios, Jamaica. Retrieved January 31, 2008, from http://pcf4.dec.uwi.edu/viewpaper.php?id=309

Walcott, P. A. (2007). *A Web-based tool for learning extensible markup language.* Proceedings of the 6th WSEAS International Conference on Data Networks, Communications, Computers (pp. 413–417). Trinidad & Tobago.

NOTES

1. "I Have a Dream" is the popular name of a famous speech by Martin Luther King Jr., wherein the phrase was the dominant theme. It was delivered on the steps of Lincoln Memorial in Washington, DC, on August 28, 1963.
2. The 1992 U.S. Summer Olympic basketball team was called the "Dream Team" because it was made up of the best professional players from the National Basketball Association (NBA). This was considered "a dream come true" because NBA players were previously not allowed to play in the Olympics.
3. REM or Rapid Eye Movement is a normal stage of sleep, which is characterized by much brain activity.
4. The book, *Alice's Adventures in Wonderland* (commonly referred to as "Alice in Wonderland") is a children's book written by Charles Dodgson in 1865. Wonderland was a fascinating dreamworld in which Alice interacted.
5. The concept of being bowled is associated with the game cricket. A good delivery may often result in the opponent being "bowled out."
6. Back in the days of the Microsoft Disk Operating System (MSDOS), this command would format a floppy disk.

7. Hannibal Smith was a character in the popular TV series, *The A-Team* in the 1980s. His favorite catchphrase at the end of a successful mission was, "I love it when a plan comes together."
8. The trademark opening line of the U.S. soap opera, *Days of Our Lives.*
9. The trademark line in advertisements for Energizer batteries.
10. Based on the song "High Hopes," popularized by Frank Sinatra.

9 781607 523147

Printed and bound by CPI Group (UK) Ltd, Croydon, CR0 4YY
15/09/2026
14962368-0006